International Perspectives on Social Work

International Perspectives on Social Work

Global Conditions and Local Practice

Karen Lyons

Kathleen Manion

and

Mary Carlsen

palgrave
macmillan

First published 2006 by
PALGRAVE MACMILLAN

Palgrave Macmillan in the UK is an imprint of Macmillan Publishers Limited, registered in England, company number 785998, of Houndmills, Basingstoke, Hampshire RG21 6XS.

Palgrave Macmillan in the US is a division of St Martin's Press LLC, 175 Fifth Avenue, New York, NY 10010.

Palgrave Macmillan is the global academic imprint of the above companies and has companies and representatives throughout the world.

Palgrave® and Macmillan® are registered trademarks in the United States, the United Kingdom, Europe and other countries.

ISBN 978-1-4039-3951-7

This book is printed on paper suitable for recycling and made from fully managed and sustained forest sources. Logging, pulping and manufacturing processes are expected to conform to the environmental regulations of the country of origin.

A catalogue record for this book is available from the British Library.

A catalog record for this book is available from the Library of Congress.

Printed in Great Britain by the MPG Books Group, Bodmin and King's Lynn

Contents

Preface

This book had its origins in the happy coincidence of the three authors sharing an office in 2002/2003. Our backgrounds and positions varied – Karen had worked at the University of East London (UEL) since 1978 and a significant aspect of her teaching responsibilities since the mid 1990s was in relation to international social work; Kathleen had come to UEL from Canada (via other places) to undertake the MA in International Social Work and stayed to undertake PhD research, together with some teaching and research assistant duties; Mary was enjoying a sabbatical break from her usual role leading a social work programme in the US, and carried out some teaching as well as her own research. But, as so often happens in collaborative projects in the 21st century, having completed the proposal while physically close, we have undertaken the bulk of this project in different locations relying on one of the main stays of globalisation, information and communications technology for many of our drafts and exchanges.

We shared a common enthusiasm for the 'international social work project' but also a recognition that globalisation increasingly impacts on social workers in their local, day to day practices. While there was beginning to be some acknowledgment of this idea in the social work literature, we saw the need for a new text which would develop material illustrating this thesis in some of the areas which we regarded as topical, novel and/or requiring re-examination in the light of globalisation. We were also concerned to identify further ways in which some people might develop some specialist forms of 'international social work' in relation to our selected topics. Of course, choosing some topics for attention meant excluding others, so for instance, we have not included great detail about some of the international conventions mentioned, on the grounds that these are available in other texts or (more readily for many) on the websites of organisations, such as the UN, from which they derive. It could also be argued that the approach taken offers breadth, rather than depth. However, we hope to encourage readers to explore areas which may be new to them further or to re-examine more familiar material from a different perspective. Given our different backgrounds (including nationalities), expertise and research interests, we have drawn on a wide range of academic literature as well as grey literature (often from INGOs themselves), websites and, not least, press and media reports. We have aimed to provide examples from a range of countries – partly to illustrate that 'the local' takes on a wider meaning in a global context, but also in the expectation that this book will be of interest to an international readership. Accordingly, we have tried to avoid too great an Anglo-American bias, but, given our nationalities, access to literature and experience as white, western women (albeit all with some experience of living and/or working outside our own countries and/or working in multi-cultural localities), perhaps this is unavoidable.

Finally, as is customary, we take responsibility for all the material in this text and for our interpretations of events and literature – but we apologise for any errors of fact or misunderstanding. We also extend our sincere appreciation to our partners and other family members for their forbearance and support when this project conflicted with the demands of other work, relative to personal commitments. We are very pleased to see the completion of this text, which signifies different things for each of us as we go our separate ways. We trust that it will have relevance for a range of readers – in different places and at different stages of social professional development – as we all adapt to living and working in societies affected in various ways by globalisation.

Karen Lyons
London, England

Kathleen Manion
Wellington, New Zealand

Mary Carlsen
Minnesota, USA

1 Introducing International Perspectives on Social Work

Introduction

Globalization is a topic that has received growing attention in the press and media as well as in the economic, political and social sciences. However, it has only more recently been acknowledged as constituting several processes affecting the welfare sector and, more specifically, the work of social professionals. The focus of social work on the relationship between individuals, families, groups or communities and their environments has emphasized the 'local' nature of intervention and the importance of developing services and practices which are appropriate to a given context and culture (Webb, 2003). We do not contest this emphasis but argue that social work across the globe is now operating under different conditions, which produce new social problems – or exacerbate old ones. Social professionals therefore need to review services and practices in the light of international events and perspectives. For some, this entails working in international settings, but for others it means incorporating internationalized perspectives into local practice.

In some respects, international relationships and activities are not new in social work. The contacts between the pioneers in social work over a century ago have been well documented (see for instance Healy, 2001), and the major international organizations of social workers had their origins in a conference held in Paris in 1928 (Lyons, 1999). However, there was perhaps an assumption that international activities were restricted to the leaders in the field or were at best an occasional and marginal interest for a minority of social professionals. Global interdependence means that global events and processes now impact on individuals,

1

communities and societies worldwide. We suggest that *all* social workers need to have some appreciation of international perspectives and feel better equipped for social work activities, which are increasingly likely to have cross-cultural and possibly cross-national dimensions (Hokenstad and Midgley, 1997). Additionally, a minority will continue to be involved in an area of work more specifically described as *international social work*.

In this book, we aim to provide readers with a better understanding of some of the theoretical concepts and themes relevant to developing international perspectives, or perhaps even embarking on more specialist practice in an international setting. The central theoretical constructs of 'globalization'; 'inequality', 'human rights' and 'poverty'; and 'loss' (presented in Part I) will be used to analyse how these concepts affect particular populations globally and locally. In Part II we focus on selected topics that have been relatively neglected (or are only recently coming into view) in existing social work literature; and overall we aim to illustrate the 'interconnectedness' of the local and the global in particular ways. Within social work theory and practice, globalization represents a new, dynamic perspective; inequality, human rights and poverty represent both residual and emerging themes; and loss represents a perennial underlying factor within social realities.

We neither presume to provide a comprehensive account of a wide-ranging and changing field nor to duplicate material presented in earlier texts, but aim to introduce material (including in areas with which some readers will already be familiar, for instance in relation to loss and health) from a fresh perspective and in ways that will inform and stimulate new thinking and practices. We suggest that social professionals increasingly need to recognize the international dimensions of many situations. Conceiving social work practice and social problems within an international framework allows us to see that 'global issues' matter to this profession. Although some authors have begun to develop the concept of *international social work* (see for instance, Hokenstad and Midgley, 1997, 2004; Lyons, 1999; Midgley, 2000; Penna *et al.*, 2000; Pugh and Gould, 2000; Healy, 2001), corresponding fields of practice are scarce or, as yet, little documented. Within this book, where practice examples have yet to be developed, arguments are made for the potential value of internationalizing social work.

Definitions, Assumptions and International Associations

Some organisations have for some time acted as champions and identifiers of social work at an international and regional level. At the global level, we find the International Federation of Social Workers (IFSW), the International Association of Schools of Social Work (IASSW) and the International Council of Social Welfare (ICSW), as well as the Inter-University Consortium Council on Social Welfare (IUCISD) (see for instance, Hokenstad and Midgley, 1997; Lyons, 1999). These along with regional groupings and some specialist international organizations are provided with contact details in the Appendix. It is perhaps appropriate, initially, to introduce and define some of the terms which we shall frequently be using in this text, not least concerning social work itself. It is relevant here to note a 'new definition' of social work adopted in 2000 at a joint Congress of the IFSW and the IASSW.

The core definition is contained in a one-page document on the websites of IFSW and IASSW and reads as follows:

> The social work profession promotes social change, problem solving in human relationships and the empowerment and liberation of people to enhance well-being. Utilizing theories of human behaviour and social systems, social work intervenes at the point where people interact with their environments. Principles of human rights and social justice are fundamental to social work.

We would identify some terms such as 'problem solving', 'human relationships' and 'well-being', the phrase 'where people interact with their environments' and the 'fundamental' principles as probably uncontentious and reflecting commonalities in extremely diverse examples of practice across most countries of the world. As an indication of the diversity, globally, national associations affiliated with IFSW exist in 80 countries (with over 470,000 members), and according to the IASSW's 2000 census there were an estimated 2000 schools of social work worldwide. Schools of social work are well established in almost all countries in Europe, and North and South America, and have developed more recently or irregularly in Asia and Africa and the countries of the Former Soviet Union (FSU) (Garber, 2000).

However, Hare (2004) has discussed some of the challenges faced by the joint working party in the process of producing this short statement, and, even since its adoption, it has been critiqued as reflecting a 'Western' understanding (and it is true that all but three of the 12 people associated with devising this definition were from North America or West European countries). Thus, Yip (2004) has suggested that in China and some other societies where Confucian values are strong the terms change. Empowerment and liberation could be contrasted with the more dominant values of maintaining stability, respect and harmony expected of social workers in many Asian countries. This both reflects a tension within the profession as to how far the aspirations of some social workers match the societal expectations of them and the actual modes of practice, and reflects another debate common in international forums about the difficulty of agreeing 'universal' definitions or standards without apparently imposing 'Western' (or even Anglo-American) assumptions and expectations. We shall return to the concept of imposing 'Western' ideology on international social work in the context of developing international perspectives and practices.

We have also utilized the term 'social professions'. This term was coined in the context of a conference marking the evaluation of a decade of Erasmus (university) exchange programmes in the European region (Seibel and Lorenz, 1998). Social work participants in European networks had become increasingly aware of the range of occupational groups with different titles and qualifications across countries, undertaking broadly similar work in the social sphere and the term was given wider exposure through the inception of a new European journal (Otto and Lorenz, 1998). The funding provided by the Erasmus (and later Tempus and Socrates) programmes for the establishment of European networks laid the basis not only for the development of joint education and research programmes (Lyons and Lawrence, 2006) but also for published and unpublished comparative accounts about welfare contexts and social work practices in a range of European countries. These reflected the national differences in education and training traditions; views on the role of the state, voluntary, private and informal sectors in providing 'welfare'; and ways of organizing social and community services for particular user groups (see for instance, Lorenz, 1994; Adams *et al.*, 2001; Hamburger *et al.*, 2004).

We suggest that 'social professions' is also a useful term in the wider global context, considering the different emphases in training, organization of services and practice embraced by the global definition and reflected in comparative study of particular national provisions. We therefore tend to use the term 'social professions' instead of 'social work' in many places, particularly since a wider understanding of what constitutes 'social work' (than would be familiar to, for instance, many British social workers) is appropriate when discussing social work in a comparative or international context. Similarly, we sometimes use the term 'social professional' as opposed to the narrow and, for some, alienating term 'social worker'. We should make it clear at this stage that we do not intend to present a comparative account (which would detail similarities and differences across a range of countries according to similar criteria) in the following chapters but rather to elaborate on the idea of international social work as a perspective or specialist activity (see later); we therefore take a thematic approach, using examples of local practice (either actual or anticipated) drawn from many countries or taking place at regional or international levels.

We should also clarify here our use of the term 'welfare' and stress that patterns of 'welfare provision' vary widely, even between countries apparently sharing a common language (including the United States [US] and the United Kingdom [UK]) or with similar economic status (for instance, Sweden and Japan). Ideas about 'welfare' in wealthy countries generally presume free education (up to school-leaving age) as a universal right and include some access to free health care (although the level of entitlement and means of funding such provision vary widely). Additionally, there is some provision of social security/welfare payments to people who are unable to support themselves through paid work for some reason. Other measures sometimes include subsidized housing and provision for personal social services, although whether these are provided by the state through local authorities or by the independent (voluntary and private) sectors again shows wide variation. The extent to which different countries can be said to have a 'welfare state' and the different models of welfare states (using comparative examples) have been widely discussed in the social policy literature since the late twentieth century (see for instance, Esping-Anderson, 1990; Deacon, 2002; Cohen *et al.*, 2002; Midgley, 1995, 1997a).

Assumptions about the nature of welfare, social care and social services in relation to family and community responsibilities are even more varied when we consider the needs of, and provisions in, countries with less developed economies (as discussed by Mwabu *et al.*, 2001), and again a word on terminology is appropriate. Countries with well-developed (capitalist) economies have sometimes been described as 'advanced industrial countries' (AICs) (Lyons, 1999), although it can be noted that, with changes in patterns of extraction and manufacturing industries (related to globalization), many West European countries might now be classified as post-industrial, with more emphasis placed on the knowledge economy and research and design functions. Such countries are predominantly located in the northern hemisphere (referred to as the 'North' or sometimes the 'West'), with the exception of Australia and New Zealand/Aotorea. Meanwhile, poorer countries (or less developed countries – LDCs) are predominantly located in the southern hemisphere and are sometimes referred to collectively as 'the South'.

Healy (2001) provides a useful section on how terminology has changed to reflect changed political realities since 1989 and the widespread shift towards market economies (relative to command economies of communist countries) globally. This has made the previously used terms of 'first world' (advanced capitalist economies), 'second world' (communist countries) and third world (LDCs) largely redundant. However, Healy noted that such usage also suggested a (distasteful) prioritizing of groups of countries, although (with the decline in the number of countries which could be categorized as 'second-world countries') the gap between 'first world' and 'third world' countries usefully emphasized a gulf which has widened between relatively wealthy countries and those which experience widespread poverty. It is appropriate at this point to introduce some initial discussion about the concept of globalization and why this might be relevant to social work.

Globalization and Poverty: Understandings and Implications

'Globalization' has become an overused term and one that is frequently poorly defined or used loosely to suggest a range of processes at many levels which impact differentially on countries across the world. There are also differing views as to whether this is really a new phenomenon and whether it can be seen as a 'good' or a 'bad thing'. As also suggested, some have seen it as something remote which has little or no relevance to their daily lives and work – and this might include many in the social professions. We do not advocate for or against globalization as such but consider that it does constitute a new phenomenon, the processes of which have profound – but differing – implications for the lives of people across the globe, and that, in so far as there are negative effects, these are most likely to fall on individuals and groups who are marginalized or excluded – who are also most likely to be the focus of social work and community development activities. As such, we consider that all social professionals need to have some basic knowledge about the nature of globalization to better understand the effects of the various processes on their own countries and practices. Additionally, globalization is reflected in some new social problems which require responses across national borders and often at an international level.

Much of the literature about the phenomenon called globalization emphasizes its economic aspects and the way in which countries are increasingly linked by international commercial networks rather than through bilateral trading arrangements. Indeed, a significant aspect of this process is the role of multinational or transnational companies (MNCs or TNCs) in decisions about location of manufacturing and extractive industries and their influence on the economies of countries in both the North and the South. Indeed some see their undemocratic power as a threat even to the role of nation states, and many agree that individual countries have less autonomy and national boundaries have less relevance than was true a generation ago (Held *et al.*, 1999).

Although we will be focusing more on other aspects of globalization, it may be useful at this point to highlight (international and national) social movements, including antiglobalization movements, which seek to challenge existing power structures, both state and corporate. Evidence of the effectiveness of this may be seen in the increased use of trisector partnerships (also known as threefolding) between private, public and civil society in decision making on small and large projects (see Carmen, 1999; Perlas, 2000). These movements may be dominated by a push from civil society, but the public sector is also reacting in a variety of ways. For instance, in what could be equated to a redefinition of citizenry, in 2003 the Indian government endorsed the development of a *Non-Resident Indian Day* (9 January). This is a state recognition of the achievements of the Indian international diaspora. Through this celebration, the government has invited former residents back to India and in doing so is attempting to capitalize on these successes by encouraging collaboration between current and former residents.[1]

Whatever the impact on the economies of particular countries, there are certainly implications for the ability or willingness of countries to spend money on welfare resources, although as mentioned, there may be an increasing need related to greater differentials between rich and poor people, both within and between countries. For example, in the US, tax policy rhetoric has changed to 'it's your money – you can choose how to use it'. There are thus greater demands on social professionals, almost regardless of the sector or type of agency in which they are based and the user group or community to which they relate.

But globalization is not only an economic phenomenon – it also has other dimensions, including political, demographic, technological, cultural and environmental, which interact both to increase the diversity within societies and to promote uniformity in, for example, social policies across national boundaries. It can also be seen as both a holding together and a bursting apart of traditional hierarchical structures. We have seen a restructuring of social justice in recognition of a reorganization of criminal activities, with an International Police Force (Interpol), a transnational court system, but also an increase in extraterritorial jurisdiction in some countries for some crimes (e.g., paedophilia). More immediately recognizable to many global citizens are the cheaper, more convenient transport networks and telecommunications services (e.g., the Internet).

An American social work educator has defined globalization as 'a process of global integration in which diverse peoples, economies, cultures and political processes are increasingly subjected to international influences' (Midgley, 1997a, p. xi) and others have identified the increased extent of *interdependence* between different societies (Barry Jones, 1995). A Canadian analyst has discussed the decline in the 'welfare project' across a range of countries, related to the rise to dominance of a political ideology which favours a free market (Teeple, 2000). In countries such as the UK, where a welfare state and universalist principles were widely accepted until the late 1970s, this ideology has led to serial restructuring of health and social services into a 'mixed economy of welfare', in which the rhetoric of consumer choice is placed above the value of solidarity, as reflected in some former provisions, including community development thinking and practice.

To date there has been relatively little resistance to the dominant ideology, and indeed the power of MNCs and the interests of wealthy countries have combined to influence the direction of global bodies such as the International Monetary Fund (IMF) and World Bank to discourage dissent. However, there are signs that this may be changing, as divergent interest groups are solidifying their goals to effect change, for example, in the Seattle riots and debates about the cancelling of national debts (the latter debate being current at the time of writing in response to the catastrophic effects of the tsunami on countries around the Indian Ocean) and, perhaps more significantly, the 2005 international campaign for trade justice. The Global Call to Action Against Poverty is a loose alliance of groups working towards poverty alleviation through forcing leaders to live up to their commitments. One criticism of the global campaign has been its lack of recognition of 'home-based' poverty, but Canada, along with Scotland, has been noted for linking issues of local poverty to global poverty (www.bond.org). The Canadian coalition has succinctly stated their demands as 'More and better aid. Trade justice. Cancel the debt. End child poverty in Canada', further stating that 'poverty exists because we have an unwillingness to invest in social development'.[2] Many of the national campaigns affiliated with the global campaign are fighting for three main issues – more aid (at least 0.7 per cent of gross domestic product [GDP] as promised at the UN General Assembly in 1970, which few countries have lived up to), debt cancellation, and fair trade practices. It is interesting to note that, in the UK 'Make Poverty History' Campaign, the most problematic area of consensus and commitment has been on trade justice (personal communication).

We are living in a time when there are real and impending concerns about global food security, freshwater resources, energy availability and pandemics, as well as an increased incidence of civilian casualities in conflicts and trafficking (and exploitation) of women and children. Additionally, the increased mobility of people at both ends of the poverty/wealth continuum, and the hitherto unprecedented level of interconnectedness of people and communities around the world, means that it is in the interests of the rich to pay attention to the poor. In fact, it may be shrewder to say that the boundary between the rich and poor may be more complex than previously thought, making it increasingly apparent that more attention needs to be paid to the issue of poverty as a pragmatic approach, rather than as an altruistic one.

Additionally, as previously discussed (Lyons, 1999), and as more recent examples have illustrated (e.g., the Asian tsunami or serial Caribbean hurricanes, including Hurricane Katrina, which destroyed several US cities, including New Orleans, in 2005), the destruction caused by extreme weather has emphasized that we can no longer afford to ignore the warning signs about environmental damage, global warming, or planetary vulnerability – neither can we see these as country specific in terms of their origins or effects. Air and water do not recognize national boundaries and, just as the 'man-made' disasters of the explosion of a nuclear reactor at Chernobyl (1986) or of a chemical plant in Bhopal, India (1984), have had lasting effects in particular locations, so the tsunami in the Indian Ocean on December 26 2004 has caused devastation which will have a long term impact on the island and shoreline communities of up to 12 countries bordering that sea. The tsunami also illustrated our global interconnectivity not only in terms of the devastation, where citizens of more than 50 different countries died, but also in terms of response. The tsunami elicited unprecedented giving to international and grassroots NGOs in the affected regions and a desire in many people to give in more substantial ways. A similar phenomenon was illustrated in the 11 September 2001 attacks (hereafter 9/11).

We can reflect that there was a time when social workers had a greater say in the policies of the UN and other international bodies, but as economic development superseded social (and environmental) development their role has been neglected (Drucker, 2003). However, we suggest that the values of social work are akin to those of many of the current global social (and environmental) movements and we need to see an end to the way in which social, economic and environmental issues are decontextualized and individualized. These components are inter-connected. In the words of Nelson Mandela at a Make Poverty History event in London in 2005,[3]

> Overcoming poverty is not a gesture of charity. It is an act of justice. It is the protection of a fundamental human right, the right to dignity and a decent life. While poverty persists, there is no true freedom. Sometimes it falls upon a generation to be great. You can be that great generation. Let your greatness blossom. Of course the task will not be easy. But not to do this would be a crime against humanity, against which I ask all humanity now to rise up.

International Social Work and International Perspectives in Local Practice?

In such a context, it is perhaps not surprising that the past two decades or so have seen a revival of interest in the idea of interna-tional social work – whether as a lens through which to view local practice or as a form of practice in its own right. Indeed, Ahmadi (2003, p. 14) suggests, '(i)nternational social work can and should play an important role in consolidating democracy, social justice and the implementation of international conventions such as human rights, elimination of discrimination against women, rights of children and so on, as well as preventing conflicts and supporting peace by promoting global cultural integration.'

Both Lyons (1999) and Healy (2001) have discussed some of the events and literature that predated or have marked this devel-opment and have summarized some of the attempts to demarcate or define the field of international social work in particular. Healy cites a definition of international social work by Warren included in the (American) *Social Work Yearbook* of 1937 – it 'includes the exchanges of ideas by social workers at international meetings as well as inter-country work, intergovernmental work, and relief work' (Healy, 2001, p. 6). Lyons cites a study carried out by social work educators from Sweden and the US (Falk and Nagy, 1997; Nagy and Falk, 2000) in the mid-1990s in which they gathered data from 96 social work educators from 20 countries about their understanding of the notion of 'international social work' and from which they identified 12 core aspects (Lyons, 1999). These can be grouped into four main themes:

1. international seminars and conferences, opportunities for exchanges and international practice and consultancy;
2. comparative study of social policies, values, practice approaches, etc.;
3. knowledge about the role of international organizations, financial institutions, MNCs, and international conventions;
4. struggles for social justice and human rights which recognize the increased relevance of international events and interdependence of populations.

Healy advanced her own definition as 'international professional action and the capacity for international action by the social work profession and its members' and identified international action as having 'four dimensions: internationally related domestic practice and advocacy, professional exchange, international practice, and international policy development and advocacy' (Healy, 2001, p. 7). These discussions and other literature form a useful basis for developing our ideas about what constitutes international social work, which will be pursued to some extent in this text. However, we are also concerned to identify the ways in which social workers (who would not necessarily wish to be engaged in international social work as such) can nevertheless have their practice and professional development enhanced by adopting an international perspective in their local practice (in line with the first dimension of Healy's definition). We take this to include having an increased understanding of global events, influences and problems; recognizing the international and cross-cultural dimensions of local issues; and utilizing comparative or internationally derived knowledge to inform their analyses of problem areas and evaluation of possible strategies for intervention.

Ahmadi (2003) sees international social work as cross-national or comparative in nature, but also more broadly suggests it can be seen as a vehicle for rethinking social concepts and social work methods in the wake of the changes brought about by postmodernism and globalization. He accuses international social workers of hiding from the international community and failing to champion the rights of the poor; and he also critiques the euro-centric and ethno-centric view of 'international social work'. He warns that it must remove itself from its euro-centric and ethno-centric milieu and embrace 'a multidirectional web having the character of a decentred practice' (Ahmadi, 2003, p. 16). The crux of his argument strongly reflects the assumption that social workers have become too familiar with the role of 'stretcher-bearer' and are reacting to crisis and not focusing on strengths and being proactive in their efforts.

Returning to the role of international associations in developing policies and practices at an international level or with international dimensions, as well as a global definition of social work, the IASSW and IFSW have also produced a joint document on Global Standards for social work education; and the IFSW periodically issues position papers on various topics of global significance (currently including on ethics and globalization) (see IFSW and IASSW websites). The 'Global Qualifying Standards for Social Work Education and Training' was ratified in Adelaide, 2004, and was largely welcomed by members, in the interests of protecting service users (clients or consumers) and of articulating 'social work' at a global level. However, again there have been concerns raised that this could be an example of 'Western imperialism' and could suggest the possibility of 'standardization', which would be neither feasible nor appropriate. These concerns have, to some extent, been articulated and addressed in articles in a special Issue of *Social Work Education* (2004). In addition, there is also some evidence of the recognition that countries must develop education, organization and practices of social professionals which are indigenous or locality specific, whether these are well-established programmes in countries with very different cultures and socio-economic conditions (from the West, as for instance in Africa) or where these are more recently being (re-)established in countries now identified as 'the West' (as in some of the Central and East European [CEE] states).

Aims and Scope

This leads us more specifically to the aims and scope of this book, which as the reader may have gathered, addresses a wide audience. We aim to assist social professionals across a range of settings and countries to explore selected aspects of the nature and effects of globalization on social welfare and to consider the implications for the development of local and international practices and policies which enhance the well-being of individuals, groups and communities, specifically by social professionals. This includes those working in non-standard or specialized areas of social work which includes an explicit international element, but also a broader group of social professionals who, in keeping with changing times, have to internationalize their practice. The book is therefore aimed at those involved in the initial training and continuing development of social workers, including those practising in the management of staff and agencies or projects, as well as those directly engaged in service provision or capacity building (including, for instance, through community development or action research projects).

As already indicated, the book is aimed at both those who are already engaged or might wish to become involved in international social work and those for whom this seems an unlikely course but whose understandings and interventions could nevertheless be enhanced by a shift in perspective. We think the often-quoted adage, 'think global – act local' (a phrase likely to have come into being with the first Earth Day in the 1970s) has particular relevance to social workers! The overall message is that social work has changed and practitioners and commentators need to change in line with changes in the nature of social problems, social policy responses and favoured frameworks.

We have organized the material in this book into two parts, and, while individual chapters may 'stand alone' for some readers' purposes, we aim to demonstrate the interrelation not only between the two parts of the book but also between the issues addressed in each chapter. Part I addresses the core themes we have selected as providing the theoretical underpinnings of the issues discussed in Part II. As mentioned, we have identified 'globalization', 'inequality' and 'loss' as the focus for Chapters 2–4 in Part I. Apart from the centrality of globalization to this text, we see inequality and loss as universal aspects of the human experience. When these have damaging effects, they are frequently the focus of social work interventions or of collaborative work with other professionals and policy makers, who try to address or mitigate them.

Selecting topics for inclusion in Part II – where we aim to explore the more practical aspects of societal problems and how social professionals are responding to these in the light of global conditions – was more difficult given the nature of the field. However, we have identified some issues as having a particular relevance to debates about the implications of globalization for social professional activities. The topics selected by no means encompass all aspects of international social work practice, but (apart from reflecting the interests and expertise of the authors) seemed to us to encapsulate a number of areas where one could find international social professionals working or where international dimensions would assist local practice. Further, these specific topics also feature in current international social development debates. Omissions include, for instance, what George (1997) described as the 'global greying' (that is, a specific focus on the implications for social professionals of aging and of increasing numbers of elders in populations); or the role of religion in social work – but these topics must be left for another volume.

Additionally, the selected topics relate to new or topical challenges in particular areas of social work or require us to review current knowledge and practices in the light of changing conditions. We therefore consider issues related to conflict in communities in Chapter 5; natural and forced migration in Chapter 6; exploitation of children in Chapter 7; and global spread of disease in Chapter 8. These topics relate to specific vulnerable groups – victims of war, migrants, children and young people and those experiencing ill health. The following section provides a more detailed overview of these chapters.

Chapter 2 sets the scene of the book by first looking at globalization. Globalization has conventionally been seen as mainly an economic concept but the relevance of global conditions to welfare thinking and arrangements and to ideas about 'cultural convergence' have been increasingly recognized. This chapter will argue that a major feature of globalization is 'people movement', which, when combined with historical, political and economic factors and with mass communications, has particular consequences for the interconnections between states and communities. The implications for social work and related interventions are identified, including increasing scope for cross-national and international activity.

In Chapter 3, we recognize that division of people, based on factors such as gender, race, ethnicity, class and religion, is a common theme in all societies. We suggest that globalization has exacerbated the material inequalities, but has also created new forums for social movements and pushed the agenda of social justice and human rights into local and global debates. This chapter aims to analyse social divisions from an international perspective, and to explore methods for tackling those disparities that most impact on individuals and communities. Social division and oppression have significant implications for how social workers should conceptualize and place issues within a social context. Understanding the underlying power differences at all levels of society and between nations and regions is therefore important when attempting any social intervention whether at the individual, family, community, national or supra-national level.

In Chapter 4, we see that loss permeates human experience. Whether material, spiritual or psychosocial, whether caused by illness or death, natural or human disasters or on a personal or community level, people cannot escape loss and its consequences. Yet the reactions to loss and the practices related to bereavement are located in, and shaped by, the social environment and therefore vary considerably across cultures. Globalization and migration challenge social professionals to review their understanding of the impact of loss on human functioning within a person-in-context framework. This chapter therefore considers theories of loss and bereavement and discusses implications for education and practice of social professionals.

In Chapter 5, we look at the increase in (relatively local) civil and cross-border conflicts and at the extent to which these events impact on civilians and whole communities. One of the major consequences felt across the world has been an increase in refugees in neighbouring countries and people seeking asylum in more distant societies. This raises issues for policy makers and professional practitioners in (usually) wealthier countries and regions, such as Europe, and has led to some development of specialist services aimed at those whose physical or mental health has been particularly affected. However, there have also been significant consequences for many of the families and communities who have remained in sites of conflict or been repatriated to them. We give some consideration to the development of international instruments to regulate the conduct of war or to address transgressions, particularly in areas related to child soldiers and rape of women.

Chapter 6 summarizes the debates about different causes of migration; identifies some of the characteristics of migrants; and considers some of the national, regional and global policy and service responses to particular categories of migrants. This includes issues related to citizenship and welfare rights, for instance, in relation to asylum seekers or undocumented workers, and the ways in which social workers at local and international levels are attempting to intervene locally and strategically. Additionally, the chapter explores emerging knowledge about the nature, extent and patterns of recent migrations that are part of a broader problem of people trafficking and smuggling. While (public) attention tends to focus on the responses of workers in the national and international justice systems, the implications for the roles of humanitarian agencies and social professionals to 'victims' (often women and children) are also considered.

In Chapter 7, we explore the emotive and topical issue of child exploitation, which encapsulates broader concerns such as loss, social justice and human rights. Globalization has opened the door to many global companies to exploit lax labour conditions in the developing world. Internationally there have been both pro– and anti–child labour factions. It will be shown how these differing opinions affect people's livelihoods in areas where child exploitation is a reality. In addition, a closer examination will be made of what Castells (1998) called the worst form of child labour, commercial child sexual exploitation, focusing both on the loss of childhood and how this form of labour links to people trafficking. We will also explore the role of international, national and local actors in social intervention.

In Chapter 8, we explore how various forms of disease have taken on a global dimension, assisted in part by ease of travel and population mobility. We explore some current and potential pandemics and their effects on individuals, families and communities. While HIV/AIDS features as the best-known challenge to medical knowledge as well as social and health care interventions, we also identify other diseases which could develop into global pandemics with significant effects in terms of human suffering. We consider the particular implications for social professionals and include examples of how local practices address both local and global needs.

Finally, in the concluding chapter we reiterate some of the main themes of the book and consider further the relationship between the global context and local practices. We review the need for wider knowledge in the light of increased opportunities for cross-national and international social work, and the importance of local practice with a global awareness, with an additional focus on environmental concerns. We make particular reference to the implications for the education of social professionals and link this to the growing evidence that social professionals are themselves part of a mobile labour force. In line with the beginning of debates about 'global citizenship' we propose a new vision for a globally minded social profession.

Part I
Theoretical Frameworks

2 Globalization: Fact or Fiction and Is It Relevant?

Introduction

The term 'globalization' is now familiar to many people. However, there are ongoing debates about its meaning and effects, and even its relevance to some populations and occupational groups. Are the poorest populations of an American ghetto or a Peruvian village or a remote Pacific island really 'touched' by its effects (and is it therefore relevant to welfare professionals?) or is globalization only a reality for young share traders on the London Stock Market or expatriate employees of global corporations or even just people with enough time and money to engage in 'foreign travel'? This chapter aims to clarify some common understandings of the term and to suggest that its effects, although varied across and within different societies, are pervasive in ways that demand the attention of social workers.

We will also consider how the current phenomenon of globalization is different from previous periods of international activity, notably through colonization; and also the implications of globalization for the role of nation states and its relation to other processes evident at regional and local levels. We will then examine more particularly the notion of 'welfare', as a precursor to considering the possible relevance of globalization to social professionals. As Irving and Payne (2005) have suggested

> Concern about globalization has, in part, grown because inequalities between countries are emphasized by the growing pace of change. . . . This issue underlies the public debate about policy responses to globalization and professional responses to its consequences for welfare systems. (p. 155)

The chapter concludes that globalization is a reality – or perhaps has many realities – and that it is most likely to impact adversely on those who are most vulnerable. It is therefore relevant for social professionals to consider both local and international responses.

Interpretations of Globalization

Globalization is understood by many to be essentially an economic phenomenon. Indeed in a recent handbook of globalization (Michie, 2003), it seems that at least 16 out of 31 authors are economists. (Others approach the topic from a range of different perspectives – international relations; government; politics; social theory; industrial relations; management, or, rather exceptionally, an anti-free trade, pro-localist think tank.) One of the earliest exponents of globalization (Wallerstein, 1974) used the term to describe the expansion of capitalism to the point where a world economy was operational, thus creating a world system. More recently, Khan and Dominelli (2000, p. 96) have described economic activity as the 'lynchpin' of globalization. They identified it as having the following key features:

- mobility of production processes from advanced capitalist countries to developing countries;
- the spread and rising power of TNCs worldwide;
- the liberalization of international finance systems; and
- reductions in transportation and communication costs.

But another early writer on the subject, Modelski (1972) (an international affairs specialist) suggested a more broadly based definition: 'the process by which previously discreet societies come into contact with and influence each other'.[1] Richards (1997) subsequently suggested that 'globalization' now has many meanings and that these in part reflect the perspective of the user. 'To the geographer it implies the compression of time and place incurred in rapid and frequent movements of people and information; to a cultural anthropologist it signifies the world wide spread of McDonalds and Coke, and the dominance of the English/American language; while to the economist it signals

the triumph of free trade and the development of global corporations and markets' (as paraphrased in Lyons, 1999, p. 5).[2]
The idea that 'globalization' might have subjective as well as objective meanings was picked up by Trevillion, who used the term 'to embrace *both* the objective social, economic and technological changes associated with the dismantling of national and regional barriers to trade and communication *and* the subjective shifts in consciousness associated with the growth of global concerns and global sensibilities' (Trevillion, 1997, p. 1). Globalization of consciousness is a theme also addressed by Ahmadi (2003). Other authors – who have expounded on the nature of globalization since the 1970s, which has particular relevance to the theme of this book – include Midgley (2000) and Castles (2000). Midgley noted the importance of economic activities and effects but also recognized globalization as having 'social, political, cultural, demographic and other dimensions as well' (Midgley, 2000, pp. 13–14); while Castles (2000), writing about ethnicity and migration, described the increased 'interconnectedness' of societies as being related to migration patterns.

Whatever the emphasis in different 'definitions' of globalization, we can identify some particular characteristics of the late twentieth century context in which it became an established phenomenon. These include the extent to which 'world peace' and worldwide bodies, such as the UN and World Bank (both established in the wake of the Second World War, 1939–45), have enabled or encouraged international dialogue and the establishment of global corporations and trading arrangements. Secondly, we have witnessed the spectacular development of information and communications technology (ICT) and rapid mass transport systems, contributing both to the physical interchange of people (as discussed in Chapter 6) and to the spread of ideas and cultural icons. Thirdly (and related to notions of interdependence), there is a gradual recognition (perhaps not yet fully achieved) that patterns of behaviour in one country or part of the world can have profound implications for whole populations in other societies or perhaps even worldwide.

Turning to the first characteristic mentioned above, the idea that we have been living in a peaceful period, since the last quarter of the twentieth century, may seem a naïve view – or simply incorrect (and there is ample evidence in Chapter 5 of conflicts within and between states which have global implications) but in broad terms there was at least, up to 1989, a certain stability built on the basis of a 'balance of power' achieved between the two superpowers of the US and the USSR (Union of Soviet Socialist Republics) and their respective military, trading and cultural allies. But given the different politics, economics and societal controls in place in the communist countries, it could be argued that globalization – in the form of free trade – was proceeding, at that stage, minus a significant proportion of the world's population. This changed substantially from 1989 with the break up of the Soviet Union and the (re)emergence of newly independent states with aspirations to emulate the capitalist countries in terms of economic (and usually also political) systems. A similar process is now taking place in China (since the mid-1990s), although with a less marked swing away from communism as a political ideology. It might be thought that peaceful conditions are a prerequisite for capitalism to flourish and for population mobility and interdependence between states to be sustained. However, it can also be argued that in some cases capitalism itself engenders conflict and that war gives rise to forced migration. Both points will be returned to later in this book (in Chapters 5 and 6).

In relation to the development of ICT and rapid mass transport systems, it is now taken for granted that ideas, money, goods and people can move round the world at startling speed. The use of satellite technology has made information exchange virtually instantaneous and has allowed connections to be made between many individuals and organizations, irrespective of time and place. Similarly, population mobility has become a reality for a greater number of people than ever before and has brought different cultures into contact with each other in virtually all societies. This might be in the form of the daily or weekly commuting across national borders, or the work related to seasonal movements of people; or the more permanent settlement of immigrants in particular localities. It can be argued that the motivating factor in each of these cases is likely to be predominantly economic but, unlike the inter-continental migrations in the nineteenth and greater part of the twentieth centuries, it is much more feasible for the populations involved to maintain close and regular contact with home countries and extended families, both through ICT and, periodically, through visits facilitated by air travel. But if

ICT and fast, cheap travel can facilitate interconnections which advantage some, they can also be used for illegal purposes and operate in ways which further disadvantage significant sectors of the world's population, not least through a deepening of the 'digital divide', but also for instance through child sexual exploitation, as discussed in Chapter 7.

It is in relation to the third characteristic – the impact of local or national behaviour on other people in other places – that some states have been slower to recognize the reality of global interdependence. However, there are signs of a growing recognition that we inhabit 'one world' as far as resources and the environment are concerned and that patterns of consumption and legislative and technical capabilities in one country have implications for the welfare of people in neighbouring or even far-distant countries. Examples of this include the spread of diseases (as discussed in Chapter 8) and the effects of major disasters (such as the explosion at the nuclear power station at Chernobyl, in 1986) polluting air and/or water quality; destruction of hardwood forests destroying local ecosystems and also contributing to climate change; the potential for global spread of 'bird flu'; and excessive oil and gas emissions depleting the ozone layer and again threatening environmental conditions. Lyons (1999) highlighted the connection between the natural world and 'man-made disasters' and the relevance of environmental concerns to the social work task in a previous text; and this theme has also been emphasised in a recent policy statement by IFSW (see further discussion below and in Chapter 9).

Finally, we should stress that we see globalization essentially as a *process* – or rather 'a complex set of multiple processes . . . (which) operate very unevenly across both time and space and above all *are politically mediated*' (Khan and Dominelli, 2000, pp. 100–101); and that these processes take place *across interconnected systems*. Globalization is a reality and from a social work perspective one can recognize significant negative effects. However, some aspects of its manifestation may not be inevitable or irreversible and there is evidence in some recent public protests and popular movements of resistance. Although globalization seems to us to be a 'fact' (rather than a fiction), how it is experienced (in different locations and by different groups) suggests that it comprises many different realities rather than having a unitary form. However, in so far as globalization is a very current and recognizable phenomenon, it might be useful to identify how it differs from a previous process, which also established important interconnections between different parts of the world, namely, colonization; and also to talk briefly about other processes which are recognizable and which seem to be happening in parallel – or perhaps in opposition – to globalization, particularly, regionalization and localization.

Globalization and Other Processes

Population mobility has been a feature of human behaviour from earliest times, initially spurred by survival instincts but later more overtly linked to economic motives and desire to gain access to resources outside home borders. Such motivations often resulted in heroic tales of exploration and 'discovery' of distant countries in the Western literature; but also carried with them witting or unwitting violence against existing communities.

'Colonization' occurred wherever traders or raiders not only sought access to resources but also aimed to control them, often through seizure of land, settlement and 'development' – or exploitation – on the colonizer's terms (Held *et al.*, 1999). Depending on the timing, nature and scale of the colonization, incomers either became 'absorbed' and accepted as part of the history of a country (e.g., the Vikings in South East Ireland; the Welsh in Patagonia) or set up injustices and tensions which resulted in dramatic conflict with local populations or longer-term attempts to 'respond' to more persistent inequalities in societies. Relatively recent examples of the latter scenarios can be seen in various African countries, including the Congo ('Belgian'), Algeria ('French') and South Africa (Dutch, British); and elsewhere, including Chile (Spanish), Canada and Australia (both initially colonized by the British and later the Irish, but also by the French in Canada).

A significant feature of colonization has been its racialized nature, with 'white' domination of 'black' or 'Indian' communities (Castles, 2000). Nowhere was this more apparent than in the Caribbean Islands, where indigenous populations were largely destroyed and the islands were 'repopulated' by a black slave labour force (largely from West Africa) or indentured labourers (from the [Dutch] 'East Indies') under the control of white plantation owners and a hierarchy of administrators and officials. In some cases a more or less peaceful withdrawal (though often following significant local unrest) of the colonizers (often as late as the 1960s) has left a legacy of institutional arrangements and cultural practices that owe at least some of their characteristics to the political systems (and sometimes also religious beliefs) of the previous dominant group, as reflected, for instance, in present-day differences within the Caribbean region.

The difference between the nineteenth- and twentieth-century colonial arrangements and the current manifestations of globalization is the extent to which colonization, while driven by economic motives, was also a national (and nationalistic) venture related to imperialism, with the establishment of 'empires' on a competitive basis (Axford, 1995; Held *et al.*, 1999). Such arrangements promoted bilateral trading and other ties between the 'mother country' and 'the colonies'. Thus, colonized countries not only provided valuable or essential 'goods' (including minerals, timber, palm oil and agricultural products) but also became a source of (cheap) labour, including for wartime service or to plug gaps in the domestic economy (Castles, 2000).

Additionally, this last named characteristic of colonization has resulted in the temporary or permanent settlement of minority ethnic groups in various 'mother countries', predominantly in Europe, which has emphasized the sense of interconnectedness between some advanced industrial (or post-industrial) societies and particular LDCs. The extent to which such minority populations have felt 'accepted' and integrated (in the sense of having equal status and opportunities under the law and in relation to access to employment and to public and private provisions) has had significant implications for the state of race relations in specific countries and has assumed greater significance in the post-9/11 world. In this situation, perceived injustices and a gulf in religious beliefs (specifically between Judeo-Christian and Muslim traditions) has increased the sense of vulnerability and/or antagonism experienced by both host communities and minority groups.

In contrast to the colonial process, globalization is not driven in the same way by individual national governments but rather by the power of multinational (or rather global) companies, sometimes allied with the policies and requirements of global financial institutions such as the World Bank or IMF, as well as the interests of the most powerful and wealthy states (Michie, 2003). The reach of corporate organizations is highly significant and there are concerns about both their power to 'negotiate' with (and sometimes ignore or bully) national governments and their lack of accountability to all but their shareholders. Similarly, there are also concerns that the World Bank and IMF are themselves too influenced by capitalist principles and markets of powerful, wealthy nations at the expense of smaller and/or poorer countries. A possible intermediary or international regulatory body, in the form of the United Nations (UN), is also seen as lacking teeth or being too much influenced by the large, rich countries or power blocks (Held *et al.*, 1999).

The foregoing illustrates one of the accompanying features, namely the extent to which the role and power of nation states have changed with the progress of globalization (Held, 1995; Held *et al.*, 1999). Again there are debates about the extent to which national sovereignty has been diminished and it is also clear that some countries maintain significant power, including through their involvement in international regulatory bodies (Lyons, 1999; Khan and Dominelli, 2000), but there is also evidence that an increasing number of countries are influenced by international or regional conventions or directives in their framing of legislation and development of policy – including in the welfare field – as well as being influenced by dominant political ideologies and economic strictures.

Similarly, the mention of regional influence reflects the way individual states have sought alliances with neighbouring countries, often corresponding to alliances within a particular continent (in the case of the European Union [EU] or Asia Pacific region) or spanning two continents (notably between North and South America). The relationship between such arrangements and globalization is variable since some of the regional bodies were established before the onset of globalization. However, it can be argued that regionalism is developing as a form of defence either against the influence of one superpower (as the US has now become) or against the most damaging excesses of globalization (and perhaps both, in some cases). The origins, form and extent of powers of these arrangements are varied but the EU can be taken as one example.

The EU (comprising 25 member states at the time of writing) had its origins in concerns in the 1950s about creating a peace based on shared industrial output and economic agreements initially between six countries. These formed the basis for the later expansion of the European Economic Community (to 15 countries by the passing of the Single European Act in 1986), and a gradual shift in focus to the development of workers' rights as a precursor to a broader concern with social policy issues. These have been articulated since the 1990s as encouraging harmonization across a range of services (including education) and strategies (ranging from poverty reduction to military intervention) (Cannan *et al.*, 1992). More recently, aims to create a shared cultural space and sense of 'European identity' alongside specific measures aimed at curbing immigration, have increased concerns about the exclusionary purpose and outcomes of EU policies, alongside the more often cited aims of enhancing social inclusion.

The extension of the EU from 15 to 25 countries since 2004 has also given rise to various concerns, including that the accession countries (eight from the CEE states plus Cyprus and Malta) will have 'second-class status' (relative to the existing membership); or, conversely, that low labour costs and poorer socio-economic conditions in the new member states will detract from the benefits of membership previously enjoyed by smaller, peripheral countries (such as Greece, Ireland and Portugal). A major challenge facing the EU at the time of writing is to convince national voters of its relevance and to reduce bureaucracy while promoting more effective democracy. However, a number of the EU policies have had direct relevance to national policies and provisions for marginalized populations and for social professional education (Lyons and Lawrence, 2006 and see later).

Finally, we can turn to the trends towards 'Balkanization' and 'localization', both closely associated with the establishment (or reassertion) of national or ethnic identities and perhaps both understood as, in part, a reaction against the tendencies towards cultural imperialism (or westernization) associated with globalization.

In the first case, 'Balkanization', we mean the splitting apart of countries that had previously functioned as one unit. This might be a relatively peaceful and only partial process (at least with conflict mainly expressed through Parliamentary and local politics), as in the case of the UK. Here, some powers have been devolved since 2000 from England to the Scottish Parliament, a Welsh Assembly, and (in due course) a Northern Ireland Assembly; and already differences are emerging with regard to a range of policies and institutional arrangements. Some of these are relevant to social workers, for instance, in relation to elder care policies and provisions; and the establishment of separate regulatory (including professional accreditation) bodies for England and Wales, relative to those for Scotland and Northern Ireland, respectively.

However, the term also refers to the more dramatic disintegration of a country, possibly involving armed conflict, such as occurred in the 1990s with the break-up of the former Yugoslavia, and the (re)emergence of a series of smaller countries in the region. Some of these, such as Slovenia, managed to extricate themselves with relatively little conflict and have since established a stable political and economic context for public and private developments (including meeting the criteria for admission to the EU in May 2004) and for continuing with social professional education. Meanwhile, other countries, notably Kosovo, were the scene of relatively prolonged and bitter ethnic conflict and (at the time of writing) they continue to call on UN peacekeepers in attempts to re-establish a viable political economy and civil society. Establishing welfare programmes and social projects are essential, but still difficult, in the latter case.

Localization generally refers to a process that takes place within a country and usually refers to the delegation of powers and budgets to administrative units at 'local level', on the assumption that these will be more in touch with local needs and capacities and that resources will be used more efficiently and effectively if 'managed' in conjunction with local voluntary agencies and community groups. In the US this process is referred to as 'devolution' and has been underway in policy and welfare programmes for about the last 20 years. Within Europe, Poland is an example of a country pursuing an active policy of localization, not least in development of a range of social care services (Krzyszkowski,

2003). In this context, 'localization' was seen, in part, as a way of 'gearing up' for integration into a regional forum (the EU in 2004), rather than being a response to globalization specifically, but in other respects we can note a changed relationship between the global and the local and an increased need for people to feel 'connected' to a locality in the face of globalization.

Relevance of Globalization for 'Welfare' and Social Work

Given an assumption that social work is essentially a local activity (Webb, 2003) – and that arguments for its extension to include international perspectives and practices have only been advanced relatively recently – the relevance of globalization to social work has not yet been fully explored. Indeed, some have called for a new research agenda which would enable systematic explications of the implications of globalization for social work (see for instance, Khan and Dominelli, 2000). However, the IFSW initiated a paper on globalization in 1996 in response to a resolution at the World Congress (in Hong Kong) expressing concern about the social impact of neo-liberal economic policies and structural adjustment programmes across the world. This was later developed and combined with other drafts in relation to environmental concerns to constitute the IFSW Policy on Globalization and the Environment, accepted at the General Meeting (in Adelaide) in 2004 (see IFSW website and also later discussion). This statement and the development of some literature in the social policy and social professional fields provide a basis for further consideration of the implications for social professionals. However, first we should clarify what we might mean by 'welfare'.

Use of the term 'welfare' has been closely tied to the notion of 'welfare state' in much of the literature emanating from north west Europe and some English-speaking countries such as Canada and New Zealand. The term encompasses public provision across a range of services, usually including at least pensions and other kinds of state subsidies (in cash or kind), health and education; and sometimes also housing and social services. The extent to which services are universally available or only accessible on a means-tested basis varies, as does the way in which such services are financed (for instance, through taxation or insurance

schemes); and the likelihood or not that they will be complemented by services provided by the voluntary or private sectors.
It is also a term which is invariably only used in the context
of advanced industrial (or post-industrial) societies, although
political ideology seems more important than national wealth in
determining whether or not a welfare state exists – and cultural
factors play a significant part in the form it takes.

Using a comparative approach to social policy, Esping-
Anderson (1990) produced an important typology of welfare
states (drawing predominantly on the examples of Germany,
the Scandinavian countries, UK and US) – an analysis that has
subsequently been critiqued and revised to some extent. More
recently, Mishra (1999) has written about the way in which
welfare states have been changed by (or had to adapt to) globalization (using examples from a range of countries, particularly
Sweden, Germany and Japan). In writing about the 'hollowing
out' of the welfare state he suggests that, in Anglo-Saxon countries in particular, 'globalization and strong neo-liberal tendencies
in policy making have come together to erode social citizenship
and to weaken . . . an earlier commitment to a social minimum as
a right' (Mishra, 1999, p. 51). Teeple (2000) also identifies the
negative effects of globalization and neo-liberal policies on the
social reform project (as previously represented in some countries
by commitment to welfare states). Teeple draws on examples from
around the world, and makes important connections between the
changes being experienced in 'western democracies' relative to
the impact of globalization on LDCs.

This suggests that it is useful to conceptualize 'welfare' more
broadly. Van Wormer (1997, p. 4) provides a very broad definition – 'the state of collective well-being of a community or
society' – while Midgley (1997a, p. 5) expands on this in relation
to 'social welfare', describing it as 'a condition of human well-
being that exists when social problems are managed, when human
needs are met, and when social opportunities are maximized'.
However, as in any comparative or international context, we must
be aware that the term 'welfare' also has very specific meanings in
some national contexts, for example, its use to describe assistance
to lone mothers in the US or to ensure that people with a variety
of needs claim their 'welfare rights' in the UK (Bull, 2000). It
is also apparent that the conception of welfare (as well-being);

the development of welfare systems; and the role (and resources) of social professionals in low income countries are likely to be very different from those of their counterparts in wealthy nations.

However we understand the term 'welfare', and whether social workers in a particular location are involved in its delivery as state employees or as community development or project workers in a non-governmental organization, it seems likely that globalization will impact on their work in some way. The investment, location and pricing decisions of global corporations constitute a major factor shaping the socio-economic conditions of particular societies and communities, affecting employment opportunities and working conditions as well as the availability (literally and in cost terms) of particular goods and services. These include provision of information technology and pharmaceuticals, in turn affecting the opportunities for societies to participate in the information revolution, and to offer adequate health care to individuals and particular groups (such as those suffering from HIV/AIDS), respectively (see also Chapter 8). These factors therefore form part of the overall picture of increasing inequalities, both within and between societies, attributed to globalization (see for instance, Hoogvelt, 1997; Gregg *et al.*, 1999; Jordan with Jordan, 2000; Palma, 2003). Given these differences within and between states, globalization impacts differentially on the demands and expectations placed on social professionals.

Whatever their particular roles locally, it seems likely that social workers are well placed to identify the 'costs' of globalization to particular individuals, families, groups and communities and to contribute to the challenges to economic liberalism which Pugh and Gould (2000, p. 135) suggest might flow from a 'broader awareness of the effects of untrammelled capitalism'. This also suggests the need for macro-analysis of oppression and disadvantage and attention to national and international policies and frameworks as well as local contextual knowledge and initiatives (Ife, 2001b). These suggestions require social professionals to go beyond the implementation of selected social policies (which many see as their role) to playing a greater part in identifying gaps and malfunctioning in national and international policies, and developing their skills in advocacy and lobbying. Healy

(2001) makes the point that, increasingly, national policies are 'rarely purely domestic in impact' (p. 220) but have international implications, either because they impact directly or because of 'social policy emulation'. So for instance, in the first case, it can be argued that US policies, as reflected in the 'war on drugs' and the 'war on terror', have had implications for welfare and immigration policies around the world.

With regard to social policy emulation (the attempted transfer of policies), reforms resulting from the 1990 National Health Service and Community Care Act in the UK gave rise to changes in both organizational contexts and forms of practice for British social workers. The shift to 'care management' (mainly in relation to social work with vulnerable adults) was considerably influenced by US thinking and in turn was seen as influencing (negatively) developing forms of social services and styles of intervention in Greece (personal communication). Community care has also been taken as a case example by Harris and Chou (2001, p. 161), who suggest that 'the global economy will continue to act as a major constraint on social welfare development'; that welfare discourses will be increasingly 'globalized'; but that local policy and practice will nevertheless be influenced by national contexts and 'mediated by country-specific institutional arrangements' – a process they describe as 'glocalization'. Thus, they see community care as an example of a global discourse but one which is differentiated when examined at national levels, for example, in Taiwan and the UK.

Additionally, it has been suggested (Healy, 2001) that social professionals are increasingly developing local services and interventions in the context of 'global social regulation, redistribution or provision of social resources'. For instance, the national welfare developments of some countries, such as Peru or South Africa, have periodically been affected by requirements imposed by the IMF or World Bank. Countries of the South are also particularly vulnerable to changes in global trading arrangements and are reliant on the 'goodwill' of powerful governments (for instance, in relation to proposals for debt relief being suggested by some member states of G8 at the time of writing); or the policies of INGOs (confronted by more demands on their resources than can be met by the donations of distant publics or sympathetic governments). However, at a global level, bodies like UNICEF, UNDP and the World Food Programme do raise money from wealthy nations to assist in establishing relief and development activities in poorer countries, demonstrating both the redistribution and provision elements of social policy. It can be noted here that projects established either directly by these bodies or through INGOs (following consultation with national governments and often in conjunction with local communities) sometimes employ social professionals from the locality or foreign nationals working for an INGO.

We would also add that the policies framing social work activities may be regional, and not necessarily aimed exclusively or particularly at social professionals. For example, the EU, in efforts not only to promote worker mobility but also to 'regulate' standards, issued a Directive in 1989 concerning recognition of qualifications across a range of occupational groups which has become a benchmark for the social professions, regionally. Thus, most European countries had already established, or have since implemented, education and training programmes which met the criteria of a qualification gained after at least three years higher education as the basis for national registration (which can be seen not only as an exclusionary device but also as a mechanism for ensuring public accountability). It seems likely that the impetus to achieve regional standards will also assist social professionals from some countries to meet standards required elsewhere in the world and we return to the issue of professional mobility and 'global standards' in Chapter 9.

Meanwhile, the IFSW policy statement (after preliminary material defining globalization and stressing the 'integrated' nature of the world community) suggests that social workers are, by definition, most likely to engage with people who are adversely affected by the processes of globalization and proposes that they should draw on human rights perspectives in formulating their analyses and responses to the impact of globalization. The supporting material describes an approach to globalization that includes five elements with which, the Federation suggests, social professionals should be engaged at local and international levels:

1. ensuring the availability of universal education for children up to 16 years of age;

2. promoting employment opportunities (particularly for those likely to be discriminated against in an 'open' labour market);
3. lobbying for and contributing to social protection (fiscal) programmes for people who are unable to support themselves (e.g., due to age or incapacity);
4. protecting children through supporting and implementing policy measures based on the UN Convention on the Rights of the Child; and
5. developing all new initiatives on the basis of citizen participation and empowerment approaches.

We discuss the issues raised in this statement in greater depth in the following chapter.

Pursuing the question, 'why might issues to do with globalization matter to social professionals?' Irving and Payne (2005) suggest three reasons to do with 'knowledge transfer, the labour market and cultural awareness' (p. 154) and these also provide a useful framework for considering the relevance of globalization to social work. For instance, in relation to knowledge transfer, policies and practices in relation to 'family group conferences' in the childcare field have become increasingly widespread in northern countries and these are recognized as emanating from service developments in New Zealand/Aotorea to respect the cultural values of the Maori population. Fox (2005) has also pointed out how similar ideas from First Nation people in Canada can be recognized in policies and practices developing in the UK juvenile justice system. Also in the childcare field, an increased emphasis on kinship care initially in the US and more recently in UK services owes much to practices in the Afro-Caribbean communities in both countries and can be related back to African traditions (Lyons, 2006).

Issues of transferable knowledge also arise within the context of labour market mobility, and it is suggested that while social work is still predominantly recognized as a local activity (and, as noted, one which must be culturally relevant), increased numbers of social workers are themselves migrating, and requiring knowledge and skills to function in an international and cross-cultural context. (The phenomenon of international labour mobility among social professionals is further discussed in the concluding chapter.)

In some respects the need for cultural awareness (and more proactive strategies to address discrimination and oppression) by social professionals is not new, nor is it necessarily particular to the conditions of globalization. For instance, the New Zealand policies of biculturalism had their origins in the 1980s and it was in that decade also that some UK schools of social work began to develop anti-racist training (in the wider context of acknowledgement of continuing discrimination in a multi-cultural society) (see for instance Dominelli and Thomas Bernard, 2003). The need to develop opportunities for inter-cultural learning and anti-oppressive practices has also been recognized subsequently in countries such as Germany and the Czech Republic, in relation to the Turkish minority population or the Roma people, respectively. However, it seems likely that globalization has increased the scale and complexity of migration, and that social workers will increasingly need to utilize cross-cultural knowledge and skills to engage effectively with minority populations in local communities or across national borders (Lyons, 2006).

Concluding Comments

Globalization has important, and some would say overriding, economic dimensions. However, there are other aspects which also have significance for the lives of vulnerable populations and thus for the roles and responsibilities of social professionals. Pugh and Gould (2000, p. 125) have identified fragmentation of old arrangements; damaging effects upon general living standards and economic security; and pressure to reduce expenditure on welfare (in order to be competitive) as consequences of the various processes associated with globalization which are relevant to social workers. Dominelli and Hoogvelt (1996) suggested that globalization has influenced a process of technocratization and resource reduction in social services; and we suggest that these processes can be linked to wider trends, including 'delayering', 'downsizing' and 'outsourcing' frequently found in other forms of organization, and impacting on people's employment opportunities. We would add the tensions associated with pressures towards cultural homogenization inherent in globalization relative to the desire to maintain national or ethnic identities as having particular implications for social professional activity in many places.

There has been some analysis in the policy field of the consequences of globalization for welfare systems but to date relatively less empirically based material about how globalization has impacted on the activities of social workers. However, we espouse a view gaining wider support that social problems are becoming increasingly globalized and that, consequently, social workers (whether practising and developing services locally or involved in the development of trans-national or international policies and provisions) must take account of events, institutions and policies beyond national and even regional borders. The need for a new international orientation in social work has been advocated by a number of authors, including from Australia, Sweden, the UK, and US (e.g., Elliot *et al.*, 1990; Hokenstad and Midgley, 1997; Lyons, 1999; Ramanathan and Link; 1999; Healy, 2001; Ife, 2001a; Ahmadi, 2003) and is supported in some countries through requirements regarding qualifying education (e.g., by the Council on Social Work Education in the US), as well as through the statements of international professional associations. Penna *et al.* (2000, p. 109) identified the need for a 'dual configuration' (to both the local and the global level of policies) by social workers, while Ife's (2001b) call for a global-local dialect also resonates.

A number of the authors identified above have joined others in calling for attention to macro as well as micro analyses; and to the need for preventive and community development strategies as well as more individualized and reactive interventions which characterize social work in many Western countries. Reference to international conventions and standards have been identified as useful frameworks, both for viewing local developments and for shaping international initiatives. We would also stress the need to recognize the interdependence between nations associated with globalization; the different (but sometimes related) implications for social professionals in different locations; and the ways in which social professionals can be seen both as having their own areas of expertise while also sharing concerns with other occupational groups and with civil movements associated with social development and with the promotion of human rights and social justice. The technological revolution (another facet of globaliz-ation) has opened up important opportunities for social workers to seek allies and work collaboratively at the international level as well as at local levels, in relation to a wide range of areas, including those discussed in greater depth in Part II of this book.

3 Towards a New Equality: Social Divisions in a Global Context

Introduction

Midgley (1997b, p. 19) suggests '(i)f social work is to survive as a profession, it needs to transcend its narrow concern with remedial practice and promote activities that make a positive contribution to social well-being'. He further suggests that this may be established through a development perspective, which we would endorse. However, here we draw more on sociological perspectives to analyse 'difference' and the effort to promote more egalitarian relationships.

What is the new equality? How do we see others and ourselves? How does this reflect in our actions and inactions in a globalized era? These are the central questions of this chapter. Division of people based on gender, race, ethnicity, nationality and religion is a common theme in all societies and differentiation takes place at the micro, mezzo and macro levels. However, the degree to which people identify with or distinguish themselves from different groupings has become disparate in post-modern society.

Within broader debates of sociological theory, the erosion of the nation state, both politically and socially, has complicated the search for a single unifying (sociological) theory. Further, globalization has created new forums for social movements that have pushed the agenda of social justice and human rights into local and global arenas, while at the same time exacerbating divisions due to material inequalities. As a result, attempting to find a cohesive and single sociological definition, much less theory, that encompasses the diversity of a globalized society is increasingly meaningless. With that in mind, social professionals must look at both social division and social cohesion and embrace concepts such as capabilities and tolerance in order to make sense of the world they are studying and realize that these concepts are dynamic and require constant interrogation. Bearing in mind the inevitability of multiple subjective points of view, social professionals should engage with these various opinions, while recognizing the dangers intrinsic in creating all-encompassing theories that are strong on compromise, yet questionable in substance.

The following chapter analyses social divisions from an international perspective, and explores methods for tackling the disparities that impact on individuals and communities. We will first discuss some of the building blocks of social theory, social division and social cohesion and how we conceptualize 'the other'. From there, we explore different perspectives on power and hierarchies, preparing us for a brief discussion of the ramifications of equalities and inequalities. Turning our attention to issues of social justice and human rights, we look at some of the current dialogue for working with the *new equality*, including *trust*, *accountability* and *participation*, but we also explore rights-based and capabilities approaches. Finally, we conclude by discussing how the concept of a new equality affects social professionals within international social work.

Understanding Social Division and Social Cohesion

Division and cohesion have significant implications for how social workers conceptualize and place issues within a social context. Further, this conceptualization impacts on the formation of strategies that work with social division and best maximize social action and social cohesion. Appreciating the underlying power differences at all levels of society and between nations and regions is therefore important when attempting any social intervention – whether at the individual, family, community, national or supranational level. Working to increase tolerance within cosmopolitan communities is an evermore important task for social professionals. Some argue for the need to understand multiculturalism and provide culturally and ethnically diverse practice (see for instance Lum, 2000), while others argue for avoiding implicit and explicit racist practices and developing overtly anti-racist strategies

(Dominelli, 1997, 2002). Human rights, social divisions, power and hierarchy all have a common link forged by how we conceptualize others and ourselves.

One way to examine the mechanics of difference and solidarity is to deconstruct the notion of identity. Various fields within the social sciences can help us to clarify the concept of identity and how it factors in the conceptualization of social division and cohesion. Identity provides us with an understanding of who we are (as individuals or as members of groups) and how we are constituted, as well as what makes us distinct from others. Identity is a tool or a label that utilizes the precepts of sameness and difference to create the foundations for both social division and social cohesion. In this sense, identity is the interrelationship or tension between an individual's agency and societal structure. Identity gives us a link between how one sees oneself and how others see us (Woodward, 2000).

The 'other' takes many forms. We can see it reflected in differences in gender, race, age, physical and mental abilities, ethnicity, class, religion, political affiliation and so on but it is also evident in the food we eat, the places we live, the way we play, the work we do, the learning we participate in, and how we get from place to place. Some groupings are inherited and fixed, but others are not. For instance, whether we are meat-eaters or vegetarians may be inherited and fixed in some cultures but not in others; and there may be a certain animosity between vegetarians and meat-eaters in some societies. Anthropologists and developmental psychologists would say that it is within human nature to try to create and be part of the 'in-group'. This, by default, automatically creates an out-group. We do not seem to tire of creating these divisions. A similar concept, although more intimately tied to access to resources, is social inclusion and exclusion. The struggle between these groupings is what results in the creation or definition of the 'other'.

However, within groups, individuals possess multiple identity facets related to nationality, religion, ethnicity, class, work status, family/community position and so on. Indeed, Oakley (2002) discusses the difficulty in defining self as only a gender, a sexual orientation, a career and so on. Each element adds to a cohesive whole, and although any one facet may be dominant in specific situations, it becomes inaccurate or partial if used to label an individual under a single heading. This is particularly important when elements of identity appear contradictory.

Our cultural identity is one form of group identification, where we generally share beliefs and behaviours (ideas, habits and customs). An important part of our cultural identity is defined by juxtaposing our culture in opposition to the *other*. It helps us to delineate our differences and bonds us to people with similar characteristics. The same juxtaposition and delineation take place with all aspects of our multiple identities, finally arriving at the mix of characteristics that define our individuality.

Movements in many Western countries towards multiculturalism have partially addressed the multiplicity of divisions within society, potentially failing to grasp the inherent plurality evident within individuals. This is particularly apparent in countries or areas that promote either egalitarian or 'melting pot' views. In addressing some of the challenges facing the cultivation of ethnically diverse practice, Lum (2000, p. 74) suggests, 'To bridge the gap between individuality and collectivity, social work must incorporate a cosmological orientation that accounts for the importance of family, spirituality, and nature.'

However, identities are not fixed but dynamic, responding to the socio-political and psychological environments in which individuals find themselves. This fluidity raises important problems when considering identity politics such as racism, sexism and other stereotyping. These 'isms' are not necessarily fixed or uniform, for instance Dominelli (1997) has suggested that there are three components of racism: personal, institutional and cultural. At different times in our lives, different aspects of our identities come to the fore. For instance, one's skin colour may only be relevant when one becomes a visible minority or when one is in the presence of visible minorities. In other words, when an individual becomes the 'other', their identity is solidified as a result of being different. John-Baptiste (2001) argues that fluidity (or hybridity) is simply a renaming of earlier forms of colour-blindness or assimilation and calls for an end to the euro-centric chains that still operate in social work. He argues that ' "Beyond racial divides" must incorporate the potential for broadening practice possibilities to include interventions based on aspects of cultural specificity that assist in the understanding of definitions of social well-being and distress' (p. 277).

Laing (1990, pp. 25–26) stated that '(e)ach of us is the other to others'. One example of how this can manifest itself through identity politics was offered by DeBeauvoir who studied the issue of racism between the 'white' and 'black' populations in the US in 1948. DeBeauvoir argued that the racial tension present in the US was manifestly a white issue, not a black issue, because it was the majority population conceptualizing how the minority population was different (cited in Cord, 2003). This may be increasingly obvious today, but at the time it was revolutionary. Further, this has particular contemporary relevance when we consider events such the destruction caused by Hurricane Katrina in New Orleans (in 2005) and the subsequent eruption of perceived institutional and personal racial bias in the provision of aid. Put simply, racism exists in the mind of the racist. However, the effects do not only exist in the mind of individuals or groups. Dominelli (1997) has argued that redressing racism requires participation of everyone, recognizing his or her differing relationship to racism. For instance, in Britain she suggested that 'white people have a different relationship to racism from black people' (p. 15). Despite equal opportunity policy and rhetoric, racism (through both indifference and hostility) is endemic in social work and the wider world (Dominelli, 1997, p. xv). In contemporary society, this *us and them* duality has been institutionalized. Equal opportunity exercises have attempted to address these differences. However, this will be discussed in more detail later on.

As social workers, having an appreciation of the concept of identity is of vital importance. It allows us to appreciate the effects of labelling and to understand when and how people begin to identify with those labels. Social professionals have long recognized the danger of labelling, not least because labels are rarely accurate (Laing, 1990). According to Laing (1990, p. 11) '(t)here is little truth between labels and "social reality"'. For example, a young person who has been labelled as anti-social may grow to fit that role – or he or she may not. As pointed out by Szasz (1970), classifying someone's behaviour with a label can be a form of social control, and can also incur a loss of dignity.

Lum (2000) suggests that social professionals need specialist knowledge/training in multicultural practice, with competency-based practice founded on cultural awareness, knowledge acquisition, skill development and inductive learning. Gutiérrez and Lewis (1999, p. 12) suggested that social work approaches to social diversity and oppression have included three main types: ethno-centric (whose main goal is to reject identity in favour of dominant values and behaviours), ethnic-sensitive (whose main goal is to encourage a sense of pride in identity, taking into account individual needs of diverse groups) and ethno-conscious (whose main goal is to create affirming social structures, removing barriers to 'full development').

The Impact of Globalization on Identity

To understand how the conceptualization of identity in post-modern society takes place, it is important to appreciate the impact of globalization. In the last chapter we saw how globalization is overwhelmingly seen as an economic process. The language of globalization is steeped in contentious geopolitical labels or global divisions such as West–East, North–South, advanced/industrialized–rural/agrarian, capitalist/communist; developing–developed–undeveloped; first–second–third world. More interestingly, over a decade ago, O'Gorman (1992) split the world economically into one-third of the 'haves' and two-thirds of the 'have-nots', reminding us that while these 'labels' apply significantly to particular societies there are also 'haves' in poor societies and 'have-nots' even among the most affluent populations. As poverty creeps up the development agenda, this is an interesting way to envision the world because it illustrates the networks of people across nation state boundaries. Glissant (1996) argued that the increasing variants of contact made between cultures across these boundaries inevitably lead to creolization, a process to which, he argues, we are all subject. However, Vergès advises caution and hypothesizes that 'processes of creolization will exist alongside other processes produced by contact and conflict, such as indifferent multiculturalism, apartheid, segregation and the creation of ethnic enclaves' (cited in Gane, 2004, p. 195).

Another approach to the conceptualization of division and cohesion of people during the process of identity formation has been proposed by Castells. Castells (1998) talks about the rise of

the *Fourth World* or *information capitalism*. Information capitalism is the '(p)rocesses of global social change induced by interaction between networks and identities'. According to Castells,
forming new networks through new technology across nations
and cultures creates the Fourth World. This will inevitably lead
to multiple 'black holes' (his term) of disenfranchised individuals
linked by an inability to access these new networks. These black
holes, he argues, will be a result of poverty and will only lead
to more poverty (pp. 166–167): they will be linked to issues of
drug addiction, mental illness, delinquency, incarceration, and
illegality; and will lead to increased social exclusion and global
criminality. Social workers therefore have a role in ensuring that
their clients have access to networks (and other resources) based
on the use of ICT.

Power, Hierarchies and Social Capital

So far, we have examined how individual identities are complex,
fluid and influenced by external forces that exist on a number of
different levels from the micro to the macro. However, what is
missing is a change agent, a reason for identity to be influenced or
even formulated in the first place. For some, power and hierarchies
encapsulate that change agent. However, power is not necessarily
a negative force and can be used as a positive agent for change.

The French philosopher Foucault has revolutionized the way
we think about power and hierarchies. His theory of micro-power
maintains that power is crucial in all of our interactions. Previously
(a euro-centric view of) power was seen as a hierarchy with the
white European male at the top, but Foucault believed that power
struggles were endemic in our everyday lives and interactions and
therefore more complex than as represented in straightforward
hierarchies (Rabinov, 1991).

Power has been part of our social fabric for so long that the
act of obeying has become almost instinctive. In the 1950s, a
psychologist, Milgram, explored the impact of power on 'normal'
individuals when conducting his famous and controversial experi-
ments on obedience and authority in the US. Participants believed
they were being segregated into teachers and learners (the learners
were in fact actors). Teachers were instructed to ask learners a

series of questions. When learners answered incorrectly, teachers were ordered to inflict electrical shocks on the learners with increasing intensity. The experiment was set up to test the conflict between an individual's conscious ethics and morals and the degree to which they would obey someone in a position of power. It found that two-thirds of 'teachers' followed the instructions to the end, even though they believed they were inflicting significant pain on the other person. Milgram helped to show that power, even when it is ill-used, has a potent ability to nullify individual senses of right and wrong (Blass, 2004).

Subsequently, Arendt (1970) looked at the power of consensus within pre-war Nazi Germany and made strong arguments for the existence of an 'I was only doing what I was told' mentality. She formulated theories of how 'normal' men could be turned into 'weapons' of war. This was a powerful theory that looked at social cohesion and its potentially destructive force when influenced by a source of power seen to be unquestionable.

The work of feminist researchers has also greatly influenced our conception of power and hierarchies. Through the deconstruction of accepted sociological 'norms' of hegemonic, euro-centric, male-based theories of social construction, these researchers were able to question the status quo. Theories that were assumed to function in an egalitarian way were in fact shown to be further entrenching power hierarchies within and between societies. The actual and/or assumed changes in (patriarchal) power structures as a result of feminist movements have been experienced differently in different societies (for further discussion see, for instance, Pease and Pringle, 2001).

Power can also be examined between networks, as operating laterally rather than hierarchically. This relates to a concept that is gaining wider recognition, namely 'social capital'. Social capital has different (and sometimes conflicting) meanings depending on the source. The central premise of social capital is that social networks have value. It was modelled upon Bourdieu's notion of symbolic capital (Bourdieu, 1977), but was also discussed by Loury (1977). As previously stated, we define our identities through identification and differentiation. It is these identifications and differences that act as the fuel for social capital. Social capital refers to the collective value of all 'social networks' (who people know) and the inclinations that arise from these networks to do things for each other ('norms of reciprocity') (Putnam, 2001). Benefits associated with this concept include trust, reciprocity, cooperation and community. Social capital is dependent on social networks and information flow, collective action and broader identities, and encompasses ideas of inclusion and exclusion. It is often thought of as the social glue that binds us together and is one way to envision social cohesion in an increasingly globalized context. When such social cohesion is threatened or eliminated, for instance by natural disasters or disease outbreaks, social professionals may be called upon to intervene. We revisit the notions of power and social capital when we examine the growth in research and practice of participative approaches later in this chapter.

Equalities and Inequalities

As we have mentioned, the divisions within society are many and have become more complicated as globalization forces us into contact with new ideas and different concepts of identity. In essence, we face a growing list of 'others'. Race, gender, ethnicity, class, wealth, religion, education, technological understanding, and language form just some of the factors that influence individual access to resources and power. Inequality is brought to life when we see that the life expectancy at birth in 2002 was 34 per cent in Sierra Leone and 81.9 per cent in Japan (WHO, 2004b) and where the gross national income per capita with purchasing power parity is $490 in Sierra Leone and $35,840 in Norway (UNFPA, 2004). Unlike a 'loss' (of affluence, power, status and so on) as discussed in the following chapter, this is a case of millions of people 'never having had'. However, in a new world where identities are complicated, fluid and highly mobile, how do we define, much less work with, the concept of equality? And how can poverty eradication schemes, as mentioned in Chapter 1, actually work?

We can see material inequalities throughout the world and in any community, but particular groups have additional difficulty accessing either resources or power to attain equality. These include children and elders, people with physical or mental illness, and those with physical disabilities or learning difficulties. Additionally, women generally have fewer assets, greater reproductive burdens, less power and status, less mobility and less defence against violence (see, for example, the effects of HIV/AIDS on women in Chapter 8). Similarly, people referred to as the underclass or socially excluded often live on the margins of society and lack equal access to the services and resources that enable them to exercise their human rights.

Perhaps one of the best known and recent examples of institutionalized inequality existed under South African apartheid, where social divisions were codified in law. Even after the implementation of full democracy, the entrenched social norms make true equality a distant dream for many South Africans. South Africa still has one of the most unequal economies, with 51.2 per cent of the economy reserved for the richest 10 per cent and 30 per cent for the poorest 40 per cent (Noyoo, 2004). More importantly, in an identity context, the divide is 'neatly' visual between black and white (ibid.). Social unrest is clear as the crime rates continue to shock, although the murder rate has fallen (from a high in 1994 of 70 in 10,000 to 39 in 10,000 in 2000). Noyoo, argues that social workers were key in overthrowing the apartheid era, but have now lost their voice in efforts to realize the aspirations of the democracy initiated in 1994.

So why do these situations persist? Arguably, many of us live in meritocracies but these are still divided between the deserving haves and the undeserving have-nots. This view supports the belief that those living in poverty deserve their fate, or that their poverty is a result of their own personal shortcomings. Similarly, those with wealth have earned this due to hard work and wise decisions. This division has proved attractive because it is both simplistic and exonerates the haves from making sacrifices on behalf of the have-nots. Such beliefs allow the haves to watch dispassionately from the sidelines while disasters such as AIDS, famine and war ravage those who apparently lack the initiative to better themselves. Such a standpoint seems antithetical to the underlying ethos of (international) social work, at least one that is built upon the bedrock of social justice. British Prime Minister Blair, along with Giddens, advocates the 'third way', which seeks to find a balance between equality and meritocracy (Giddens, 2002). Whether the inherent contradiction in this approach is workable is yet to be seen.

Impact: Social Justice and Human Rights

Social justice and human rights can both be seen as frameworks for social action that counter the negative effects of inequality, power imbalances and social divisions. Social work is a practical profession with a strong value system, arguably one predicated on social justice. According to the American National Association of Social Workers (NASW) '(s)ocial justice is the view that everyone deserves equal economic, political and social rights and opportunities. Social workers aim to open the doors of access and opportunity for everyone, particularly those in greatest need' (NASW, 2004).

Social Justice

Social justice is based on various social contract theories, many of which endorse an ideal of social welfare (including human rights) provided by government. Put simply, it is a contract people make with their government for mutual benefit (Nussbaum, 2000a). Dominelli (2002), writing about anti-racist social work, suggests that

> Social workers have a responsibility to...(bring) to public notice the strengths of those who battle to transcend social exclusion, to work to empower those who are engulfed by the weight of circumstances in which they are embedded. Promoting social justice and human development in an unequal world provides the *raison d'être of social work practice*.... (p. 4)

The fair and equal distribution of wealth and resources to all people are at the core of social justice, but this also entails the equitable distribution of burdens. Those promoting social justice therefore are fighting for the eradication of poverty and biased, racist policies.

Discussions about social justice often include reference to equal opportunities and these constitute a contentious aspect of this theory. Opponents of social justice often argue that equal opportunity policies are contradictory because they can promote favouritism, while colour-blind policies and practice can conceal racism (Dominelli, 1997). Dominelli (2002) calls for anti-oppressive practice as a framework for egalitarian relations. Using employment-hiring practices as an example, equal opportunity policies often allow a greater chance of employment to groups who are less represented in the given field, possibly putting more weight on minority status than qualifications. This of course disallows a meritocracy. The counter argument is that in order to rectify historical power imbalances and unjust 'isms', enforced equal opportunity policies constitute a necessary mechanism to achieve balance and are one way to counteract poverty.

Poverty, as seen from the point of view of social justice, is antithetical to human rights. Every human being should have equal access to the same resources and world wealth. It is their right. Social justice, according to Tyler *et al.* (1997), can be separated into two main schools of thought: identity-based or resource-based. Identity-based social justice posits that 'people interact with others to feel good about themselves' (p. 185) and that these social interactions are at the core of injustice as well as justice. Resource-based social justice speculates that 'people enter into social interactions to gain resources for themselves' (p. 181) and that these interactions are the core of injustices and justices.

Turning to the legal framework, there are three main avenues of social justice: distributive, procedural and retributive justice. Distributive justice refers to the assurance of just results or outcomes and can be exemplified by pay disputes and equal opportunity debates. Procedural justice refers to the construction and support of fair procedures and good governance. The concept of good governance has formed an important framework for development in recent years, creating a new avenue for donors such as the World Bank and IMF to engage with recipient governments to ensure that development assistance has a greater impact and long-term effect. Retributive justice refers to fair retribution or punishment (Tyler *et al.*, 1997). It is the most common form of criminal justice, and encapsulates the idea of imprisoning lawbreakers, as both punishment and protection for the population at large. At its most extreme, we see the use of the death penalty in some countries, including the US and China. All three avenues are relevant to service development by social professionals in the West, as well as to social and community development programmes in countries of the South.

In the context of social welfare and criminal justice systems, there has been increasing international focus on a fourth area, that of restorative justice (Lawson and Katz, 2004). Restorative justice is an approach borrowed from cultural and justice-based practices, for instance in New Zealand and Canada (Fox, 2005). It is changing the way that some police forces are dealing with crime, particularly juvenile crime. The idea is that perpetrators are asked to repair damage with their victims through face-to-face, safely mediated conferences, where the victim has the opportunity to discuss the impact of the crime (e.g., loss of property, emotional burden). In conferences, a jointly created restitution agreement may be created instead of detention. If it is effective, it can not only deter recidivism, but also help young people understand the greater implications of their crimes (Lawson and Katz, 2004). The impact can be threefold: reconciliation, reparation and transformation (ibid.). Another use of restorative justice principles and practices can be seen at the macro level, for instance in the *Truth and Reconciliation* trials in South Africa and Rwanda.

Capabilities Approach

The capabilities approach is related to human rights and promotes greater equality. Both Sen (1982) and Nussbaum (2000b) focused their attention on individual social agency while discussing human capabilities. Sen (1982, 1999) sees human capital as being the skills, knowledge and effort needed to be productive, human capability as focusing on the ability to add value to personhood, and 'functionings' as the things people accomplish. A capabilities approach can be thought of as understanding the *whys* of people's actions. This entails not only understanding the outcomes ('functionings'), but also taking into account the process of obtaining the outcome. This can include the injustices of procedure; the freedom of choice of the individual; and the structural or systemic inequalities. Sen (1999) suggests that in the current global climate, we should enable people to have space within socio-economic development to create their own personal capabilities (or actions which they value), regardless of what is dictated by society. As an example of a capabilities approach, imagine two young men living on the street. One of them has chosen to live on the street because he does not like the constraints of conformist society and feels more comfortable and free living on the streets. The other man has no money, has lost his job and his place of residence. The two young men have had the same outcome and live under the same welfare policies, but the reasons behind their choices are different. A capabilities approach recognizes the different motivations and provides services better tailored to their individual needs, using a framework of both tolerance and participation.

Nussbaum (2000b) also espouses a capabilities approach, but her focus is on the centrality of gender differences in international politics and social justice. She also added value to the approach by advancing the idea of the 'humanness' of a capabilities approach, by recognizing the importance of human dignity. For both Sen and Nussbaum, a capabilities approach is an alternative position from which to understand welfare. Nussbaum's capabilities approach also postulates a basic set of entitlements, not unlike human rights (2000a).

Human Rights

Human rights can be seen as a set of unifying social principles, an antidote to a multitude of discourses of division. As such, they form an important toolkit that allows us to explore how the negative aspects of social division, such as institutional and endemic inequalities, can be countered or addressed directly. Much effort has been made by organizations such as the UN to arrive at universally applicable and inalienable human rights that form the foundation for our understanding of how humans should socially interact. However, as a toolkit, human rights are only as good as our ability to utilize them.

The concept of a universal set of human rights is not without its critics. Some reject the idea as a leftover of the imperialist world order. Others point out that post-modernism, with its multiple voices and fragmented world view, has no room for universals (a view discussed by Ife, 2001a). Further, human rights, especially as denoted by the UN Declaration of Human Rights (1948), are criticized for their Western-industrialized cultural bias or their degree of generality and difficulties around implementation. As a result, some regions have enacted their own declarations. For instance, African leaders came together and made two significant human rights charters, taking into account their unique African characteristics – *The African Charter on Human and Peoples' Rights* (1981) and the *African Charter on the Rights and Welfare of the Child (1999)* (Sewpaul, 1994). In Europe, individuals of the many countries represented in Council of Europe (a geographically larger and longer-established grouping than the European Union) have for some time been able to bring cases of denial of human rights (as represented in the European Convention on Human Rights [1950]) to the European Court of Human Rights and many countries have more recently established national legislation in this area.

However, what constitutes an inalienable human right is also contested. There is little consensus on how human rights are defined, or which human rights have precedence, for instance, individual or collective rights; or economic, social, cultural, political or civil rights. Indeed our understanding of what constitutes a human right has adapted and grown over time. Ife (2001a) envisioned three generations of human rights that have led to our present understanding. The first generation looked at civil and political rights and had its roots in the eighteenth-century Enlightenment period. This generation of rights is practised through advocacy, and has shaped many modern legal systems. The second generation includes economic, social and cultural rights. These were influenced by feminism and are practised in a variety of settings, including social work. The third generation of human rights attempts to present a set of universalities, largely seen in broad based initiatives (ibid.) such as the Millennium Development Goals (Sewpaul, 2004) and Global Action Against Poverty. Interestingly, the generations have grown to encompass more philosophical areas of social interaction, as well as increasing in scale of application, so that they are designed to apply to all living humans.

The third generation of human rights have been born from a century that saw wars of incredible scale, as well as the dismantling of global empires. While noble in their goals, it is important to question the usefulness and viability of anything universal. The act of drafting universal human rights (based on consensus) can have the effects of silencing dissenting voices, ignoring diverse points of view and creating watered-down sets of laws that are easily agreed to and also easily sidestepped. The UN, as the driving force behind the creation of these principles, has earned the reputation of being tokenistic and powerless. 'Human rights, which we venerate today, are more often gestured at than they are seriously argued for' (O'Neill, 2002). If we take, for example, the case of the most basic right, the right to life, many states have enacted various caveats to this 'right'. Such caveats have implications for policies related to birth control (in the context of disagreement about when life begins) as well as to assisted suicide or capital punishment, at the other end of the life cycle, giving rise to variations in state and national laws which have proved to be controversial at both local and international levels.

As suggested, universal human rights are, by their nature, generalizations. As a result, it was recognized after the Declaration of Human Rights in 1948 that it was necessary to specify the rights of particular groups. To date, various sets of rights for particular groups exist, including children, women, and trafficked persons (see also Chapters 6 and 7). Manderson (2004) has examined the need for a convention to protect the rights and conditions that determine the well-being of the estimated 600 million people with disabilities worldwide and 80 per cent of whom are living in resource-poor societies and are particularly disadvantaged in terms of access to health, education and employment.

In addition, there are also implications for how individuals interact in a society dominated by inalienable rights. '. . . the underlying difficulty of any Declaration of Rights is that it assumes a passive view of human life and citizenship. Rights answer the questions "What are my entitlements?" or "What should I get?" They don't answer the active citizen's question "What should I do?" ' (O'Neill, 2002). Ife and Fiske (2006) argue that an unequal emphasis is placed on articulating human rights, relative to responsibilities. Furthermore, human rights cannot be and are not granted in communities or nations where human duties do not underpin their success, such as in countries where there are high rates of corruption or autocracy. Perhaps what is needed is a corresponding Declaration of Human Duties (ibid.).

Interestingly, in the *African Charter on the Rights and Welfare of the Child* (1999) the child's rights are set in the context of their responsibilities to the family.

Human rights can provide a useful set of principles important in ensuring social development agendas are adhered to, but they are not without limitations. Having said that, they provide a foundation and a focus for the formulation of international social work ethics (Reichert, 2003; Ife, 2001a); and also lay the basis for rights-based practice approaches, which move them from theoretical tenets to practical implementations. Ife and Fiske (2006) argue that employing a community-development perspective could help in the realization of human rights.

The Rights-Based Approach

The concept of human rights aims to overcome divisiveness and sectarianism and unite different people by codifying a universal human value system. One result of this has been the emergence of a new development ethos called a rights-based approach. The key aspect of a rights-based approach is the right to participate, which includes the right to vote and the ability to advocate for one's own rights. This approach turns our understanding of development from one of a 'charity–benefactor' relationship (or alms giving), to one where access to services and resources are viewed as basic human rights in themselves and inherently involve participation. The result is an approach that empowers the people who are participating in 'development', raising their status to the same level as those in developed countries. It is founded on the premise that all human beings are equal and should be accorded certain human rights, often pointing to the UN Declaration of Human Rights as the basis for its methods. Women's rights and other 'autonomous' rights movements have inspired the development of rights-based approaches. Rights-based approaches have helped to drive debates on legitimacy of action, power hierarchies and accountability, especially as these issues relate back to development agencies such as the World Bank.

Social workers often advocate on behalf of those whose rights have been abused or ignored, such as children, disabled people or prisoners. Framing social work as a human rights profession has opened new avenues, as well as creating a new form of identity as a global citizen. A rights-based approach sees individuals as citizens, not stakeholders, clients or beneficiaries of welfare. The 'client' is discursive and implies a different professional meaning than citizen or partner. Similarly, development agencies are beginning to view people in developing countries as partners and citizens, not faceless recipients of aid. This change has opened many debates, as a change in power hierarchies is implicit in the adoption of a rights-based approach. As such, development practitioners, including social workers, have had to be prepared to meaningfully share power and control. This is a significant change.

Many social movements employ a narrow definition of civil and political rights, but a more holistic approach includes less tangible aspects such as cultural and social rights, which are seen as interdependent. Within, for example, the EU and North America the rights that are stressed are individual rights, whereas other areas stress community and societal rights and responsibilities above those of the individual. In a broader view (socio-economic) development itself may be considered a legally binding right (although many governments do not subscribe to this view). Finding consensus has proved difficult and possibly not desirable. However, this does bring up other interesting questions: which rights supersede others and more significantly whose rights are more important? For example, are the rights of the community or the individual more important? When might the rights of children take precedence over the rights of parents? The new rights-based approach can offer the potential for positive change, but some fear its impotence. For instance, many social change agents, including agencies that have helped formulate what is meant by a rights-based approach, seem unable or unwilling to put into practice what they champion. They appear to have adopted the terminology, but have not fully implemented, or even considered, their meaning, and made the organizational and practice adaptations which should follow their acceptance (Eyben, 2003). In a 1997 study (ongoing), Wallace criticized British NGOs as degrading their ties with grass-roots organizations in the South and reverting to rhetoric (cited in Sunderland, 2004).

As an example, we can examine government policies pertaining to prostitution. In many countries prostitution or prostitution-related offences are illegal, although many such offences are thought of as victimless crimes. This makes it an interesting example through which to juxtapose the rights of the individual against those of the community. Governments have to tackle several complex issues: Do the individual rights to choose to sell sex weigh up against the (alleged) risks to public safety and public nuisance associated with prostitution? Complicating matters, there is the question of whether prostitution is a choice at all or whether underlying social structures exist that narrow the choices of people engaged in selling sex. Of course, the issue is complicated by the violence or addictions that are sometimes associated with sex work. As a result, it exemplifies the potentials of a capabilities approach, where each case is unique and attempting to identify universalities is not helpful. From the point of view of a human-rights approach, the focus would be on ensuring that equal rights were given to sex workers and that they were at the heart of the activism/advocacy and therefore empowered to speak on their own behalf (see Chapter 6).

A powerful example of a rights-based approach in practice can be seen in Canada's struggle with domestic violence. Domestic violence has not traditionally been seen as an issue for the state, but rather a domestic issue, a private matter. However, activists were pushing for legislative and grassroots change in how domestic violence was seen and dealt with. The crux of this argument was that it is an individual's right not to experience violence. In Canada huge gains have been made in the fight against domestic violence (Women's International Network, 2001). The (international) White Ribbon Campaign, began in Canada as a public means of illustrating commitment to end violence against women, specifically by including men (Kaufman, 2001). In addition, more and more individuals, organizations and governments are realizing the links between social problems, with domestic violence being related to many other social ills. A rights-based approach allows us to illuminate social problems, previously taboo, by focusing on the rights of individuals.

A rights-based approach can be useful, but it is not without its theoretical and practical problems. However, when it is effective, it should empower people, giving them a voice and agency regarding their own futures. The much-maligned concept of empowerment has been overused; yet at its core it is a key concept when dealing with issues of inequality, power hierarchies and rights. Gutiérrez *et al.* (1998) suggest specifics ways of incorporating empowerment into practice, based on the central principles of providing a safe and supportive environment, understanding the whole person, providing a helping process that facilitates self-confidence and demonstrates a 'power-with' (not 'power-over') relationship model and, finally, recognizing the multiple roles that workers must take on in empowering practice.

Participation

Participation in itself is both a tool and a goal. Participation works with and enhances social cohesion and aims to equalize hierarchical power. The democratic principles of power sharing and shared decision making are keys to understanding participation, but authors such as Cornwall (2002) have also stressed the equality (particularly gender) agenda in participative approaches.

Within the development field, community participation came into popularity in the 1970s when fundamental questions were being asked, which included who should define development's outcomes, and to what degree should local knowledge be harnessed. This was a time when Freire's (1970) ideas of education as emancipatory were influencing different professional paradigms. Community participation was a crucial switch from 'top-down' to 'bottom-up' approaches that emphasized the use of local knowledge and participation in the fundamental design and decision-making processes of development. Chambers is often held to be one of the founding fathers of participative approaches in development. He argues that democratic and participative methods are necessary for social sustainability, and states that poverty is not inevitable, but rather a matter of social actions (Chambers, 1997). Chambers postulates that professionals have a tendency to oversimplify complex issues that consequently lead to mismatched programme development in rural communities. Participative approaches have now become mainstream, adopted by such diverse groups as the World Bank, and community-based organizations, and have even made their way into government and private sector policy. Few organizations that want to be taken seriously on a diverse range of social agenda will put forward programmes or policies that do not emphasize (at least on paper) their support for a participative approach.

Critics of participative methodologies, such as Craig and Porter (1997), argue that many participative approaches are only inclusive on the surface, and actually entrench pre-existing systems of control. In essence, if participation means giving added voice to community leaders, the approach neither has made a difference to the power structure within a community nor has elicited the views of those most vulnerable. Chambers (1997) himself pointed out that one of the downfalls of participative approaches is that they can strengthen pre-existing power structures. He asks how the voices of the suppressed can be heard and taken seriously and what the consequences are of changing power dynamics. Chambers questions whether an outsider can understand the internal dynamics of a community. He also questions the impact on power hierarchies when they have been tampered with through the use of consensus-building exercises (Chambers, 1997).

Conclusion: The New Equality and Social Professionals

What effect does the formulation of the *new equality* have on social professionals and the ideal of international social work? How social work is envisioned is important. According to Healy (2001) (drawing on the work of Hokenstad), social work takes on a broad range of roles and responsibilities in each country where it is present. There are shared values of 'promoting human dignity and social justice, empowering poor and vulnerable peoples, and encouraging inter-group harmony and goodwill' (Hokenstad *et al.*, 1996, p. 182; also cited in Healy, 2001, p. 99). Similarly, if we look to the IFSW (2000a) international definition of social work (see in Chapter 1), we find a corresponding resonance.

If social work is an emancipatory profession, working to promote human rights and social justice, then it is imperative to look at and understand both the social divisions and cohesions within our societies, with all of the micro and macro power structures and imbalances and inequalities. However, we must be careful when 'practising in the best interests of the other', as this could take on the characteristics of cultural domination. Having explored the possible impact on individuals of globalization in

Chapter 2 and examined ideas of divisions and cohesions in this chapter, we must ensure that our practice is in harmony with the lived experience of those who need the support of professionals. The global citizen may face an increase in social division with its resulting fragmentation, but convivial tolerance and respect can prevail.

If our world is to be a decent world in the future, we must acknowledge right now that we are citizens of one interdependent world, held together by mutual fellowship as well as the pursuit of mutual advantage, by compassion as well as self-interest, by a love of human dignity in all people, even when there is nothing we have to gain from co-operating with them. Or rather, even when what we have to gain is the biggest thing of all: participation in a just and morally decent world. (Nussbaum, 2000a, p. 18)

Social work educators, argue Chan and Ng (2004), are increasingly required to be researchers and practitioners, as well as educators. These different arenas are well placed to advance the social justice agenda, particularly through advocating an anti-discriminatory framework. This contemporary reality can herald the role of social professionals in encouraging dialogue between local and global levels, as well as between policy and practice arenas.

4 Loss: A Core Concept with *Universal* Relevance

Introduction

Loss permeates human experience. It is present in any situation encountered by social professionals working with people to improve social functioning and enhance life situations. Loss can affect individuals, families, groups, communities and nations. Grieving people are found in schools, immigration centres, programmes for the aging, health-care settings, and any other place where social and emotional support could occur. While the presenting concern of a person is often something else, for example, poverty, exploitation or social exclusion, loss can be an underlying issue that must also be addressed. The well-prepared professional will assess for loss in many situations and if professionals are not open to discussion of loss and grief, they may miss an important opportunity for service.

'Loss' is a global term that encompasses many different causes and consequences. The key point for social professionals practising worldwide is to develop awareness of loss and its potential emotions and responses. Such knowledge, coupled with skills in varied cultural contexts, can enable social professionals to better collaborate with individuals, groups, families, organizations, and communities to improve their social functioning in the light of their loss experiences. The most obvious loss is that experienced through death, but loss also underlies many other life changes. Is it helpful, or even accurate, to generalize about loss or grief or mourning as global, international phenomena? Are they universal? Can social professionals educated and working in one cultural context be of any assistance to a grieving individual or community from a different cultural context? These are important questions for social professionals.

This chapter defines grief, loss and mourning, discusses different categories and types of loss globally, and describes the relationship between loss and recent processes of globalization. The variable impact of loss on individuals, families and communities is described, as are social responses of human beings to loss in groups, organizations and communities. The chapter concludes with implications of loss for the work of social professionals worldwide.

Relationship of Loss to Globalization

As referenced in Chapter 1, Nagy and Falk (2000) (among others) have confirmed the need for social professionals worldwide to better understand the impact of increasing global interdependence. They refer to the influence of television and the Internet, which carry the impact of social problems such as social unrest, terrorist actions, ethnic conflicts and brutal wars into our homes. Such social problems flow back and forth unimpeded across national borders and can lead to increased international migration, disasters and conflict. We cannot separate economic forces within nations from global socio-economic forces.

These changes can result in increased awareness on the part of social professionals of the universal nature and presence of loss and grief in an era of globalization: war, famine, genocide, bombing, torture, natural disasters, and movement of people across borders can all result in loss, sometimes multiplied in unimaginable ways. Visual and auditory communications media might remind migrants of what they lost – identity, home, possessions, freedom, childhood. This may result in 'loss at a distance' due to interconnectedness of communication and the graphic images available at our fingertips via the Internet or television and radio. So our awareness of loss is increased, both for those experiencing loss and for those providing social assistance.

In addition, globalization sets the larger context in which social professionals practice. Awareness of international perspectives on social problems with examples from local practice can help social professionals function more effectively and compassionately as professionals within their own locales. 'Think globally, act locally' is an important idea (Chapter 1), where practising with global awareness can mean acting differently in the local context. This means social professionals must have the knowledge and skills to work with people whose human concerns – poverty, disease, discrimination, identity, exploitation and conflict – transcend borders. This chapter illuminates loss as a fundamental human experience that crosses borders, language, culture, age and social location. It offers suggestions for education and practice with people who have experienced loss, particularly losses linked to the processes of globalization.

Loss, Grief, Bereavement and Mourning

Academics and practitioners use a variety of definitions for loss, grief and mourning. In this chapter, we use the following definitions. *Bereavement* is the process surrounding the loss of a loved object (Lloyd-Williams, 2003, p. 150); *loss* is defined as the harm or suffering caused by losing something or someone; *grief* is the psychological reaction to bereavement; and *mourning* is the public display of grief (Parkes *et al.*, 1997, p. 5). Mourning is the behavioural, emotional and cognitive expression of grief (Lloyd-Williams, 2003). Grief and mourning rituals are heavily influenced by cultural and gender-specific contexts.

While there is some debate about the universality of grief and expressions of mourning, Harvey (1998, p. 346) concludes that grieving is biological and mourning is cultural. How individuals respond to loss varies considerably; there do exist some general explanations about what individual and social responses are likely to occur. Crying, fear and anger are so common as to be virtually ubiquitous, and most cultures provide social sanction for the expression of these emotions in the funeral rites and customs of mourning, which follow bereavement. For instance, Wikan (1988) studied crying, and found it present as part of grieving in all cultures they studied except the Balinese, though the Balinese still grieve. In this respect, Western cultures, which tend to discourage the overt expression of emotion at funerals, can be seen as somewhat deviant. They differ from most other societies and from other societies as they were a hundred years ago (Parkes *et al.*, 1997, p. 5).

Rosenblatt (in Parkes *et al.*, 1997) completed some of the earliest studies of grief and mourning across cultures. He states,

> (t)here are no pan-human categories for understanding death; how people think about death is everywhere culturally imbedded.... we might consider others to be uneducated, misinformed, superstitious, less developed, or in some other way faulty. But such ethnocentrism is unhelpful ... there is no justification for privileging one's own reality over that of the people one wants to understand and help. The more useful course is to become adept at listening, responding and dealing with another person's reality, no matter how discrepant it is from one's own. (p. 31)

He provides an example of how embedded in larger and well-articulated aspects of culture and society are cultural approaches to dealing with death. He describes highland Ecuadorian peasants who believe that the cause of death was 'connected to relations with land owners and officials of local development agencies, differential integration of men and women into wage labour and speaking Spanish, the uses of modern medicine and Catholicism as political forces, and traditional patterns of exchange in the community' (p. 39). While it is true that responses to loss are culturally embedded, it does not excuse social professionals from the necessity of learning basic theories about loss and grief. Some of the better known theories and models are described in Lloyd-Williams (2003) and Bruera *et al.* (2004).

Developmental or stage theories imply that one experiences discrete stages of grief in response to loss. The focus is on intra-psychic processes, the ability to control one's responses, the importance of 'grief work'. They also imply failure if 'moving on' through or past the grief does not happen. They also generally imply that loss of attachment is necessary to give rise to grief (for further discussion see Harvey and Hofmann, 2001); therefore, some losses cause distress, but not necessarily grief. The most influential theorists in this class of theories include Freud, Bowlby, Parkes, Kubler-Ross and Worden (discussed further in Harvey, 1998).

The best known of the *stress and coping theories* are those of Selye (1956) and Stroebe and Schut (1999). Stroebe and Schut's 'dual processing model' of bereavement provides helpful understanding that people suffering loss have two emotional/psychological processes happening simultaneously; loss orientation and restoration orientation. This model might be useful when working with immigrants, refugees and asylum seekers who are both grieving all they left behind and working to adapt to new surroundings. It also has appeal in the developing-world context, where people are simultaneously grieving a loss and coping with basic survival issues (Bruera *et al.*, 2004, p. 54). However, one must recognize the different degrees of loss in situations where people migrate against their own will (e.g., to escape rape in wartime or use as sexual slaves).

Continuity theories propose that people who experience loss of a person or many people wish to maintain feelings of continuity with the loved one(s) and believe that relationships may be transformed but remain important within the individual and in communities. An example might be the efforts in Britain to keep alive the losses of the Second World War through memorials and rituals; we may be seeing similar examples of this type of grieving among some of those in the US whose loved ones were killed in the attacks of 9/11. One of the more common of these theories is articulated by Klass, Silverman and Nickman (in Bruera *et al.*, 2004, p. 53).

Theories of complicated grief (Rando, 1984) explore grief that is complicated by additional factors such as multiple losses in a short time or grief in a person with severe mental illness. These theories might have real relevance for the social professionals who work in areas where whole communities, including the professionals themselves, are experiencing loss, for example in areas struck by natural disasters or the crime of genocide.

Post-traumatic stress (PTSD) and trauma theories ask social professionals to recognize that individuals and communities interpret loss and trauma differently, depending on timing, identity of target populations (in situations of violence), dosage of exposure, and vulnerability due to socio-economic conditions. These theories, as most, still need examination (Zinner and William, 1999, p. 11). The impact of loss is greater when it results from a hostile action (the murder of Itzak Rabin in Israel or the bombing in Oklahoma, US, for example) or when prevention could have helped. It can be more difficult, perhaps, to find meaning when trauma kills large numbers, involves prolonged suffering, destroys massive amounts of property, or happens suddenly without warning (Zinner and William, 1999, p. 12). The earthquake in Kashmir in 2005 might be such an example.

Many researchers and authors have written about *cross-cultural differences in beliefs about death and dying* (Irish *et al.*, 1993; Parkes *et al.*, 1997; Fletcher, 2002). These differences are important for local social professionals to respect and learn about, particularly when working with immigrants, asylum seekers or others who might not share the majority culture rituals and interpretations. The following are some examples (drawn from the above texts and personal experience):

- *Native American (Ojibwe)*: Sage burning is important in the grief ritual, which can challenge conventional health care providers in institutions;
- *Hmong of Thailand*: At an American college, Hmong students must be absent for a whole week from classes for a funeral, as compared to one to two days for students from the majority European-American culture; this can challenge their professors;
- *Bali*: People believe that emotional control in bereavement is necessary, as gods won't heed prayers if one is not calm; a social professional might misinterpret this response as 'unfeeling';
- *Ifaluk*: People living on this Pacific atoll believe that after a good cry, grief is done and the bereaved is back to normal; this challenges the traditional Western thinking that grief lasts months to years;
- *Shona of Zimbabwe*: People here might understand the death of a child as the result of an undiagnosed disease, failure to follow proper birth rituals, incorrect burials following previous deaths in the family, anger of a spirit from a clan other than one's own, among others; these explanations might be misperceived by professionals not from the ethnic group.

Theories about grief and loss and the difference in meaning and practice across cultures can aid social professionals to better understand, and then work to improve, the lives of those affected by loss.

Examples of Loss and its Impact on Individuals, Groups and Communities

Loss can result from the absence of anyone or anything important in one's life. As one researcher stated, this might be 'anything that has personal meaning to the individual' (Lloyd-Williams, 2003). Anything with meaning attached to it by an individual, a family, a group or a community can result in loss when it is removed, destroyed or left behind. Some categories of loss include concrete (personal possessions, including pets, money, stocks/bonds, residence, job, home, country), abstract (such as dreams, faith, childhood, humour, femininity or virility, innocence, hope, identity), developmental (due to age, fertility, mobility, vision, hearing, natural hair colour, hair, skin tone, memory changes), sense of self or identity (as a result of physical illness, divorce, spouse's death, job loss or migration) and significant human relationships (for example, parents, spouse/partner, friend, sibling, child, grandparent, relative, grandchild whether through death, separation, divorce, move or retirement) (Irish *et al.*, 1993, p. 37). Some argue, however, that death is a type of loss that results in a much more dramatic life experience than loss of other kinds. 'Losing someone you love is less like losing a very valuable and irreplaceable possession than like finding the law of gravity to be invalid' (Marris, in Parkes *et al.*, 1997, p. 215).

Losses are experienced in the wake of disasters, whether natural or human-made. These can include hurricanes, typhoons, earthquakes, tornadoes, floods, as well as wars and explosions (whether related to industrial 'accidents' or terrorist acts) or slower-moving disasters such as desertification and famine. In 2000, 256 million people worldwide were affected by natural and human-made disasters – more than in any year during the previous decade (Straussner and Phillips, 2004, p. 106). The Indian Ocean tsunami in December 2004 was an example of the magnitude of such natural disasters and the incredible losses sustained by individuals, families, communities and nations. People die, suffer, or are often forced to move, abandoning their homes and former lives. People in other countries are affected by the trauma when viewing images on the Internet or on television, or if loved ones (as in the 2004 tsunami) were vacationing or working in the areas hit by disaster. Resulting tangible losses can include land, buildings, crops, income and assets. Other examples include the loss of livelihoods suffered by the rural poor as a result of Hurricane Mitch in Honduras (Morris *et al.*, 2001); losses experienced by communities in the American South with Hurricane Katrina or those by populations affected by the earthquake in the Kashmir region (affecting both India and Pakistan), both in 2005. More intangible losses can include individual and national identity, a sense of safety and community, and hope for the future. Health concerns, especially with acute, life-threatening and/or infectious diseases (such as HIV/AIDS and tuberculosis) can cause a whole spectrum of losses, real and perceived, including touch, relationships, homes, employment, child-bearing opportunity, freedom of movement and so on (Welsby, 1998, p. 1139) (see also Chapter 8).

Loss has been analysed closely for particularities that might require specialized approaches to helping. These include 'ambiguous loss', when a loss is unclear and the person is partly absent and partly present (Alzheimer's disease) or physically missing (after 9/11 or in Kosovo or the tsunami) or psychologically missing (chronic mental illness) (Boss, 2006). It also includes 'traumatic loss' (Straussner and Phillips, 2004, p. 24), which is death that is sudden, traumatic, with no preparation, no process, and no goodbye for survivors. It offers no chance to repair relationships, deal with ambivalence, or return an overdue call to the loved one.

Traumatic loss has serious effects on individuals, such as somatization and staying awake to avoid nightmares. Some survivors use drugs, exhibit increased interpersonal violence, become isolated, over-engage in work or physical activity, or have trouble sleeping. In Oklahoma City, a significant portion of the population experienced sleep problems for a year after the bombing and in Tokyo researchers saw this last for five years after the poisoning by sarin gas on the subway (Straussner and Phillips, 2004). Traumatic loss also affects families through disrupted routine, role changes, loss of community ties such as through the workplace, school or place of worship, homes, land and animals in the rural areas, and family cohesion. Trauma caused by mass violence results in 'a sense of profound helplessness in the face of overwhelming danger, anxiety, and arousal when confronted with an external situation in which there is a high risk of death or injury to oneself or to another' (Arroyo and Eth, cited in Straussner and Philips, 2004, p. 4; see also Chapter 5). Deliberate violence tends to create longer-lasting mental health effects than natural disasters or accidents. There may not be a body. In homicide, energy that would normally be spent on grieving is instead placed in legal action. For the loved ones of a person who has committed suicide, they will have many more complex emotions to deal with than just grief, for instance feelings of guilt and anger.

Particularly vulnerable to the effects of traumatic loss are those families involved in divorce or separation; people who are not legally recognized or undocumented; people suffering other simultaneous losses, and those with chronic illness or disability. Adults with poor health, immobility, isolation, or earlier traumatic experience are also prone to more difficulties in times of traumatic loss. Some have studied the particular issues of loss and grief in people with learning disabilities (McEnhill, 2004). The concept of 'intergenerational, transgenerational or multigenerational transmission of trauma' is illustrated in studies from children who are Holocaust survivors and Vietnam veterans' children. Researchers postulate that vulnerability to PTSD is hereditary (Yehuda *et al.* in Straussner and Phillips, 2004, p. 12). Social workers should be aware of this potential in immigrants, refugees, asylum-seekers and their children.

'Multiple or compound losses' are common after mass violence, including loss of loved ones, home, workplace, school, pet, emotional and physical safety, comfort in daily life, trust in the future, financial stability, sense of fairness, control, identity, meaning and hope. Multiple losses affect all survivors, including professional helpers, for example as occurred in the bombing of Hiroshima (1945) or as currently seen among the gay community in the US affected by HIV/AIDS. The predictable loss of identity, home and country due to migration may be heightened when persons are forced to flee persecution or other traumas (see Chapter 5). Political uncertainly can cause social workers to have stress about their own potential for relocation, can cause difficulties in treating clients across political opinions and can cause ethical dilemmas between obligation to the employing agency and needs of clients (Lev-Wiesel and Friedlander, 1999). Grieving during war can be complicated because issues of fear and safety are paramount during acute crises.

The increasing connections across international borders due to globalization can cause new challenges related to loss for the practice of local social professionals. Demographic changes, movement of people, capital and technology across borders can all create losses in the local populations. Some sending countries that are less wealthy experience loss of many educated people, commonly understood as the 'brain drain'. Demographic changes are occurring as many industrialized nations are expected to lose a portion of their population in the next 50 years (Russia by 17 per cent, Germany by 9 per cent).[1] People may delay child bearing or just have fewer children (for instance, as in some of the CEE countries), perhaps due to 'modernization' of an economic system built on a more educated work force; any children they have need more education. 'Some European countries have considered loosening immigration curbs as a way to help fill their need for highly skilled workers and to build a tax base to replace dwindling funds for programmes for the aged'.[2] The movement of capital – factories, jobs and money – across borders can result in the loss of jobs and a sense of community as evidenced by urban areas in the US losing industry to other countries and being unable to regain their economic bases. Movement of technology can result in changes in human interconnectedness, both increasing it (cell phones, Internet) and decreasing it (voice messaging, computerized staffing of call centres). Those in highly technological societies who are poor suffer the effects of the 'digital divide' and may feel they have lost importance as members of their own communities as they are unable to engage in the commercial and personal activities afforded those with technological opportunities.

Communities may also lose their ethnic identities when populations become more diverse, as is the case in the changing demographics of Midwestern, traditionally European-American, Christian small towns in the US with rapidly growing Latino populations. Alternatively, patterns of trans-national adoption can also lead to losses for individuals and the countries from which they originated. After the dissolution of the Soviet Union in 1992, Russia began to allow foreign adoptions. Approximately, 50,000 children have been adopted to foreign families.[3] While this strengthens families who welcome the children, it also can result in the loss of Russian identity for the children and a loss of citizens for the country. At the time of writing, Indonesia was considering a law against the adoption of Indonesian children after the tsunami until it could be determined whether the children were indeed orphaned.

Straussner and Phillips (2004, p. 71) proposed that media and technology might play a role in loss experienced by people across the globe. People in many countries have experienced the spread of gun violence in schools by young males who feel powerless, rejected and ostracized (for example, in Canada, the Caribbean, Germany, Scotland and the US); and awareness of mass violence in workplace settings has similarly increased around the world. Repeated showings of the destruction of the World Trade Centre caused some children to think many other buildings were also falling. This may result in a loss of security and safety. One can consider the worldwide awareness of the events of 9/11. Many people remember exactly where they were and what they were doing at the time, due to the omnipresent media. Many around the world were affected by the trauma, and many were comforted by the commonality of the experience – so while people remembered the devastation, they also remember the social connection and the feeling of being a part of a community, which helped them through the experience (Straussner and Phillips, 2004, p. 106).

There are many texts on the 'routine' effects of loss on individuals, and how social work practice with these individuals can be taught, learned and improved upon (for instance, Currer, 2001; Thompson, 2002). Perhaps it is the death of a spouse, or a job loss or forced migration without a family or community. If a social professional lives and works in a Western country, the techniques developed in the stage models of grief might be useful, since research and practice have been developed primarily within this context. The focus is on the individual and his or her responses to loss and how that can be addressed by the social worker in a therapeutic context. While such a focus can be useful to social professionals in other countries or communities, the need to better understand the impact of loss across cultures can enable social workers to practice with more cross-cultural competence.

Consider the special impact of loss on some individuals related to their cultural practices, for instance the Shona in Zimbabwe. If a very young child dies, the mother may be prevented from grieving extensively or holding a public funeral. Her perceived lack of fertility, or less productivity due to grief, may result in abuse, distancing, or even divorce (Parkes *et al.*, 1997, p. 37). Or consider the case of SARS deaths and Chinese rituals; funerals traditionally held with the deceased's body are now brief memorials without the body.[4] Whatever the source and type of loss experienced, individual human lives are changed. It is important for social workers to understand theories of loss, grief and mourning to better intervene with individuals, but in most contexts, the impact of grief is not only personal, but is rooted in culture and tradition of the family and community.

Another special situation occurs when migrants experience a death in their new context. Special foods, or flowers or soil from one's homeland may be missing.

> For a person far from home, a death can set off grief for deaths that occurred at the time the person was driven from his/her homeland, for the home left behind, for a lost way of life, for a time when his/her language was the only language the person could hear, or for other things related to leaving. Consequently, one of the barriers to performing rituals in a new homeland is that one may feel overwhelmed by the totality of one's losses. In a sense the prime difficulty may be that one scarcely knows what to grieve or may lack ritual to deal with the bitter losses of war, of governmental-sponsored 'disappearances', of expropriation of farmland, etc: that led to one's needing to move . . . and proper grieving may require things as well as people, and those things may not be available when one is away from one's home community. (Parkes *et al.*, 1997, p. 44)

In addressing responses to migration, IFSW holds that 'agreements and legislation on migration . . . often show little sensitivity towards their social consequences' in the lives of migrants. As a consequence, their International Policy on Migration (IFSW, 2000b) considers it important that receiving countries offer migrants various specialized services, such as those provided by psychologists, doctors and lawyers. IFSW states that social workers should have responsibility in linkage between migrants and various 'authorities', and for advising, consulting and mediating in conflicts which affect migrants (IFSW, 2000b). Among these responsibilities, we should include addressing loss issues involved with the migration experience (more on issues of loss in relation to migrants is found in Chapter 6).

Moving from individual loss to the impact of loss on entire communities is complex and multi-layered. Effects of loss on communities are most severe and long-lasting when there is extreme and widespread damage to property, serious and ongoing financial consequences, disaster caused by human intent, and/or high prevalence of trauma as a consequence of loss of life, injuries and threat to life. Chapter 5 reflects on the impact of war and other types of conflicts on communities, for instance in the Darfur region of Sudan.

In addition to concrete community losses, there may be loss of certainty in politically unstable areas (such as the Middle East). Sometimes loss has resulted in the 'scapegoating' of a portion of the population, as the Jews were in Boston in the 1940s after the Coconut Grove fire, or, more recently, as is happening to Muslims in the US following 9/11 (Straussner and Phillips, 2004, p. 13) or in the UK following the smaller-scale bombings on the London transport system (7/7/05). In some situations, voluntary community migration causes loss of tradition and ritual due to a change in the geography of place. For instance, in the Greek and Turkish immigrant communities in Berlin, home, burial ground and prayer halls have been restructured into the religious domain. Questions of where to be buried and how to respect the older women as passers-on of cultural knowledge of death and mourning arise (Jonker, in Field *et al.*, 1997). 'Communal bereavement', evidenced by sadness, distress and diminished sense of well-being and safety within their communities, is a useful description for what individuals tend to feel after a major catastrophe (Talbot, 2001, in Straussner and Phillips, 2004, p. 13). So, for example, there have been some indications of communal grief among Kahsmiri immigrant populations in the UK following the 2005 earthquake on the Indian/Pakistani border (personal communication).

Community grief is only resolved when the loss is accepted (Zinner and William, 1999, p. 11). It may even become a source of identity or pride if only for surviving the catastrophe. Communities are best able to respond well to mass violence when

their social resources, inherent social supports, level of cohes-
iveness and availability of social networks are high. Professionals
are important but cannot supplant natural helping networks.
Survivors need to continue routine social activities in the
communities that provide a natural forum for sharing experiences
and can allow a sense of social embeddedness to return after
being destroyed in mass violence (Morris, 2001 in Straussner and
Phillips, 2004, p. 107).

The social impact of losses on individuals, families and
communities can be described and analysed. They are usually
viewed by social professionals, politicians and others through
the lenses of 'problem', difficulty and suffering. However, the
responses of those same human beings can also be assessed, in
addition, from a strengths perspective that can inform interventions to enhance people's capacity and social capital to survive and
thrive despite, and perhaps due to, the losses. Social professionals
can assist in strengthening these natural networks and thus aid in
healing.

Implications for Social Work Education, Practice and Service Developments

Social professionals must have knowledge and skills in loss and
grief in the cultural context. These human concerns pervade social
work, no matter in what setting or with which population. We
consider that there is currently a lack of preparation in social work
education in the UK and US (and elsewhere) to work with grief
and loss in the lives of clients/service users (Christ and Sormanti,
1999). It is important for students to grasp the pervasiveness of
loss in human lives and as a core concept underlying trauma and
chronic illness as well (Harvey and Hofmann, 2001).

In the document that has been produced by the joint working
party of the IASSW and IFSW on global standards for social
work education (see Chapter 1), while not specifically addressing
content on loss, the standards state that social workers should
work for social inclusion of vulnerable people and respect and
celebrate differences. Of course, the preparation of social professionals, whether in a formal university course or through in-
service training, must be culturally specific and appropriate to

the historical, political and social context of the country. For instance, in Canterbury, England, a specialist MA programme in Palliative and Chronic Illness Care at the University of Kent aids multidisciplinary professionals to learn in a multicultural context, to understand differences in health-care systems, and to learn to use another language professionally (Walters, 2003, p. 6). In recognizing the pervasiveness of loss throughout human experience, programmes that prepare professionals to work with human beings to improve their social functioning can teach certain values, knowledge and skills to ensure better practice with those whose lives are adversely affected by loss and grief.

Service to others, competence, preventing harm, and social justice are core *values* that are international (Taylor, 1999). Other values can be culture-specific. Social professionals must learn what values inform work with people experiencing loss in varying contexts. In Tanzania, for example, traditional cultural values hold that the extended family ought to care for orphans. When the extended family is dramatically reduced in number due to HIV/AIDS, the grief felt by local communities associated with the building of orphanages must be understood by social professionals (see also Chapter 8).

Many theories and models are important to teach social workers. *Knowledge* required for working with loss includes empowerment approaches, resiliency theory, and attachment theory, as well as many of the models specifically related to bereavement referred to earlier in this chapter. Taylor (1999) asserts that empowerment approaches underlie all international social work practice. Teachers can stress cooperation with Koranic and other Muslim healers in learning to address mental health issues with Muslim clients (Al-Krenawi and Graham, 1999) and also stress learning to be gained from shamanic healers (Ng, 2003)

Social professionals can learn which grief rituals facilitate adjustment in their particular context (Castle and Phillips, 2003). An example from Jonker (in Field *et al.*, 1997, p. 193) illustrates how German, Turkish and Greek professionals, including social workers, act to prevent a 'corruption of morals' as it relates to burial. This included the development of a Greek cemetery and the retention of gender-specific roles for both Greek and Turkish communities, with men as protectors of cultural values, women as transmitters. Other examples encourage social workers to learn how recent immigrants view health care and healing (Culhane-Pera *et al.*, 2003) and the influence of 'place' on loss (Patricola-McNiff, 2002). For social professionals who specialize in grief work, more in-depth knowledge, for instance, about the intertwining of trauma and bereavement (Rubin *et al.*, 2003) and the dual model of bereavement (Stroebe and Schut) is important. The latter takes into account the biopsychosocial functioning of the bereavement and the relationship to the lost object (person).

While not all social professionals are clinicians, with many being community workers, all can follow suggestions from the National Mental Health Information Centre of SAMHSA about what is helpful to say when they know they are working directly with people experiencing loss (in Straussner and Phillips, 2004, p. 139), particularly as a result of disasters:

- These are normal reactions to a disaster
- It is understandable that you feel this way
- No one who sees a disaster is untouched by it
- You are not going crazy
- It wasn't your fault; you did the best you could
- It is normal to feel anxious about yourself and your family's safety

These responses help grieving people normalize and ground feelings, release some of the emotional pressure and facilitate recovery.

In the US, the National Association of Social Workers (NASW) offers continuing education on practice in end-of-life care because it recognizes that loss is pervasive. However, it is essential that social workers consider the context of such work and 'relearn the lessons of community building' (Straussner and Phillips, 2004, p. 105). The trend towards psychopathology and micro-level social work, reflecting societal focus on the individual, leaves many in the North and West unprepared for the kind of community work which would be more appropriate following mass violence or disaster. This (re)learning can be aided by an increase in cross-cultural and international research (Abbott, 1999). Abbott's study shows that social workers around the globe share some common values, respect for basic rights and often support of self-determination, but not necessarily a shared sense of social responsibility or commitment to individual freedom (p. 465). Social workers need to be aware of these differences.

Martinez-Brawley (1999, p. 335), in discussing the globalization of social work education, is 'concerned that we are able to incorporate many diverse views on caring, healing and change. In moving across continents and striving to transcend language and hemispheric boundaries, it is essential for social work to develop the position of the philosopher rather than being tempted by the ethos of the expert'. Social professionals need to be reflective in practice as we encounter other traditions.

Loss is present in all settings and populations in social work, so practice with an awareness of the global pervasiveness of loss is important to social professionals. Practitioners should always assess for the possibility of loss that underlies anger, somatic complaints, conflict in the family or community (see Chapter 5) and other concerns of social professionals. Whether the intervention is then with an individual, a family or an entire community, it is always in its own cultural context. Of course, this cultural diversity can result in difficulties for practitioners. One, as Rosenblatt says (in Parkes *et al.*, 1997, p. 27), is that knowing someone is from a certain country may not be of help at all in identifying the person's native language or culture (consider a Spanish-speaking person in the US who might be Mexican or indigenous Indian).

It is vital for the social professional not to stereotype, but to learn about a certain culture. Though some believe the best intervention with grief is done by specialists (Rosenblatt in Parkers *et al.*, 1997, p. 46), generalist social professionals should be

> good at working with a diversity of cultures, good at learning, good at finding how others can help them, good at avoiding ethnocentrism, comfortable working with social and practice standards different from the ones that would be "right" in their own cultures. In a sense, one of their great strengths is not that they know *what* to do but that they know *how* to find people who can help them to know what to do, that they know how to seek help, and that they know how to evaluate the advice they get and to learn quickly from a mistake. (Rosenblatt in Parkes *et al.*, 1997, p. 47)

A well-prepared social professional in any context knows how to discover what is culturally appropriate in relation to their practice.

Parkes and his co-authors (1997) provide some helpful suggestions for those needing to learn:

> We can be helpful to people from other cultures if we take the time and trouble to see the world through their eyes. Despite cultural differences in expression, the support all social animals give to each other at times of danger transcends culture. Emotional support can be expressed non-verbally as well as verbally, and openness evokes open responses, even across cultural difference. We need to ask clients to explain their cultures and practices to us, and invite questions' (pp. 216–217)

In societies where people do not easily show emotion, intense distress before or at the time of a bereavement is a predictor of poor outcome; but in other societies it may have the opposite connotation (p. 212).

Unlike usual grief and bereavement states, people experiencing severe stress reactions due to profound trauma do not necessarily 'recover' over time by themselves and they may need professional help (Parkes *et al.*, 1997, p. 211; Straussner and Phillips, 2004, p. 13;). Social professionals should make referral when possible. However, nearly all social professionals can work to re-establish feelings of safety, manage anxiety and anger, empower clients by seeing them as survivors (although there is some argument about this, see Straussner and Phillips, 2004 p. 14) so that they can begin to take charge of their lives, help people appreciate how their feelings may be a normal response to an abnormal situation, and intervene early with children. Intervention with children should be non-judgemental, allowing them to express their feelings and could include involving parents listening to them. Social professionals should be comfortable and competent in assessing spiritual needs in loss and letting children (and adults) know that it is normal to cry, be afraid, and be sad following traumatic experiences.

With regard to spirituality, this tends to be 'off limits' to social workers in many parts of the world (that is, seen as a personal matter which should not influence practice and/or the responsibility of another profession). However, as Angell and others have found, social workers frequently are confronted with the client's intrinsic need for and expression of spiritual meaning (Canda, 1988; Angell *et al.*, 1997;). Spirituality is a concomitant of the human spirit and a fundamental part of the client's personae. However, moving from the secular to the sacred can cause concern or discomfort for social workers who have been professionally socialized to be 'value neutral' when it comes to dealing with a client's spirituality and/or religion; this is true in much of the West and North. However, social workers need to be more confident and engaged in this respect and there are some indications of a renewed interest in this field, including as it relates to traditional knowledge (see for instance, Zapf, 2005). This need is evermore important in today's global village.

There are times in practice when social work intervention is with individuals, families and communities simultaneously. Consider the example of elderly Chinese immigrants in New York. After 9/11 the assistance of social professionals in senior centres to elderly Chinese immigrants not only resulted in assistance to those directly affected, but also helped to strengthen the larger community connection to their new country, as the elders raised $20,000 for charity to help survivors and placed memorials adjacent to Chinatown (Straussner and Phillips, 2004, p. 63). After mass violence, there is not simply one method of intervention for social workers. It moves from direct engagement at the site of devastation, to protection, provision of concrete needs and a responsive presence and then to the ongoing clinical work, including support for community engagement and social interaction (Straussner and Phillips, 2004, p. 29). However, all intervention by social workers in the aftermath of mass violence should respect and normalize the complexity of traumas and traumatic loss responses (including the fact that individual and family reactions are unique and most often occur over a long, often delayed, process) and provide additional information about expected responses, the importance of support networks, coping strategies and strategies for taking care of oneself in the future (p. 29).

Catastrophes in Northern Ireland, Oklahoma City and Tokyo and aviation disasters like Lockerbie have illustrated a crucial need to provide diverse services over time, for those immediately affected and to their communities at large (Straussner and Phillips, 2004, p. 30) Bearing witness, listening deeply and bringing an active presence to any interaction (p. 32) will aid survivors as they cope with, and transcend, the loss experience.

One role of social professionals is to humanize the institutions and organizations that deeply influence people's lives. For instance, social workers can teach 'organizational compassion', a method to assist organizations to respond to their employees' grief needs; this rewards both the employees and the organization (Cranston, 2004, p. 98). Social professionals can use 'ritual specialists', that is, elders or other adults who are connected with and respected in the particular community (Rosenblatt in Parkes *et al.*, 1997, p. 35). A teamwork model can be developed to assist social workers in politically unstable areas to prevent burn-out (Lev-Wiesel and Friedlander, 1999). A model of political intervention can be developed in conflict areas (for example, the West Bank) as proposed by Shamai and Boehm (July 2001), including elements of

> creating a clear contract of the intervention goal, including discussion of political issues . . . create a safe intervention context in which clients (individuals, families, groups and communities) and professionals feel safe and secure enough to open up and share their feelings and thoughts about the political situation . . . analyze the political context of the intervention, etc. (p. 358)

Development of palliative care services is another important role of social professionals and should not be left to health professionals alone. Apart from the development of hospices in the UK and US and many other (predominantly Western) countries, 'Almost Home Houses' in Holland provides an innovative example. Since 1986, in neighbourhoods where caregivers can no longer cope with caring for a dying relative, volunteers under the guidance of a social worker or nurse take over direct care (Jurgens, 2004, p. 12). Social workers can urge twinning/partnership relationships between palliative care efforts in developing countries and those in wealthier nations. VIAGENCO, a hospice organization in Kenya, was set up initially to care for and support AIDS orphans at home. When guardians and the children themselves started to fall ill, they decided to turn part of the administrative office into a hospice unit and to look for a partnering relationship with a hospice in a Western country (WHPCO, 2004).

In service development, social professionals need to be aware of and involved with some of the many international organizations involved with loss and grief. International Work Group on Death, Dying and Bereavement; Compassionate Friends; and Widow-to-Widow are some of the organizations with roots in Britain which now have branches in other countries (Parkes *et al.*, 1997, p. 213). Other examples include the Christian Children's Fund, who, after 9/11, translated the World Trade Center Children's Mural Project guidelines into 12 languages and distributed it to participating countries. Children in 22 countries, including Uganda, Kosovo and Columbia, sent messages and portraits to children in the US to encourage survival (Straussner and Phillips, 2004, p. 111). In addition, Voices for Hospices held the first World Hospice and Palliative Care Day (8 October 2005) to raise money for 44 hospices and palliative care programmes around the world.

Social workers must understand the collective community context of individual and family experiences after loss, particularly mass violence (Straussner and Phillips, 2004, p. 28). Active participation in a full range of community experiences links people to others and provides a sense of reconnection, restoration and recommitment to life, especially cultural and familiar rituals. Collaboration with people from the affected communities is crucial, both to assure cultural competence and to aid in the healing of those involved. Several authors provide community healing models and interventions (Zinner and William, 1999; Straussner and Phillips, 2004). For Zinner and William (1999, pp. 216–217), these include memorial services, drop-in discussion groups, and focus groups on unmet needs to de-stigmatize individual reactions and enhance long-term social support and remembering later anniversaries. Use of culture and community to promote both individual and community grieving and healing in South Africa can be described in the uniqueness of the nation's ubuntu philosophy ('We are who we are through others'). The healing power of community and culture finds expression in physical and financial support, cultural and emotional support, and spiritual support (Kasiram and Partab, 2002). Rowlands (2004) has also given examples of the use of the strengths perspective and community development approach in contributing to recovery from disaster and trauma.

In addition to such direct assistance, social professionals need to re-focus on social justice (see Chapters 1, 3 and 9). Social workers can empower communities with training in crisis debriefing, preparation in advance for losses and wise use of power by community leaders during times of loss (Zinner and William, 1999, p. 13). They can teach the BASIC PH model of assistance for traumatized children: Belief system, Affect, Social support, Imagination, Cognition, Physical (Straussner and Phillips, 2004, p. 77). They can enable people to get useful information; for example, WHO publications may be downloaded and Hospice Information provides materials to resource-poor countries at little or no cost.

Conclusion

Loss has always been a core concern for human beings. Social professionals work every day with those affected, directly and indirectly, by losses of all kinds. But global changes in human migration and travel, communications technology, and international connections have pushed knowledge about the effects of loss to the forefront of efforts to improve human lives. Even 50 years ago, a tsunami in Asia would not have affected people in Scandinavia; ethnic genocide in Africa would not have been widely known outside even the continent. As H. Marshall McLuhan (1967) foretold,

> time and space continuums, which have historically separated people and communities, have collapsed due to a combination of factors including ever-increasing waves of mass migration and advances in cyberspace technology. However, movement in the direction of a global village has not been met with commensurate advances in tolerance of human difference. (in Angell *et al.*, 1998)

Differences in how people assign meaning to loss, how they grieve and mourn and how social professionals might best intervene must be better understood. This chapter has introduced fundamental theories and concepts of loss and suggested how they might relate to global phenomena of relevance to local social work practice. In the words of Nagy and Falk (2000, p. 52), such information will help social professionals to focus on the need for a global vision of the profession of social work. Knowledge of loss as a continuing concept in a globalizing world will strengthen the contributions of social workers in disparate and varied practice settings, both local and international.

Part II
Effects of Globalization in Practice: Some Topical Examples

5 Communities in Conflict

Introduction

Conflict, whether at interpersonal, inter-group or inter-state level, has always been part of the human condition. Societies have evolved ways of managing conflict which have varied according to time and place. Traditional means (still current in some locations) rely on the personal decisions of powerful community leaders (and their supporters) and may include the use of force. Modern societies have developed democratic systems at local and national levels which aim to represent the views of all groups and reach solutions to tensions which threaten to destabilize communities or could result in overt conflict – although these do not always work in practice. Modern societies have also sanctioned interventions by social professionals and through mediation schemes in relation to disputes at interpersonal, neighbourhood and institutional levels; and international conventions and protocols have also been formulated to guide or restrain behaviour in relation to military personnel and civilians caught up in wars.

Many social workers are familiar with – and often intervene in – interpersonal and interfamilial conflict, but this chapter addresses the implications of conflicts which occur between communities within a given country or across national borders, and which sometimes are more appropriately described as wars. It is debatable how far globalization, itself, is responsible for an apparent increase in conflict during the twentieth century and indeed many current conflicts have their origins in previous processes of colonization and subsequent emancipation. However, the compression of time and space facilitated by rapid transport and the ICT revolutions brings many conflicts more dramatically to a worldwide 'audience' and they are more likely to have repercussions across national boundaries and at an international level.

This chapter is concerned not only with the effects of conflicts within societies between social groups (or communities) differentiated by ethnicity or other characteristics, but also with recent cross-border conflicts or those which have led to the fragmentation of previously united countries. It is suggested that we can identify different types of conflict and also different mechanisms for addressing them, some of which involve social professionals directly or indirectly. It can be noted that migration is often an integral part of conflict scenarios, either as cause or effect (and often both) and the role of conflict in migration is also discussed further in Chapter 6. Similarly, one consequence of conflict in some countries has been the recruitment of children and young people to serve military purposes, which is an extreme form of exploitation and child labour (other aspects being more fully discussed in Chapter 7). This chapter therefore aims to present some examples of conflicts worldwide, the effects on particular groups and the implications for actual or potential intervention by social professionals.

Locating Communities and Conflict

Before proceeding further, it may be as well to consider briefly the term 'community'. This concept provided a focus for some discussion in the Western sociological literature from the late nineteenth century but less than a century later a dictionary of sociology stated 'the term community is one of the most elusive and vague in sociology and is by now largely without specific meaning. At the minimum it refers to a collection of people in a geographical area' (Abercrombie *et al.*, 1994, pp. 75–76). After some elaboration, the section concedes that the term continues to have some normative force, and some would argue that recent years have seen a resurgence of interest – at least among politicians – in the idea of 'community', specifically as it relates to the notion of participation in the life of social groups in given neighbourhoods. This is in part a response to a felt 'loss of community' (apparently contributing to social ills such as rising juvenile crime rates and isolation of older people) and also part of the rebalancing of rights and responsibilities in relation to welfare and personal social services being witnessed in so many AICs. We have therefore seen the rise of ideas related to communitarianism in the US (Etzioni, 1993) and the development of 'community care' services, for instance, in the UK (Orme, 2001).

Additionally, the term 'community' may have greater relevance in many developing countries where traditions and economic circumstances promote or require considerable interdependence and obligations to the social group (Laird, 2004) (and such assumptions and behaviour may be carried over to AICs if members of a given social group migrate). In many countries of the South, Western individualistic values and models of welfare provision and social work practice are inappropriate (Laird, 2004) and community development approaches have more relevance. It is also worth noting here an earlier description of community as being based on a common culture, since many conflicts are rooted in enmities between groups differentiated by race, ethnicity or other aspects of culture. Whether such groups are located in the close proximity of an urban neighbourhood or rural village – or inhabit adjacent territory in different nations (actual or desired) – longstanding struggles for a fair share of material resources (including land) and political power fuel new or ongoing disputes which periodically result in overt and violent conflict.

The term 'conflict' is also one that is loosely used and it is understood, in part, according to context and one's disciplinary or professional perspective. For instance, there are a number of references to it in various forms in a recent sociology text (Macionis and Plummer, 2002), where it is cross-referenced with wars. Held *et al.* (1999) provide a useful analysis of military conflicts in a globalized world and remind us of the potentially catastrophic effects of a nuclear conflict for the whole planet. However, for social professionals, there are inevitable associations with interpersonal or inter-group violence, and many 'community conflicts' are relatively small scale and localized, receiving attention only in the local or national press, rather than on the world stage. But some forms of civil unrest or cross-border military action command international attention and, as recent events in many countries (including Afghanistan and Iraq) have demonstrated, even interventions aimed at 'democratization' or 'peacekeeping' may themselves provoke violent conflict.

It can be suggested that, even in the case of 'local events', conflicts are integrally associated with more fundamental factors which have international bases and repercussions. Laird (2004), writing about inter-tribal conflicts in sub-Saharan Africa, has suggested that competition for power and scarce resources is at the heart of specific wars and examples of community conflicts, although there are also psychological processes at work (in terms of people identifying with a particular group and building up negative stereotypes of 'the other') (Tajfel and Turner, 1979) and such divisions often also have a religious dimension. At the global level, it can be suggested that economic as well as religious and political factors are at play in deteriorating relations and actual outbreaks of violence between the Islamic world and the West. The attack on the World Trade Centre in New York and the subsequent events (such as the bombing of the Australian Embassy in Jakarta on the third anniversary of 9/11) can be interpreted in many ways but do suggest a fundamental dissatisfaction in many communities with the global economic and political power system, where US 'leads' countries of 'the West', leaving Islamic countries in particular feeling that they constitute a significant proportion of 'the rest'.

The experience of 9/11 gave rise to the American slogan about waging a 'war on terrorism', which has been significant in the subsequent development of US foreign, as well as some domestic, policies. Such policies have in turn given rise to concerns in relation to the civil and human rights of both US citizens and people in other countries deemed to be enemies of the US. The danger is that such slogans as the 'war on terror' promote a simplified vision of conflict, where clear divisions can be made between 'us' and 'them', the South and North, Islam versus Christianity.

Turning to some examples of conflicts, it might be useful to attempt a classification of different types of inter-community conflict before considering some of the effects and their implications for social work interventions. The factors which promote or sustain conflicts are complex, not uni-dimensional, and are specifically related to the unique history, geography, politics and economies (including resources) of each location. There are also likely to be international or cross-border influences (and impacts) as well as 'local' factors in most cases. The following paragraphs summarize the key determinants of some recent/current conflicts, with examples.

Many conflicts are 'civil', in the sense that they occur within national boundaries; may or may not involve physical violence; and are related to the unequal relationships of particular groups, which are differentiated by race; ethnicity, culture, religion or sectarianism, or class (socio-economic conditions) and political ideologies – or a combination of these factors. In relation to race, problems can arise where the indigenous majority population sees a minority group retaining economic power (e.g., the white population in Ivory Coast/Cote D'Ivoire or Zimbabwe); or where an aboriginal or first nation people constitute an oppressed minority in a country (e.g., in Australia or Canada); or where people have migrated (often from former colonies) and form a minority in another society (as for example, Africans in many EU countries including UK and France).

Other civil conflicts are related rather to ethnicity and different cultural characteristics, which may include religion and sectarianism. So, for instance, there are serious conflicts related to ethnicity (tribal identities) and religion (e.g., in Nigeria); and to various forms of sectarianism (schisms within a particular religion) (e.g., in Northern Ireland and Iraq). Of course, such divisions can be exacerbated by the political goal of a separate national status or unification with another country (as in the case of Chechnya, and some of the countries in the former Yugoslavia). Finally, civil conflict can also be (primarily) related to issues of class (as related to economic power) and opposing political ideologies (as in the case of Guatemala or Nepal).

Alternatively, as previously noted, conflict can be *inter-country*, that is, occurring across national borders. Such conflicts have complex roots related to political struggles for a country's independence as well as (often) access to economic resources. Current 'border disputes' between India and Pakistan (focusing on Kashmir) and the long-running conflict between Israel and Palestine are examples of such conflicts: they have both origins and ramifications beyond their immediate vicinities and boundaries. Some of the examples mentioned in this classification are examined in greater depth in the next section.

Causes and Consequences of Conflict: Some Examples

Notwithstanding the earlier establishment of classical empires (e.g., Greek, Roman, Ottoman, Manchu [Chinese], Russian), many current or recent conflicts owe more to the patterns of colonization established by European powers (Spanish, Portuguese, Dutch, British, French, German, Belgian and Italian) from the fifteenth to the nineteenth centuries (see Held *et al.* [1999] for a brief summary of the history of – and shift from – empires to nation states). In the case of North America, Australia and Aotorea/New Zealand, relatively small indigenous populations were initially displaced or destroyed by increasing numbers of Europeans settling over increased areas of the landmass from the seventeenth or eighteenth centuries (North America and Australasia respectively). Local populations were subject to very harsh treatment if they resisted white domination and/or were decimated by the introduction of previously unknown diseases.

In South America and Africa, the numbers of, initially, white 'traders' and then settlers arriving from the fifteenth century on (South America) or mainly in the eighteenth and nineteenth centuries (Africa) were much smaller relative to the indigenous populations, and, while similarly subjecting local people to brutality and infection, they failed to shift the population balance in numerical terms. However, the economic exploitation was at least as significant. Additionally, as Laird (2004) has described, the European 'scramble for Africa' (pp. 1885–1895) resulted in 'arbitrary territorial units' which defied 'geography, ethnicity or economic rationale', invariably resulting in the displacement of ethnic groups from their tribal lands (as also happened in the other continents) and throwing disparate groups together within administrative and political boundaries (pp. 694–695). These unsatisfactory boundaries were 'frozen' by the Organization for African Unity (OAU) in 1963, when a number of countries were aiming for independence from colonial rule, in an attempt to avert 'massive violent confrontations' but in fact had the effect of ushering in 'decades of bloody factionalism' (Laird, 2004, p. 695), as apparent in many of the recent and current conflicts in the African continent.

The period since the onset of globalization has seen continuing forms of economic colonization and exploitation of developing countries by MNCs. These corporations draw their management personnel from – and return their profits to – Western countries, while utilizing developing countries for cheap labour and materials, yet deny indigenous commodities fair access to global trading markets. Additionally, we have seen the disappointing results of decades of assistance via 'aid' or 'trade' packages (Held *et al.*, 1999). While individual governments (including of Argentina, Nigeria, the Philippines and Peru) have periodically played a shameful role in mismanagement (if not outright corruption) in relation to such assistance, countries have also been subject to the direction of the World Bank and IMF in how they utilize their resources. It is apparent that such bodies also represent the interests of Western powers (often businesses) rather than of developing countries themselves.

Additionally, a number of countries, including the US and China, are directly involved in the supply of arms, military training and other means of support for specific regimes – for both economic and ideological reasons. In relation to this, a recent news report stated that 43 US allies were at risk of losing aid (including military) because of their refusal to sign a bilateral agreement giving immunity to American military personnel, following the enactment of a domestic law (American Service Members Act, 2003) which claims immunity from prosecution by the International Criminal Court (set up in July 1998 to try war crimes).[1]

So what are the effects of these violent histories and continuing exploitation in terms of community conflicts? In relation to countries where civil conflict is related to racial conflict, Ivory Coast can be cited as a case where, despite the formal ending of colonial rule, a white minority (in this case, French) retains economic power, giving rise to a recent example of serious conflict. Although independent since 1960, the subsequent history and development of Cote d'Ivoire has been influenced by its previous experience of exploitation for slaves and ivory and the effects of conjoining 60 tribes under French rule in 1893. Up until the time of writing, the official language remains French and the currency is still the Franc. Additionally, approximately 14,000 French expatriates maintain control over economic and trade activities, while France has continued to meet the 'defence needs' of the country and supply bilateral aid. France has maintained military bases there and has played the role of political arbiter since a civil war and effective partition of the country in 2002. This followed a military coup to depose an autocratic president who had been in power for a relatively short period of time (1993–99, relative to the longer reign of the first president, in power for 33 years) and political polarization and growing xenophobia against the population in the north. These are mainly Muslim economic migrants, relative to the 60 per cent of people in the south who are largely Christians or adhere to indigenous religions. The main source of income for the country has been coffee and cocoa but falling prices on world markets have led to a failing economy.[2]

In terms of French intervention (4000 peacekeepers) (and notwithstanding the presence of 6000 UN peacekeepers) the Ivorians have seen recent interventions as a renewed attempt by France (the West) to exploit the country's natural resources (including off-shore oil and gas), although the UN perspective is that troops provide a buffer between the warring north and south of the country. In November 2004, attempts to guard a major hotel, which could be used to assemble French nationals should their evacuation be necessary, led to riots resulting from Ivorian suspicions that the French were aiming to establish full rule through taking over the nearby Presidential Palace. It has been suggested that an alternative way forward could be a mediation mission by the African Union (led by President Thabo Mbeki of South Africa).[3] Meanwhile, the conditions of the civilian population since 2002 have deteriorated rapidly, with individuals caught up in violence, destruction of villages and livelihoods and increased pressure to seek refuge in neighbouring countries or further away if means can be found.

In relation to the second category (where an indigenous minority is oppressed), in Australia, some efforts have been made to recognize the land rights of Aborigines and to 'compensate' the remaining very small minority for past persecution and more recent discrimination or neglect. However, Aboriginal groups continue to occupy the least favoured land areas, to suffer economic hardship and to be over-represented in a range of social problems, including alcoholism and juvenile crime. As well as accounts of inter-personal violence within communities there are periodic accounts of more widespread conflict directed against the people they perceive as racist. For instance, in February 2004, the death of a teenager (in a traffic accident when being chased by a police car) in a suburb of Sydney inhabited predominantly by Aborigines, sparked 'Australia's worst race violence'. Commentators suggested that the press response identified the problem as one of 'law and order' rather than reflecting the serious social problems of the area and the sense of racial discrimination and even persecution felt by the Aboriginal residents.[4]

Another perspective on racial conflict in local communities – and how these affect immigrants and might be related to wider social tensions – is provided by an example from the Netherlands. The murder of a Dutch filmmaker, Theo van Gogh, apparently for his critical stance on some aspects of Islam in November 2004, was followed by a series of attacks on Muslim buildings, for example, damage to mosques in Utrecht, Rotterdam and Breda and to an Islamic primary school in Eindhoven.[5] Although aimed at the symbols of Islam, it can be speculated that such attacks increase the feelings of vulnerability and exclusion commonly experienced by ethnic minority immigrant groups in many societies, feelings exacerbated since suspicions and fears have grown among white populations of their Muslim neighbours following 9/11. While the attacks reported from the Netherlands have clearly been targeted against the Muslim community, it is also the case that other 'Asian' groups have also been subject to more suspicion and hostility since 2001, and perhaps this partly lies behind a call reported in the UK media, at the time of writing, for greater differentiation between different 'Asian' communities (into respective religious groups including Sikhs and Hindus), rather than a blanket 'labelling'.

In relation to civil wars related to class and supported by external countries, the example of Nepal can be cited. Despite the heralding of democratic elections in Nepal in 1990, the failure of the new governments to address the dire poverty and lack of infrastructure resulted in a Maoist insurgency dating from 1996 which by 2003 was threatening to escalate into an all-out civil war. It was reported that the Nepalese army (now more answerable to the King than a democratic government) was receiving massive military aid (including training in counter-insurgency techniques and 5000 new MI6s) from the US and there were mounting reports of human rights violations against the civilian population by the army. The US apparently justified this support as part of the 'war against international terrorism'; and the UK (which has had close links with Nepal for a century) has played at best a passive role, but India is concerned about the increased availability of weapons in the region and the possible effects of an overspill across its own borders.[6] This snapshot perhaps illustrates the interconnections between countries and conflicts that are not always obvious to a casual or uninformed observer.

The first example of intra-country conflict due to race (Cote D'Ivoire) suggests the possible circumstances underlying migration and applications for asylum; while the Australian and Dutch examples might resonate with social professionals in many other countries where minority groups (whether they are indigenous, or established or recent arrivals) feel themselves subject to racial prejudice and tensions lurking just below the surface of apparently liberal and well-regulated societies. The fourth example (Nepal) illustrates how the policies of major players on the world stage can impact on distant nations that are often small and desperately poor. The use of a pseudonym by the author of the article from which this example is drawn (normally a worker with an international development agency) also suggests that there are potential 'risks' (either personal or in terms of support for the organization) in publicizing such views. As well as requiring national policy measures to address discrimination and persecution, it is likely that cross-national or international actions will be necessary in some cases, and that social professionals will need to consider their own responses at local, national and international levels. These will be discussed later, but first it might be appropriate to consider further the effects of conflicts which can be termed 'wars'.

The Effects of War

Wars can be considered as a form of 'disaster', albeit ones that are essentially 'man-made', and as such, they show similarities with 'natural disasters' (such as earthquakes) in some of their effects (Lyons, 1999), while also having some distinctive features. As discussed in Chapter 4, loss in many forms is – of family members, homes, livelihoods and perhaps even one's country (if the effect is seeking asylum outside the country – and/or a change in national boundaries or perhaps even the dismantling of nation state in its previous form) – is inevitable. In relation to the last possibility, it can be speculated that loss of one's country will for some people be as traumatic as loss of family members through death – with which it is, in any case, commonly associated in the case of war.

Most wars result in a greater or lesser degree of disruption of societal infrastructures (including water and power supplies and means of transport) and, if occurring in rural areas, agricultural production is also disrupted (with both short- and longer-term implications for food supplies). Whether war is being waged across rural or urban areas, there is usually widespread displacement of civilian populations (Laird, 2004). For some, this is a 'short-distance' relocation, perhaps to a known place outside the zone of military conflict, but for many this may be the start of the process of becoming 'a refugee'. Some will find themselves in refugee camps, probably across the nearest national border, for example, Liberian people in Ghana (Kreitzer, 2002), for what they hope will be a temporary period. But for others it will be the start of a longer-term process of seeking asylum, often in a more distant country (discussed in Chapter 6).

Those who remain in war-torn areas may find themselves affected by 'collateral damage' (the euphemism coined to describe destruction of buildings not identified as military targets, with resultant injury and death of civilians); and for those injured, whatever the standard of previous medical resources, these will be damaged, depleted or non-existent. As well as having to make their homes in temporary shelters (sometimes communal) or buildings deprived of any amenities (or even on the streets or in the forests), people are likely to face shortages of the most basic necessities (potable water and food). For instance, the Executive Director of the United Nations World Food Programme estimated that 40 million Africans were at risk – of hunger, spread of HIV/AIDS and of becoming displaced persons – because of war.[7] In many cases, people are unlikely to be able to maintain their normal routines, for instance, going to work or school or shopping, or may do so in the face of risks – not just from military attack but also from the breakdown in normal legal or societal codes and sanctions – resulting, for instance, in kidnapping, break-ins and looting of premises. Children may face abduction and conscription; and women may be raped. Men may be tortured or killed and women and children may be forced to watch or even participate in attacks on family members or neighbours (see for instance reports and publicity material from Medical Foundation for the Victims of Torture, UK, 2004).

While couched in 'hypothetical' terms (clearly, not all civilians experience all effects or to the same extent) there are numerous reports and articles in the popular press and from major INGOs (such as Amnesty International, CARITAS, Oxfam) and the UN detailing the particular effects of specific recent and current conflicts, in countries as different as Kosovo and the Sudan (Darfur region). Laird (2004) cites references from UN reports and the literature to suggest that in a 25-year period at the end of the twentieth century 4.5 per cent of the total population of Africa (over 6 million people) were killed as a result of inter-ethnic conflict and 8–13 million people became refugees or were internally displaced.

'Atrocities' of various kinds, whether committed against civilians or members of the opposing military forces, are a 'fact of war': some quickly become known and receive wide publicity (and often international condemnation) while others may lie dormant for years. The effects, both physical and psychological, may also be immediately apparent or may be masked, surfacing at a future point in the lives of individuals and communities. An example of the latter situation concerns the effects of the defoliant, 'Agent Orange', widely used by the Americans in Vietnam in the 1960s, and still having repercussions on the physical attributes and life chances of children born in the last few years (Harrop, 2003, p. 7). It is also apparent that there are differential effects on people caught up in conflict situations, not least related to gender and age. We will focus on two particular breaches of international codes concerning human and children's rights which are frequent in war – rape and sexual exploitation (usually of women but sometimes of quite young girls and even boys); and conscription to the army of children (usually boys, but sometimes also girls).

Women in War
Whether or not they are involved in military service (or covert resistance) in particular conflicts, women are at particular risk of sexual crimes in situations of conflict. Rape is now recognized as a

'weapon of war' (Van Wormer, 1997). It has been systematically used to humiliate, intimidate and subjugate the women (and often the men) of particular communities but also to weaken or prevent the re-establishment of ties of family and ethnicity. In many ethnic or tribal groups, women who have been raped have been shamed: they may be too frightened to tell members of their own family or ethnic group and if they do they may not be believed or they may be punished.[8] They – and any babies they produce – may be stigmatized and excluded, whether or not the rape(s) resulted in lasting physical damage. Additionally, rape has been used as a tactic in attempts at genocide or ethnic cleansing, where a more powerful force seeks to drive the inhabitants of a particular ethnicity out of a specific region or country.

A doctor who has treated nearly 1000 victims of rape aged from 12 to 70 over a one-year period (2003/2004) in Bukavu (Eastern Congo) distinguished different forms of rape, ranging from actions based on sexual attraction (where individual women become the 'wives' of individual soldiers), through abduction of young girls to become sex slaves in the army, to mass rape and mutilation, when even physical repair may not be possible.[9] Another recent article details the longer-term effects of rape resulting from a previous conflict, namely that between Hutus and Tutsis in Rwanda in 1994, when a million people were killed. Apart from lacking husbands, homes and incomes, many women have been too frightened to go back to their villages in the face of ongoing local conflicts and fears of retribution as men implicated in killing, looting and rape have returned. Additionally, some are now suffering from AIDS as a result of multiple rapes and the country does not have the resources to pay for the anti-retroviral drugs needed to treat them.[10]

Child Soldiers

The issue of child soldiers can be considered both as an extreme form of child labour and exploitation – and as a fact of war in some countries: for the purposes of this text we are considering it in the context of conflict. Of course, some children (under 16 years of age) and young people (under 18) do volunteer for military service (although it could be argued that the conditions prompting such behaviour may leave them little choice) but others are enslaved or kidnapped. For instance, in Uganda the Lords Resistance Army is reputed to have abducted at least 14,000 children, some as young as 7 years (CSUCS, 2000). Rwanda similarly has been accused of 'recruiting' children as young as 7 years to military service (CSCUS, 1999a) and by 2001 it was estimated that 200,000 children had taken part in hostilities in Rwanda (Global March, no date). A UNICEF research study in 1997 found that 34 per cent of 2134 children associated with the military in Rwanda had army numbers, indicating direct involvement in war, while the remainder had 'served' as 'kadogos' (cleaners and servants).

On the matter of children being conscripted, a UN report identified this violation of children's rights in 1996 (Machel, 1996) and reiterated it in 2000 (Machel, 2000). Subsequently, 84 states have ratified (and a total of 116 states have signed) the Optional Protocol to the Convention on the Rights of the Child concerning the involvement of children in armed conflict. However, a survey carried out by a Coalition to Stop the Use of Child Soldiers and reported in the Child Soldiers Global Report (2004) indicated that 'Boys and girls under the age of 18 have fought in more than 20 of the world's major conflicts since 2001.'[11]

The same report claims that while some children have been engaged in active fighting (for instance, in Burundi, the Democratic Republic of the Congo and Myanmar), others have been used informally as spies, informants or collaborators (by Israel, Indonesia and Nepal); and points out that young men of 17 years have fought for the US military in Afghanistan and Iraq, while Germany, Ireland, the Netherlands and the UK continue to recruit 17-year-olds to the military forces. In relation to the UK, CSUCS (1999b) reported that 51 peacekeepers sent to Balkans were under 18 years; that 200 minors were involved in the Gulf War; and that others of a similar age had been involved in the Falkland and Northern Ireland conflicts. The government now claims that minors are no longer engaged in active duty.

The effects of involvement in war vary according to the child or young person's previous life experience, the circumstances under which he or she has been 'recruited', the type of training received, and the actual tasks and behaviour expected of such individuals, relative to their age, abilities and temperament. As indicated, some children and young people will have been unwillingly (and probably forcefully) separated from their families and communities, and conscripted into local armies. One such example comes from Darfur (an area in Western Sudan, the size of France and Spain), where an estimated 50,000 people have already been killed and more than 1.5 million people have been displaced in the conflict between the (Arab) Janjaweed Militia (supported by the Sudanese government) and the (black African) rebel forces.[12] A report in 2004 by an INGO, Save the Children, accused Sudanese government troops, militias and police of having committed 'serious violations against children', including conscription into the rebel army. Concerns have also been raised about the ability of African Union troops and police (albeit backed by Western, largely American, funding and with their remit extended from monitoring to protecting civilians) to provide security for people in villages not yet destroyed or in the vast refugee camps which have been established within Sudan's borders or in eastern Chad.[13]

There is also some evidence from previous conflicts that in the post-war situation, such young conscripts may be rejected by their families or villages because of their previous behaviour (even if this was under duress), adding to the possibility that some will be too traumatized to adapt to peacetime conditions. It is just worth stressing here that violence in the company of peers will have become a way of life for some young men (in particular) and the very difficult economic and employment conditions facing most countries in the wake of war make it even more essential to devise specific programmes that involve former participants in war in the active rebuilding of communities and societies.

Developing the Social Work Role in Conflict Situations

Given the nature and extent of some of the conflicts described above, it might be assumed that social workers have only a peripheral role to play in relation to conflicts, many of which – to many Western social professionals – may seem remote, in terms of both geography and professional experience. This view is strengthened by the limited number of references to education and strategies for intervention in conflict situations, in the conventional social work literature. Major recent texts about social work, and about international social work specifically, barely mention 'conflict' as a topic, although Van Wormer (1997) notes briefly the effects of war on children, the environment and women. Healy (2001) makes one reference to conflict avoidance and resolution (p. 273) in the context of initiatives which need to be developed (see later) and in an earlier text, Hokenstad and Midgley (1997) included a chapter by Mehta about ethnic conflict and possible forms of intervention (also discussed below). Lyons (1999) includes a number of references to the effects of war in a chapter about responses to disasters and suggests that there is some overlap in the range of knowledge and skills identified as appropriate for intervention. But in terms of policy and international developments, Ahmadi (2003) (in line with an earlier view expressed by Mehta, 1997) has suggested that social workers have a part to play in 'preventing conflict and supporting peace by promoting global cultural integration' (p. 14).

Additionally, if we assume that (Western) social workers are likely to have some understanding of the psychosocial effects of loss (including possible stages in grief reaction or alternative somatic manifestations), as well as knowledge of theories relating to crisis intervention and post-traumatic stress disorder (as previously discussed in Chapter 4), it could be argued that social professionals are well placed to respond to those affected by conflict situations. In addition, expertise has been built up in organizations such as the Medical Foundation for the Victims of Torture, which suggests that the traditional social work values of being alongside people and validating their experience (with which many social professionals are familiar) are important aspects of counselling and rehabilitation services for the individual victims of war.

But, as suggested previously, theories and models related to loss and interventions are often framed in Western and individualized terms and, as such, they might not form a useful basis for assessments and interventions with all population groups or in the context of, or the aftermath of, conflict. Developing understanding of how reactions to grief, crises or stress are manifested in different cultures is essential; but it is also becoming clear that more specific attention is needed to theories about conflict, conflict avoidance and conflict management in professional education programmes. Laird (2004) has noted this lack of curriculum development as relevant for countries of sub-Saharan Africa, specifically. Drawing on her experience of social work education in Ghana (a country which, because of its relative stability and proximity to sites of conflict, has attracted people from other African countries), she found that among social work students surveyed (at the University of Ghana), a proportion had directly experienced some of the effects of tribal conflicts described earlier.

Laird concluded that, in the African situation, all students need to consider their own attitudes and future professional practices in the light of their ethnic identity and tribal loyalties. However, she also suggested that literature related to anti-racist work (as developed in the US and UK) seemed less relevant than models developed in the context of sectarian violence in Northern Ireland for informing social work educators in Ghana, and possibly other African countries (although she also urges the development of indigenous models and material relevant to local circumstances).

The realities of migration (see Chapter 6), whether as a result of war or not, also suggest that responding to the effects of war on individuals – or strategies to contribute to the prevention of conflict in local ethnically diverse communities – must be a concern for social professionals in countries which seem far removed from the actual sites of violent conflict. In the European context, development of anti-oppressive education which includes a strong emphasis on the rights of minorities (whether, for instance, they are long-established immigrants or recent asylum seekers or 'indigenous' Roma people) is essential, as is the development of cross-cultural communication skills (including becoming proficient in other languages) or skilled use of interpreters (as discussed for instance in Kornbeck, 2003). In practical terms, in the UK for example, social professionals have found themselves working in asylum-seekers teams (see Chapter 6) or in projects in the voluntary sector where there may be more opportunity to address the psychosocial needs of asylum seekers who have been particularly traumatized by war (including women who have been raped).

However, perhaps more fundamentally, social professionals need to attend to non-majority perspectives, develop links with the representatives of local minority ethnic groups and devise or link in with broader strategies aimed at strengthening minority communities to advocate for their own interests. There is already anecdotal evidence about the initiative shown by some groups of asylum seekers in the UK in developing their own resources and establishing their own networks, both within the country and with their country of origin (for instance, by Somalians or Sierra Leonians), and of the significant role which some individuals can play in mediating between a minority group and the host community (including through acting as interpreters). In this context, it is important for social professionals to utilize the strengths perspective (discussed in Chapter 3) and not to 'pathologize' behaviours which may be serving as adaptation and coping mechanisms.

However, there is also a need for institutionalized efforts to identify, mentor and train those able to play a professional role in addressing social problems. An example from France (Tasse, 2001) demonstrates how schools of social work can be part of schemes aimed at bringing socially excluded youth into education and training programmes which would equip them for real jobs, including in the social professions. Unfortunately, the riots by disaffected minority youth in France late in 2005 suggest that there is still a need for further development of national policies and practices which make social and economic integration a reality for many minority ethnic communities.

France has been one of a number of European countries where there have been initiatives (some part-funded by the EU) aimed at preventing the onset or escalation of conflict within diverse communities through tackling social exclusion and/or racism. Such projects are often aimed at youths (particularly young men) whose experiences of school failure, unemployment and 'gang culture' are most likely to result in violence aimed at other ethnic or racial groups. Two books produced in the 1990s (Aluffi-Pentini and Lorenz, 1996; Hazenkamp and Popple, 1997) illustrated a range of projects in different countries aimed at addressing racism among young people. Many usefully demonstrate the role of social group work in challenging assumptions and providing space for the development of more constructive activities and identity formation. However, despite the efforts of some voluntary agencies, there tends to be less evidence of advocacy and lobbying for the needs of particular groups or in relation to national or regional policy and legislative changes relating to migration and race relations (see also Chapter 6); and even less attention to international events which might be contributing to local tensions.

Turning to wider policy and practice implications, former General Secretary of IASSW Vera Mehta (1997) urged social workers to engage in 'preventive diplomacy' and in reconciliation and reconstruction to address the consequences of conflict. Mehta's suggestions as to how social workers might develop such interventions include 'alleviate insecurities and material conditions that tempt violence' (p. 101) and 'monitoring violations of human rights; . . . fostering interethnic dialogue; . . . national capacity building in all spheres; and promoting education for peace and non-violent conflict resolution' (p. 103) and it is worth considering some of the ways in which these activities are already in evidence in different localities.

In some parts of the world social professionals already see the value of social and community development programmes (see for instance, Kaseke, 2001 re Zimbabwe) aimed at mitigating the circumstances of poverty and social injustice which can provoke civil conflict. Arguably, these approaches should also receive greater attention in the training and practices of social professionals in AICs and there has been some indication of adoption of at least one community development strategy in the US. For instance, it has been reported that micro-credit schemes modelled on the Grameen Bank have been established in some poor inner city areas of the US. The Grameen Bank is a micro-credit scheme pioneered in Bangladesh (since 1984) through which small loans are made to women with little or no means of support, so that they can purchase equipment or supplies which can provide them with a livelihood (Lyons, 1999). However (as noted in Lyons, 1999), while this addresses the specific needs of individuals and families, and may well feed into local community development and national capacity building, it does not of itself lead to a significant shift in wealth and resources, either within specific societies or between the world's nations, so may not address more fundamental causes of conflict.

Hessle and Hessle (1998) have suggested a four-stage model of the sites and phases of social work intervention in relation to conflict, which was developed as a result of their involvement in childcare project work in relation to Bosnia-Herzegovina. In the first 'during conflict' situation, they describe the important role of Bosnian social workers based in pre-established social centres in providing material assistance to the people worst affected by the war, as well as some psycho-social assistance to individuals and families (though staff numbers were depleted by about 50 per cent and not all centres could remain open). In their second stage, services were provided to asylum seekers and refugees (in this case located in Sweden) aimed at addressing the problems associated with flight and the process of integration. In the third stage, the uncertainties related to the possibility of repatriation in a post-war situation need to be addressed (also discussed in the context of work in a Swiss accommodation centre for asylum seekers by Mlczoch, 2002), while in the fourth stage, local and international social workers need to devise plans for redevelopment of services, including addressing the particular needs of returning refugees.

It is clear that this model relates to a situation where there were already some pre-existing social work services and in the case of many of the examples of conflict presented earlier, humanitarian aid agencies may be the only source of help to civilians. This is sometimes offered during the period of military conflict but, whatever the level of local need, these agencies sometimes judge that the risks faced by workers and volunteers are unacceptable and withdrawal is necessary. This can be the case even in the post-war period when an apparent military victory has been resisted by at least a proportion of the country's nationals, as has been the case in Iraq where Médecins Sans Frontières (MSF or Doctors without Borders); CARE International, and Action Contra la Faim (action against starvation) had all withdrawn by late 2004.[14]

But, INGOs often play an invaluable role in refugee camps set up during and after wars, which often continue to house the victims of war long after the formal cessation of hostilities. Examples include the long-established refugee camps housing Palestinians in the West Bank, the more recently established camps for Rwandans in Tanzania and the Afghan refugee camps in Pakistan, as well as refugee camps in some European countries (e.g., Greece) which house refugees from a variety of conflicts. Such INGOs sometimes employ (foreign) social workers and an example of practice in this situation is provided by a Swedish author (Segerstrom, 1998) drawing on experience in the Yemen with Somali refugees through the Swedish branch of Save the Children. Following some assessment of needs and provisions in the camp, the project focused on improving the psychological well-being of mothers through their involvement in community development activities, including establishing some educational provision for the children and support for the activities of a Women's Union (which some of the women had already formed). However, Segerstrom does not gloss over the difficulties and disappointments associated with the lack of participation of many women in this potentially valuable resource and the low impact of the project overall (p. 163).

Similarly, disappointing results were found in a study of the involvement of women in planning camp programmes more generally, in this case by Liberian women in a refugee camp in Ghana (Kreitzer, 2002). It may be that the expectations of Western women about the active role of women in public life does not 'fit' the experience of women from more traditional societies, particularly when such women have been made homeless (and effectively stateless) and either been subject to, or terrified about the possibility of, death, rape, mutilation and/or starvation for themselves and other family members. However, the psychological effects of such experiences are far more likely to be expressed somatically (ibid.), suggesting that increased emphasis on development of health-related programmes aimed at women might be more effective, at least as a precursor to other projects geared to social needs.

There are other examples of how social professionals may be involved in efforts to redress the effects of human rights violations through work in refugee camps (usually through major INGOs such as Save the Children or the Red Cross), and these may include ongoing efforts to protect women from sexual exploitation, since the scale and nature of some refugee camps can make them less-safe places than might be hoped. For some social professionals, such activity is likely to constitute a form of international social work in a country distant from their country of origin. However, in other cases, refugee camps exist inside the boundaries of countries where Western social workers are being trained, and these camps may be a site for both practice placements and employment for some social workers, as is the case in Greece (personal communication).

It is usually in the post-war period that we can see a shift from humanitarian aid (effectively concerned with survival) to community development projects and other measures to assist local populations to adapt to what is often a 'fragile peace' and to engage in rebuilding communities both physically and socially. Such efforts may be established and maintained with the backing of the World Bank or western governments, as well as charitable and corporate donations. The strategies devised and interventions utilized will partly depend on location and resources available (both human and physical), as well as the needs identified, as the following examples illustrate.

In Europe, following the 1990s Balkan war, a Greek social worker was among those participating in a pilot project co-sponsored in Kosovo in 2000 by a Greek NGO (Institute of International Social Affairs), UNICEF and OSCE (Organization for Security and Co-operation in Europe). This project was focused on a primary school serving both Albanian and Serbian communities in a village in the Obiliq Municipality and aimed to promote tolerance in a community still divided by suspicions and threats. Children from the different communities were attending the school in separate shifts and the project involved direct work with teachers, who in turn were expected to increase understanding (and thus tolerance) of the children and parents from the other community (Soumpasi, 2003).

In the context of a developing country, a recent initiative in Sierra Leone by Voluntary Service Overseas (VSO) suggests the sort of work and skills required in the 'reconstruction phase', which can be provided (at the request of a national government) by an INGO. Following an 11-year civil war in which nearly half the country's population was displaced and 100,000 people were mutilated,[15] VSO's personnel (paid and voluntary) are assisting local people in developing services in relation to HIV/AIDS and promoting community health education, community development and micro-enterprise schemes.

With reference to interventions geared to the needs of children who have been soldiers, an example can be provided from Uganda. Children (mainly boys) found in the Lord's Resistance Army are taken to UNICEF-funded rehabilitation centres where possible (by social workers), often arriving in poor physical and emotional condition. Some are 'addicted to violence', having endured and even inflicted various horrifying acts. The children receive one-to-one counselling and group work support and are gradually re-introduced to education or vocational training and are re-united with their families, where possible. The task of re-integration is often difficult due to the aggressive behaviour of the boys and some need psychiatric assistance, but the key, as always, is building trust and providing an environment which can be experienced as safe and accepting – and, in this case, more overtly offering forgiveness. Follow-up of the children when they leave the centres is difficult in a country where resources are stretched, but a multi-disciplinary approach is taken with teachers taking on a significant role. Rehabilitation programmes of this kind are sometimes controversial and seen as a Western imposition, failing to utilize people's innate coping skills. However, counselling has been found useful and there is a view that more work also needs to be done with families and communities to assist in the re-integration of child soldiers.

The above examples all suggest forms of direct practice or service developments with members of communities potentially, actually or recently caught up in conflicts with others differentiated by race, ethnicity or class. However, apart from direct engagement, often utilizing skills in mediation and group facilitation, social professionals may be operating in other forms of indirect practice. These include 'active membership' or representation in local interagency forums and/or democratic and civil organizations. Such participation can contribute to information exchange and modification of preconceived assumptions as well as furthering the development of local resources and policies aimed at counteracting racism or other factors contributing to conflict.

Additionally, the voices of social professionals (or their representative professional associations) need to be heard at national level, giving feedback about the impact of particular legislation or policy implementation on specific groups and communities and monitoring and commenting on proposals for new legislation, particularly as it is likely to impact on migration, race relations and minority ethnic populations. So, for instance, the Australian Association of Social Workers (AASW) issued a media release in 2002 calling on the federal government to demonstrate commitment to adequate resourcing, comprehensive training and collaborative relationships between government agencies and Aboriginal communities;[16] and a comparative approach to analysis of patterns of social work education suggests that there is wide variation in the extent to which social professionals are being trained for these wider roles in planning and political arenas, whether through the academic curriculum or through placement opportunities. For example, Australian social work students are placed in a much wider range of agencies (including in the offices and surgeries of Members of Parliament) than their British counterparts (personal communication).

Finally, there is scope for increased activity at international level in relation to situations of conflict. Some leadership has been provided in this direction by the IFSW and by national associations. For example, the IFSW issued statements of concern to the US President and other governments about the possible escalation of violence following 9/11 and later about the possible invasion of Iraq. It was subsequently a signatory to a joint statement presented to the UN Commission on Human Rights (at which the Federation has observer status) on the occasion of their 59th session, condemning the invasion of Iraq without UN backing and asking the UN to monitor the human rights situation in that country as a result of the war.[17] It has also been suggested that ICT offer a wealth of new opportunities for social professionals to engage in online advocacy about relevant international issues (Queiro-Tajalli *et al.*, 2003).

Concluding Comments

This chapter has sought to provide insights into a range of conflict situations and to illustrate their relevance to the work of social professionals, operating locally but within a globalized context. The use of examples of wars and conflict from a wide range of countries aims both to disseminate information about the situations which may have led some people to become the users of social work services in AICs or refugee camps, as well as to raise the profile of an area of work which has received little attention in many countries to date. Additionally, the use of some comparative material about education and practice may contribute to efforts to develop broader curricula and more relevant practices at local and national levels, while we also urge that, in an interdependent world, social professionals also need to consider the international implications of particular conflicts and related possibilities for professional interventions beyond state boundaries.

Healy (2001), in writing about international social work, while not providing a specific focus on conflicts around the world, concludes that 'the profession... needs to work on conflict avoidance and conflict resolution strategies that can be applied *at micro and macro levels*' (p. 273, my italics). Acknowledging that some experience has been gained in relation to the former (and that many western social professionals would feel better equipped to work at the micro level), we can only concur with Healy's view that social professionals need 'to work collaboratively across nations and with other disciplines to develop and apply macro-level strategies for encouraging ethnic harmony and ethnic justice' (p. 273). Stated thus, and given some of the examples above, it is clear that intervention in relation to potential or actual situations of community, national and international conflict accord with the values of protecting and promoting human rights and social justice.

6 Natural and Forced Migration: Causes and Consequences

Introduction

As previous chapters have already indicated, there are many reasons for migration. Additionally, population mobility is a complex process, where migration patterns are often rooted in the historical connections between particular countries or continents. It is a field of human activity which has increasingly given rise to both political responses and the need for practical interventions by social professionals. Hoogvelt (1997) has identified the movement of people from one political area to another as a clear symptom of the growing interconnectedness and mass deepening of globalization. Facing an increasing disparity of wealth, as well as natural and human-made disasters (including armed conflict), some populations have had to relocate – in search of employment, or respite, or basic protection. On the other hand, a new elite has emerged who are able to take advantage of the mechanisms of globalization (ICT, transport) to loosen their ties to particular geographical locations: they are willingly and globally mobile. Coincidentally, people in both these categories have influenced the global spread of disease, HIV/AIDS in particular (see Chapter 8).

In recent times there has been a movement towards closing the doors on immigration in industrialized countries. As discussed in the previous chapter, the events of 9/11 and the ensuing wars in Afghanistan and Iraq have given governments an excuse to 'crack down' on immigration, both legal and illegal, under the guise of 'security'. The idea of migrants posing an imminent threat to local societies is not a new one and public xenophobia is often politically more powerful than any real threat caused by migration, as evidenced in emerging policies in Europe and the US. As Bauman postulates, we see

> (o)n the one hand, promotion of an unbridled freedom of movement for the dominant elite (and for what it stands for – capital, commodities, information). On the other, imposition of ever tighter restrictions on movements of the rest (as manifested most spectacularly, though not exclusively, in the evermore severe anti-migration policies, coupled with the hiving-off of the job of human waste disposal to global men-smuggling mafia). (Cited in Gane, 2004, pp. 24–25)

We also find greater reference to migration in the social work literature (compared with conflict) since social work with minority groups – whether described as immigrants, refugees or asylum seekers – has long been recognized as an area of professional concern. Indeed some of the major voluntary organizations currently involved in international social work, such as Save the Children and International Social Services (ISS), had their origins in the responses to the needs of refugees in the period following the First World War (1914–1918) (Lyons, 1999), while more recent developments have provided a spur to local agency initiatives aimed at addressing the particular needs of minority ethnic communities or new groups of asylum seekers. Apart from references in the major recent internationally oriented books, there are also articles in the professional press and national and international journals (see later) as well as recent British and American texts focusing on social work with migrants (Potocki-Tripody, 2002; Hayes and Humphries, 2004), although a limited number of comparative studies (for instance, Lyons and Stathopoulos, 2001; Huegler, 2003) in this field also illustrate the variable extent to which countries have developed specific services or specialist training for this area of work.

This chapter therefore aims to present a brief overview of the causes of migration as well as identifying some common characteristics and categorizations applied to migrants. Migration is often described as 'natural', suggesting choice and commonly accepted ways of living, relative to 'forced'. The latter category may cover a wide range of reasons for and forms of migration, and we shall pay particular attention to people trafficking or smuggling. We consider that migration can be seen as both a logical and healthy coping mechanism and a process which, for some, may result in danger, exploitation and loss (see also Chapters 4 and 7). We then consider some of the particular examples of interventions in this field by social professionals and suggest that increased knowledge of global events and cross-national responses can encourage both improvements in local practices and development of international policies.

Migration: Some Causes and Characteristics

Current debates about migration tend to focus on the negative impact of forced migration, both on the people who leave their countries and, often in the public imagination, on the host societies to which they migrate. However, as De Haan (1999) has emphasized, historically, many communities were not sedentary, and migration, as a natural movement of people, became an established and effective livelihood strategy in response to local situations (environmental and demographic) in many societies. In addition, it was common in some cultures for females to move (permanently) to the homes of their husbands after marriage, sometimes at some distance from the maternal family (De Haan, 2000). Moreover, much of the recent focus has been on rural–urban migration, but more common movements are still between rural–rural locations, often for short, non-permanent durations (De Haan, 1999). In addition, Soyden (1998) stressed the functional and even essential nature of much migration and challenged the 'problematic' label often attributed to immigrants.

The complexity of migration as a process and phenomenon is such that theorists have had difficulty in encapsulating it within a working model. However, a theory proposed by Giddens includes an analysis of migrants' motivations, attitudes and their understanding of the structures within which they act, as well as repetitive and historical patterns of behaviour (cited in De Haan, 1999, p. 12). Currently, one of the common assumptions regarding migration tends to focus on its use as a political tool to attract people to jobs, and economic factors have been seen as both 'pushing' migrants from one country or area (away from poverty at individual and collective levels), as well as being one of the factors 'pulling' them towards other localities (with increased earning opportunities). (For a wider discussion of push and pull factors in migration, see Lee, 1966, cited in De Haan, 1999.) Such migration may be across the rural–urban divide in a home country (as happens in South Africa, Palmer, 1985) or across a local–national border (for instance between Mexico and the US, Walter *et al.*, 2004) or across a continent (for instance between Pakistan and the UK, Martin, 2003). In some cases, migrants are often also 'catapulted' from a rural and/or developing country into an urban location in an industrial society, posing particular challenges to adaptive behaviour for both immigrants and 'hosts'. While such migrants may often be referred to collectively as 'economic migrants', the extent to which such migration is voluntary or forced and permanent or temporary is variable. Perhaps even more variable is the extent to which such migrants have legal recognition and economic status in a new area or country, relative to the possibility for some that such migration is 'illegal', consigning them to the status of 'undocumented worker' (see for instance, Chapter 6, Held *et al.*, 1999).

Other political factors in migration are those aimed at moving people forcibly, including the relocation or expulsion of individuals or minority groups who are considered alien, disruptive or deviant from the mainstream society. This could include people of Romany descent or a wider group of 'travellers' who may or may not be ethnically different from the settled population. Again, there are both historical and recent examples of migration policies that targeted specific groups through intimidation, coercion and forceful ejection from an area and, in extreme cases, deliberate policies of genocide. Well-documented cases of abuse have occurred even within and since the last decade of the twentieth century, including in Sri Lanka, Bosnia, Kosovo, Angola, Sudan and Afghanistan (see, for instance, Kelly and Regan, 2000; UNHCR, 2000, as well as Chapter 5).

In terms of the characteristics of migrants, there are demographic differences between sub-groups, based on age and gender. Conventionally, it is often younger (single) people seeking work and/or different lifestyles who migrate (though this may be different in the case of the global elite). Historically, males comprised the majority of economic migrants, but this has changed for a number of reasons: 'surplus' males may no longer be present in a given society or community (for instance, because of war or disease) or, alternatively, employment opportunities arise that favour women. For example, there has been an increase in the number of women migrating from the Philippines to the UK or US to become housemaids or health workers (Anderson, 2003), as well as increased concern about women from Eastern Europe coming to West European countries as sex workers (discussed later). Some of the previous rhetoric surrounding gender differentiation has focused on the problems that are caused for those left behind, including the double and triple burden for women when men leave (Palmer, 1985). However, contemporary gender analysis of migration has failed to recognize underlying and pre-existing power differentials within communities and singular causation is likely to be flawed.

Men and women also face different struggles related to migration. For instance, females are generally lower paid; or they may have difficulty re-establishing rights over land when they return. It is also likely that, while economic motives may be significant for both, men and women migrate for different reasons: for example, Adepoju (2002) suggests that males may migrate to escape from dominant elders. Migration also has different impacts on the communities 'left behind'. So, for instance, in cultures where migration is not a new phenomenon, an established coping pattern may exist, while in other societies, the absence of males opens new doors for females to exercise control – either as the new 'head of the house' or as migrants themselves (Palmer, 1985).

Migration can also be analysed according to the 'costs and benefits' for individuals and also for both the sending and receiving countries. The positive effects of migration (for all three parties) vary depending on the reason for leaving, the degree to which skills match employment demands and the perceived reduction in risks and costs associated with leaving the home country. Examples of this include policies that relax international borders or migration legislation to take advantage of genuine employment opportunities, such as in West Africa during the Nigerian oil boom (Adepoju, 2002), or, more recently, in European countries where migrants with particular qualifications (e.g., in the healthcare field) are granted entry visas. Also, positive effects are enhanced if the migrant is able to meet family needs through sending money home or because they have removed themselves from a complex situation (De Haan, 2000). Remittances represent a significant national income for many countries (Martin, 2003). Some states, such as Sri Lanka, increase the likelihood of a positive experience, through offering support for nationals working abroad and making remittance transfers safer and also by offering re-integration support when migrants return. Finally, migration of one or more family members may be less risky than staying in the home area, making migration an important tool for survival (De Haan, 2000).

On the negative side, migrants may become a liability to their family. Palmer found that 'among the poorest migrant families, as in Pakistan, net remittances may not be large enough to relieve wives of additional burdens for a couple of years' (Palmer, 1985). While they are 'away', migrants may lose their jobs, run out of money, become sick, experience legal problems or even be jailed if the host country considers them a threat to employment of local people, a drain on public resources, or as involved in criminal activity. In relation to the economic conditions of 'receiving countries', a downturn in the local employment market is likely to lead to redundancies of migrant workers first and might even result in the mass expulsion of workers, as happened from the Ivory Coast and Gabon in the 1980s (Adepoju, 2002). Migrants who fail to achieve (for whatever reason) the goals they set for themselves and/or their families are likely to face significant psychological and practical problems and, in many cases, returning home may not be an option.

Wider social costs also cannot be ignored. Even in cases where migration was seen as a temporary event and return was preferable to 'settling', not all states offer support for returning migrants, and socio-economic conditions may continue to provide few opportunities. For instance, a study in Kerala (India), found that half of all returnees remained unemployed and this was partly attributed to a lack of state support (Nair, 1999). Migration is an expensive, variable, time-consuming and risky process: men (or women) may be separated from their families for years due to the high costs of returning home, even for 'holidays'. For those societies in which migration is relatively new, cultural-coping mechanisms (such as sharing labour across communities or neighbours) may not exist, making the social effects on families more difficult to predict. From an economic point of view, risk to the family is proportional to the amount of time between the family member's migration and their sending a beneficial remittance that offsets the family's labour shortage, as demonstrated by Palmer's (1985) findings on the effect of male out-migration from the Middle East and Africa during the 1980s. However, and importantly for social professionals, this analysis is one of economics, and does not take into account the emotional and social effects of family dispersion which may also be costly.

Migration also affects society (i.e., culture, collective identity, tradition) and the state (government) differently: the relationship between the two may not be complementary. Thus, development policies may be agreed which have a bearing on the migration abilities of individuals while at the same time ignoring its role in society. De Haan (2000) has identified this as a problem of some recent agricultural and development programmes, including in China. De Haan states that migration is a historical livelihood strategy in China, although since the communist revolution in 1949, there have been very restrictive migration policies. The government is wary of the threat of 'flooding' of the cities by rural poor people, a belief supported by fears of greater overcrowding in urban centres expressed in the popular press. De Haan (1999) has suggested that this fear is unfounded and that most migration, if allowed, would occur between rural areas as mobility of agricultural labour, and would re-establish a livelihood option now denied. Unfortunately for China, wealth has tended to concentrate in the new economic (urban, industrial) zones and the view that the wealth would 'trickle down' has not been supported by the evidence (De Haan, 2000). (For a different view on urban poverty in China, see Hussain, 2002.)

The extent to which migration both influences and is impacted upon by other development initiatives varies. Ignoring this relationship may have adverse effects that could complicate both aspects, including, increased nationalization and secession (Olofsgard, 2003). De Haan states that most planners do not recognize the potentials and realities of migration, and therefore do not incorporate migration into developmental policies. However, he makes the case for recognizing migration as part of a complex livelihood strategy (that varies enormously across regions and cultures) and suggests that development policies that work with, rather than against, established livelihood strategies will be more successful in terms of alleviating poverty and increasing well-being.

It may be interesting to consider the impact of migration and its possible relation with development strategies in relation to a particular country. Although part of the 'Western world', for many years (and for reasons related to history, geography and politics) Ireland lagged behind other West European states in terms of economic growth and social infrastructure. Following mass emigration and decimation of the population triggered by famine in the mid-nineteenth century, it continued to be a 'sending country' through to the late twentieth century. For many years, the country faced challenges associated with a population dominated by older people and children, with a relatively small base of wage-earning and/or tax-paying adults. However, its emergence as 'the Celtic Tiger' in the 1990s (as a result of both its position in the EU and its own economic development strategies) resulted in its ability to retain a young and well-educated workforce in new 'high-tech industries'; a need to 'recall' emigrant workers to meet its own needs in a booming building industry; and a shift to becoming a 'receiving country', employing migrants (including from South America) in the agricultural industry, admitting some asylum seekers (notably from African countries) and being open to inter-country adoption (for example, from Romania). However, the idea that countries, including Ireland, which have experienced significant emigration might be receptive (sympathetic) to immigrants has been seriously challenged[1] (see Christie, 2002).

Another aspect of the Irish example illustrates that migration can be an important issue for sending countries in terms of the loss of human resources. This phenomenon, when applied to the educated population, is known as the 'brain drain'. It is not new but it currently represents a significant concern for many countries. Apart from the high-profile cases of eminent scientists or businessmen being tempted to higher paying posts in better resourced countries, evidence suggests that young people sent abroad to study often find more lucrative employment opportunities in their new destination or do not return for other reasons, such as preferred lifestyle or personal relationships. This is an issue for some AICs, for instance, Canada, but is arguably of greater concern to countries of the South, such as the Philippines

or Sri Lanka. It is also an issue directly affecting the social
profession as Western countries (such as the UK) recruit staff
from less wealthy countries (including South Africa or the accession states of the EU), depriving them of newly trained or
experienced personnel in the health and social care sectors (see
Chapter 9). However, as in the case of the Indian example
mentioned in Chapter 1, some countries are beginning to look for
ways (in addition to remittances) to capitalize on the success of
emigrants.

Forced Migration Including People Trafficking and Smuggling

The term 'forced migration' can be applied to people who migrate
for a variety of reasons and in a variety of ways. While it is
sometimes assumed to apply to people who might be called
refugees or asylum seekers, the very specific meanings given to
these terms in international law preclude many people who nevertheless feel compelled to migrate and who, in so doing, may
experience fear and/or exploitation. Additionally, while migration is often assumed to mean movement from one country to
another, Korn (1999) declared that internally displaced people
(IDPs) are the most vulnerable migrant group in the world. While
some such migrants will be moving under government direction for economic reasons (for instance, to vacate land needed
for industrial development or a dam project) (Lyons, 1999),
others will be fleeing from civil war or seeking respite from xeno-
phobic government policies in a particular region (as identified
in Chapter 5). Since they do not cross a national border, they
are not officially classified as refugees and therefore, they may not
be eligible for aid from international organizations such as the
UNHCR.

However, the UNHCR does include IDPs in its efforts to
monitor the scale of migration and estimated that there were 5.3
million IDPs around the world and millions of stateless persons
(UNHCR, 2005), a proportion of whom are likely to suffer a
high risk of mortality. For instance, Cambodia saw one quarter
of its population of 2 million die between 1970 and 1979, due
to war, ethnic cleansing, lack of health care and famine, not least

among IDPs; the civil war in Rwanda (1994–1997) resulted in the internal displacement of a million Hutus and Tutsis (apart from the greater numbers of refugees who managed to cross national borders); and deaths among IDPs in Somalia in 1992 were estimated at 16.7 per 10,000 people in 1992; and at 8.2 per 10,000 in Angola in 1995 (Reed and Keely, 2001). Their status as IDPs rather than refugees partly explains the lack of international aid to the people (mainly women and children) gathering in 'refugee camps' in the Darfur region of Sudan, exercising world concern at the time of writing.

The number of IDPs can be contrasted with the number of people (10 million) officially classified as refugees (UNHCR, 2005). Refugees formally come under the protection of the 1951 Refugee Convention and are likely to be offered assistance by the UN and a range of bodies, including UNHCR, UNDP, UNICEF, WHO, The Red Cross/Red Crescent; and other INGOs. Some reference has already been made to the international and local responses to refugees (including those who formally seek asylum and are granted citizenship or leave to remain in new countries) in Chapter 5; and there has been some growth in the professional literature related to these groups in the past few years (see for instance, Hessle, 2000; Meuse, 2003; Briskman and Cemlyn, 2005; Choi and Choi, 2005; Rosenberg *et al.*, 2005). We therefore concentrate in this section on an area of migration which has been receiving comparatively more attention since about 2000 – but as yet, little in social work – namely, people smuggling or trafficking.

There is some confusion as to the exact meaning of these terms and, while they may often be used interchangeably, it has been suggested that there is more duress and threat in people *trafficking* relative to lesser degrees of exploitation in people *smuggling*. The extent to which people willingly seek transportation from one country to another (often over considerable distances, for extortionate amounts of money and in dangerous conditions) and the knowledge they have about the living and working conditions at their destinations are debatable. It has been suggested that 'trafficking' as a term has its roots in the so called 'White Slave Trade' of the nineteenth century. Although there were fears in the Victorian era in both Britain and the US about the trafficking of young white girls, particularly to Arabic countries, the existence of this slave trade has been disputed (Manion, 2002). Human trafficking can also be compared with the illegal trafficking of arms and drugs.

The Global Alliance Against Trafficking in Women (GAATW) is concerned with the fuzzy distinction now being drawn between trafficking and migration and clearly delineates them (Pearson, 2001), and it has been suggested that migration patterns are being redrawn by organized crime as people are transported globally (Barrett, 2000). It is difficult to get a measure of the scale of the problem, related both to definitional problems and to the illegal and therefore secretive nature of the business. For instance, it was estimated by the International Organization for Migration (IOM) (2002) that 120,000 people were being trafficked annually into 'Fortress Europe' (the 15 states comprising the EU until 2004) in the early twenty-first century. Globally, USID (2001) estimated that annually there were between 800,000 and four million people being trafficked, although in 2004 the US State Department indicated that between 600,000–800,000 people are being trafficked. They had particular concerns with the permeable borders of ten countries (Bangladesh, Burma, Cuba, Equatorial Guinea, Guyana, North Korea, Sierra Leone, Sudan and Venezuela).

Meanwhile, an INGO, Terre des Hommes, has estimated that more than 100,000 children are trafficked *each month* (Dottridge, 2004). UNICEF UK (2003) suggested that 1.2 million children may be involved in this trade annually worldwide, and that Europe (EU) may now be the biggest market, 'attracting' more than 500,000 women and children mainly from the former states of the Soviet Union. The report was released first in the UK, where only 200 children were then formally believed by UNICEF UK to have been trafficked. However, some suspect that this number may be far higher, perhaps in the thousands, with children being brought into the UK for prostitution, drug smuggling, domestic slavery, or even ritual killing (such as the boy 'Adam', see also Kelly and Regan, 2000). A later report also suggested the possibility that some child smuggling may also be related to benefit fraud (Somerset, 2004). Further, a possible connection between trafficking and private fostering arrangements which exist in the UK was also suggested as a result of the death of Victoria Climbié and subsequent enquiry (Simmonds, 2003) and this point will be returned to later.

The international nature of this activity requires increased collaboration in both detection and responses. However, the relatively recent acknowledgement of this problem is indicated by the fact that the UN Protocol on Trafficking in Persons was drawn up only in 2001 and a 'Convention on Trans-National Organized Crime' (in force since 2003) has two supplementary protocols on trafficking and migrant smuggling, which should be important instruments in protecting the rights of trafficked women and girls.[2] There are also examples of regional and national attempts to establish organizations and policies to address the problem. So, for instance, in 2003 the South East (SE) Asian States formulated the first regional instrument, the SE Asia Regional Convention on Preventing and Combating Trafficking of Women and Children in Prostitution. In addition, the Asian Women's Human Rights Council (AWHRC) and UNDP have organized a South Asia Court of Women on the Violence of Trafficking and HIV/AIDS.[3]

Taking the UK as an example of national responses, there are already measures to protect children from international trafficking (Section 2 of the Child Abduction Act 1984), and people trafficking is now illegal under Sections 145 (and 146) of the Nationality, Immigration and Asylum Act 2002, Sections 57 and 60 of the Sexual Offences Act 2003 and the new Asylum and Immigration Act 2004, while there is also some evidence of a 'toughening up' of sentences in cases brought against traffickers.

The key issue in relation to people smuggling and trafficking is the exploitative employment practices which ensue when people are vulnerable and easily manipulated because of their illegal or tenuously legal immigration/citizenship status. Additionally, in relation to people trafficking, there are some indications of greater maltreatment of the migrants and/or of threats to the safety and well-being of family members 'back home'. It seems likely that there are also gender differences in these forms of 'migration', with men being more likely to be the subjects of people smuggling, while women and children are more likely to be trafficked, although these are not hard-and-fast divisions. Thus, for instance, the deaths of 25 cockle pickers off the North West coast of England in 2004 revealed a pattern of people smuggling from

China to the UK, which included both men and women.[4] It has been suggested that the break up of the Soviet Union in 1989 has resulted in dire poverty in some areas resulting in the growth of trafficking, particularly of women and children, to 'feed' the West European sex trade (Barrett, 2000) and/or for the procurement of human organs or babies.[5] For instance, again in the UK, under public and voluntary sector pressure, the metropolitan police initiated a project to identify women trafficked into the sex industry and found that by far the most common nationalities represented among women in the brothels and massage parlours of London were from Eastern Europe (Reflex, 2004). The expansion of the EU in 2004 to include eight countries which were formerly part of the Soviet bloc has exacerbated this form of migration, giving increased mobility to traffickers with established EU citizenship.

However, trafficking of women has not been restricted to countries within the wider European region. For instance, trafficking for the purposes of prostitution has been increasingly discussed in the media in Italy, where a surprisingly high percentage of sex workers are from Western Africa, particularly Nigeria. The reasons why Italy is a destination is questionable, but apparently may entail some form of 'juju' (voodoo) rights ceremony. Once there, such women (including young women under 18 years) often find themselves in debt bondage, without recourse to public funds and without legitimate access to employment. This leaves them with few options but prostitution, even if they are not formally 'forced' into this activity by actual or threatened violence (Achebe, 2004).

In a multi-country study, Anderson and O'Connell-Davidson (2003) explored the parallels between trafficking for sex work and for domestic work. 'In both sex and domestic work, the absence of effective regulation is one of the factors that help to create an environment in which it is possible and profitable to use unfree labour' (p. 5). From a feminist perspective, they argue that it is the (sexual and domestic) labour of women of the south that have allowed women of the north to make the positional strides forward in a male-dominated society. More practically, victims of trafficking often are unable to contact local services and have little if any institutional protection, since they often lack the means (freedom of movement, language, passport, money, information) to contact any potential sources of help, including police, health and social services.

However, there is conflicting evidence about the extent to which people trafficking is as (physically) dangerous as some (European) press and media reports have suggested. For instance, Brunovskis and Tyldum (2004) conducted a study in Oslo to identify the make-up of the sex industry, establish the trafficking routes and to hear the stories of returned trafficked victims. They found that in 2003 there were 600 women, from 40 different countries, working in prostitution in the Norwegian capital. One-third were Norwegian nationals, one-third from Asia and one-third from Eastern and Central Europe. Their data also suggested that it was rare for women to be taken out of their home country against their will, but that they tended to leave because they lacked an acceptable alternative means of livelihood. Most chose to migrate and some knew they were going to work in the sex industry, but nearly all were reliant on a recruiter to assist them in migration. Although the process of recruitment, transportation and employment gave many opportunities for exploitation, the prime motivation for not exiting was psychological, not physical, coercion (not to suggest that this is less significant).

> Most women leave their trafficking situations on their own, with or without the assistance of clients, and do not come directly into contact with police or rehabilitation services. Mostly, they have contacted organizations offering support on their own, often some time after returning to their home countries, but many victims of trafficking are never registered or offered assistance. Few women want to report their traffickers to the police. This is partially explained by a fear of repercussions, but equally important is the belief that reporting the offenders 'will make no difference'. (Brunovskis and Tyldum, 2004, pp. 13–14)

The question of how national and international criminal justice and human rights organizations might respond to people smuggling and trafficking is also disputed. Two types of strategies were identified during the 2001 Second World Congress against Commercial Sexual Exploitation of Children: repressive strategies (such as tightening national immigration) and empowering strategies. Heavy-handed immigration policies that do not take into account the complexity of migration and trafficking are at risk of victimization and criminalization of people who have been trafficked, laying them open to further human rights violations and continued poverty. Such policies are likely to force the trade further 'underground' and make collection of substantiated statistics and other information even harder. Empowering strategies would explore the local and international causes of the traffic, including poverty, and evaluate programmes to prevent rather than treat the problem (see also Chapter 7).

Identifying Needs and Developing Responses

Given the varied reasons for – and forms of – migration, it is clear that there must be multi-layered and inter-professional responses to identifying problematic issues or particular needs arising from the process. Some of these will involve local strategies and interventions related to national frameworks, while others will require collaboration at cross-national or international levels to formulate policies and programmes which address underlying issues. We have already given a brief consideration to the ways in which social professionals may be involved in providing aid to refugees in camps near the site of conflicts in Chapter 5, and it is also apparent that similar resources and approaches may be needed in relation to IDPs (although the risks to personnel in humanitarian aid agencies have also been identified). The need for national and local development planning to take into account migration as an existing or potential strategy has also been discussed briefly above and it is likely that social professionals and community development workers in countries of the South (whether indigenous or employed from abroad as part of an INGO) may have a role to play in planning and/or delivering relevant programmes. Finally, there are the roles of social professionals engaged in public and voluntary sector agencies in AICs who may work either in specialist agencies or may find that factors in relation to migration have implications for their work, and it is with the local and international aspects of this work that the remainder of this chapter is primarily concerned.

There are at least three approaches which have relevance in considering local professional responses to migration. These range from *specialist therapeutic services*, through *services geared to wider user groups* where the particular needs of people who are migrants may form only part of a wider remit, to *community empowerment policies and practices*. Which of these is appropriate is influenced by assumptions – or preferably evidence – about the needs of individuals and groups from particular minorities. In addition, there is considerable scope for recognizing the cross-national and international dimensions of the work.

It can be assumed that all migrants have experienced loss to some extent (as outlined in Chapter 4) – but the extent to which this is compensated for by the gains achieved in a new situation, and indeed what resources migrants have brought with them, is very variable. In the case of refugees and asylum seekers Doña (2002) has pointed out the danger of marginalizing them by affixing them with the label *victim* and 'medicalizing' their issues. However, having said this, it is clear that some people, specifically refugees, have been seriously traumatized by their experiences prior to departure (if not during the process of flight and seeking asylum) and require *specialist services* providing rehabilitation and therapy; and social professionals are among those specialists.

Four examples can be noted of specialist services provided by interdisciplinary teams based in voluntary organizations: the Service for the Treatment and Rehabilitation of Torture and Trauma Survivors in New South Wales (Australia), the Medical Foundation for the Victims of Torture in London (UK), The Centre for Victims of Torture in Minneapolis (US) and the Canadian Centre for Victims of Torture in Toronto. These organizations primarily provide an individualized response to specific needs: these include therapeutic approaches which stress the importance of listening and accepting as part of the process of healing and rebuilding trust and some sense of worth, as well as advocacy on behalf of patients/clients (who often have ongoing problems in relation to their refugee status). However, members of such teams/agencies have also responded to invitations to work with local personnel to develop counselling and family therapy services at the site of previous conflicts, for example, in Sri Lanka,[6] illustrating how learning and experience derived from one location can be adapted and utilized elsewhere.

At the other extreme, it has been suggested that some social professionals engaged in mainstream services (such as childcare services provided by local authorities in the UK) may be ignorant of the circumstances surrounding an individual's decision to leave a particular country and/or the issues surrounding their travel and entry elsewhere. This can reduce the likelihood of sensitive and effective assessment and intervention, even when individuals could be eligible for help from established services. For instance, the ECPAT UK report (Somerset, 2004, previously mentioned) claimed that many children were suffering from the relative ignorance of social workers, police and immigration personnel of the dangers of child trafficking. When local authorities were asked to fill out reports of cases of trafficked youngsters, 68 such cases were identified across different social service teams. However, 26 of the 53 local authorities expressing concerns about trafficked children had not issued guidance to social services and it was suggested that some social workers did not know what trafficking was. Other social workers thought that it fell into the jurisdiction of immigration, not social services. This suggests both that the actual number of cases could be much higher and that there is a lack of appropriate service provision in this area, including the need for 'safe houses'.

As mentioned, there have been local initiatives to identify the scale of the problem in the UK. So for instance, Operation Paladin Child, a project by the London Metropolitan Police, was set up in September 2002 (Reflex, 2004) and it collected data on all unaccompanied non-EU minors entering the country via Heathrow airport. Anecdotal evidence from Western Africa suggested that traffickers were aware of this project and rerouted victims, but during a three-month period police identified 1738 such youngsters, 551 of whom were assessed as being at risk and referred to Social Service Departments. Most were girls from Africa (Nigeria, South Africa, Ghana, Zimbabwe) but some were from Asia (Malaysia) and all but 12 have since been located – though what actions were then taken by social workers have not been reported. This operation did not find evidence of wholesale child trafficking, but police were concerned that the large numbers of unaccompanied children left the risk of exploitation open. They also noted the limitations of the project (involving only one point of entry; focusing on non-EU passport holders;

and only on unaccompanied minors) and further research has since been set up at another major airport (Gatwick) and cross-channel rail terminal (Waterloo). Clearly, there is also scope for research into what happens to such youngsters following a referral to social workers.

There have already been concerns expressed (in the UK) about the lack of resources available to meet the needs of unaccompanied minors (e.g., Somerset, 2001), and although there is a clear duty laid on local authorities in England and Wales to assess needs and provide care (under the 1989 Children Act), many provisions in this area consist of small-scale responses in the voluntary sector, which frequently faces shortages and uncertainty in relation to funding. Huegler's (2005) comparative study of two such projects in Germany and England provides an example of the differing resources and approaches available to unaccompanied minors (in this case young people in the 15–17 age range) through voluntary sector agencies; and demonstrates how national policies, as well as the qualifications and expertise of social professionals themselves, produce variations in such provision.

Elsewhere, Hessle (2000) has provided a brief account of an action-research project, based in a transit centre established by the Swedish Immigration Board to provide temporary care and shelter for unaccompanied minors. The project aimed to offer early assessment of the mental health of children accommodated, to assist them in their transition to a new country, and help them cope with the uncertainties about their longer-term futures. It was possible that some youngsters would be returned to their countries of origin and this is also a possibility in the case of young people on reaching 18 years elsewhere (for instance, in the UK). As well as causing anxieties for the young people themselves, this can make the work of social professionals in securing or encouraging investment in, for example, educational resources for this user group more difficult and, again, it is sometimes left to voluntary initiatives to address even basic needs such as language teaching (personal communication). (The issues raised by repatriation and the need for resettlement programmes in countries of origin is outside the scope of this chapter but anecdotal evidence suggests that this is an area of work in which social professionals are involved, for example, in countries such as Bosnia and Herzegovina.)

Concerning child trafficking specifically, the voluntary sector has also taken a lead in raising awareness of the problem which has implications for statutory child-care social workers, including in the fields of fostering and adoption, as well as child-protection services. So, for instance, a British-based African organization aiming to combat child trafficking and abuse held an international conference in London in 2004 focusing on the role of the African community in combating this activity. This followed a conference held the previous year in Lagos, Nigeria, also concerned with the trafficking of children to the UK, apparently often in the belief that such children would be afforded a better life. However, as Somerset (2004) identified, there are estimated to be 8000–10,000 cases of private fostering in the UK, mainly of Western African children. Such children may be particularly at risk of exploitation and abuse, as illustrated in the case of Victoria Climbié (an African girl who died from maltreatment and neglect at the hands of an 'aunt' to whom she had been sent in London [Simmonds, 2003]). But identifying these cases is complex and many departments lack the resources to investigate effectively, even when there are grounds for concern. One response was the proposed tightening of regulations concerning private fostering under a new Children's Act 2004.

Child trafficking apart, migration may be a factor in other childcare cases where adoption or fostering opportunities are being explored in practice, or where the effects of such arrangements, when carried out trans-nationally, have been researched. For instance, there is a growing literature about the practice of inter-country adoption, where, by definition, some children are removed from their own countries and adopted by couples in often very different societies, and often of different ethnic or racial groups. The ethical aspects of such practices – with implications for the communities from which children are removed as well as for the children themselves and for the new families and societies – need to be considered as part of the wider debate about appropriate development of both national and international policies and 'best practice' guidelines (Selman, 1998; Gresham *et al.*, 2003; Ryan and Groza, 2004). Such adoptions while being trans-national are not necessarily trans-cultural, as demonstrated in a case recounted by a British social worker to one of the authors: she was involved in the assessment of a Muslim woman (herself born and reared in the UK but whose family was originally from Morocco) as the potential adopter of the baby of a cousin in Morocco, who had died in childbirth. Both families (including the baby's natural father) supported this course of action and, at the time of writing, it was likely that the legal systems of both countries (in relation to both migration and childcare matters) would approve the placing for adoption of this child with the maternal cousin.

In the case of fostering, this has increasingly been viewed in the Western world as a preferred alternative to residential care or the permanent alternative parenting arrangements provided by adoption, and replicates in a more formalized way, traditions of alternative care by relations or neighbours found in earlier times and (still) in many different countries (not least in Africa). However, with an increased emphasis in Western countries such as the UK and US on 'kinship care' (encouraging fostering arrangements normally within the extended family rather than by strangers, see Broad, 2004), and given the extent of population mobility and resettlement described earlier in this chapter, it is apparent that appropriate family members may be resident in other countries. There is already anecdotal evidence in the UK that some local authority social workers, for example, have found themselves having to liaise with family members in other countries (including, for instance, France, Ireland and Croatia) about their possible willingness and suitability to foster children who cannot be cared for by their normal care-giver(s) in the UK. This entails a steep learning curve on the part of such social workers who need to familiarize themselves with other child welfare, benefit and immigration systems. Such work may also require the use of interpreters, both in the assessment of potential foster carers and for the necessary liaison with professional counterparts across national borders (Lyons, 2006).

More general social services may have been developed to respond to the needs of minority populations, such as asylum-seeker teams in the UK, but as Briskman and Cemlyn (2005) have discussed, the harsh and suspicious public and official climates surrounding asylum seekers in both the UK and Australia have resulted in a rather minimalist response by social workers, who have tended to distance themselves from this area of work (or, in the case of the UK, become frustrated by the pressures and limitations of work in asylum seekers teams [personal communication]). As Briskman and Cemlyn point out, this area raises acutely the possible role of social workers in defending human rights and promoting social justice, for example, through advocacy at not only individual but also national and international levels, but there is as yet relatively little indication that social professionals are responding to this challenge, particularly at macro levels.

For instance, in the US, Rosenberg *et al.* (2005) discuss 'clinical' interventions with individuals and families from minority ethnic groups, suggesting that this area of work is seen by some primarily in 'micro' terms in the context of cross-cultural social work. However, Zuniga (2004) suggests the need for social workers to be well versed in social policy (with particular reference to migration and welfare entitlement policies), as well as culturally competent to meet the needs of Mexican immigrants, many of whom may be undocumented and face particular problems accessing services. The author further suggests that social workers have an ethical responsibility to assist this population, despite its illegal status, a view which might be relevant to social professionals in many other countries. Healy (2004a) goes further in identifying the international dimensions of social work with migrants, many of whom are part of 'trans-national families' and proposes the need for cross-national collaboration between social workers, as discussed above in the context of the UK.

Turning to the possibilities of social work with women who have been trafficked, there is as yet very little evidence to suggest the involvement of social professionals in this field (and indeed the Norwegian study cited above and communications raise questions about the extent to which women engaged in the sex trade as a result of trafficking would/could use the services of social workers) but again there are some indications of the growth of local 'self-help' networks and voluntary sector initiatives in some countries. For instance, in relation to the Nigerian women in Italy mentioned earlier, in response to various local, national and international NGOs demands, the Italian government has initiated a closely watched and innovative programme that offers government-supported social protection and permanent resident visas to illegal immigrants in exchange for their cooperation in the prosecution of their traffickers. This potentially gives social and health professionals greater scope to work with these women (Agatise, 2004).

It is also evident from the literature that concerns about mental health (Blair, 2001) and other health needs of migrants (not least HIV/AIDS, Duckett, 2001 and see Chapter 8) is an issue in many countries, although access to the sort of specialized services provided for torture victims (as mentioned earlier) may not be possible or may not even be appropriate. It is therefore essential that people in mainstream services (including in the mental health field) have an increased understanding of the needs not just of established minority ethnic groups, but also of the particular circumstances likely to have been experienced by asylum seekers (who tend to be drawn from a much wider range of countries).

It may also be that some people are better helped through resources in their own communities and that a third approach promoting *empowerment and community development* is more effective in providing services and informal support. Such an approach would build on the strengths of individuals by encouraging the establishment of peer support groups and advice and advocacy schemes 'staffed' in part by migrants themselves, although the need for liaison based on local knowledge and contacts and policy interventions to promote access to mainstream services and harmonious community relations between different sectors of local populations should not be underestimated, suggesting a greater role for community development workers in AICs than is currently evident in some countries (including the UK and US). Indeed, various authors have identified the need for closer co-operation between services such as health, education and housing, as well as the police and immigration authorities, to facilitate reception and integration of migrants – a process which will be improved if based on increased understanding of the reasons for migration of particular groups as well as particular cultural or other reasons likely to inhibit or facilitate their 'settlement' and integration.

As indicated, and not least because of the increase in organized crime and security threats – in which quite innocent and legitimate migrants can come under suspicion – there are particular implications for the law enforcement sector and international and national justice sectors, leaving open the question of social professional roles in the field of migrations, particularly in relation to asylum seekers or people who may have been trafficked. However, we would suggest that, apart from their established or developing work in relation to individuals, groups and communities indicated above, there is also considerable scope for more organized development of the advocacy role of social workers at national and international levels. As Caragata and Sanchez have stated, '. . . issues of forced immigration because of economic hardship or cultural or ethnic persecution require both local responses and coordinated international effort. Without action at both levels more fundamental problems will not be resolved' (p. 224).

As in other areas of practice, staff engaged in the social professions can use their experience to identify the impact of particular policies on vulnerable groups and to predict how policy changes, including in the field of immigration, will impact. In many countries it will be important to try to provide redress to a public discourse and political pressures which 'demonize' migrants and seek to push welfare professionals into additional 'policing' of this marginalized population (see for instance, Humphries, 2002 and Zimmerman and Fix, 2002, in relation to UK and US policies and practices, respectively). Additionally, alliances and collaborative action with other professionals and user movements can increase support for humane and just policies, including at international levels. This is apart from the possibility that social professionals themselves may choose to work in some of the international agencies (such as UNHCR or SCF) operating in this area, or the increased likelihood that social professionals can draw on their own experience of migration (whether as a positive or forced 'choice') in alerting them to some of the issues faced by groups and individuals. We shall return to this latter point in our concluding chapter.

Concluding Comments

Global constructs have been shaped (partially) by the Western ideological push of capitalism, democratic principles and movement towards free-market economies, while, concurrently, we have seen a continuing mass movement of people across and within national borders. Such movement has been identified as increasingly problematic in an environment in which international organized crime and acts of terrorism play a growing part in shaping public attitudes and political reactions. However, such movement must be kept in proportion. Apart from new elites who are *extraterritorial*, only a minority of people have the option to relocate, temporarily or permanently, relative to 'the rest (who) are, as before, *localized*, as are all the means and agencies of collective action, self-defence and self-government that humanity discovered/invented/deployed and learned to use in the modern era' (Gane, 2004, p. 26, citing Bauman). There are significant variations between the motivations and characteristics of those who migrate, but poverty and conflict continue to provide the major spurs to individual and mass migrations. Although there are long-established and functional traditions of migration (often seasonal or relatively short term), people who can be seen as forced migrants are the focus of current concern with regard to national and international policies and professional responses.

According to Korn (1999), success in addressing the problematic dimensions of migration has been limited. Suggested strategies for a reduction in population mobility, specifically from countries of the South to wealthier countries of the North, include a focus on prevention through such measures as good governance, strengthened legal protection, conflict prevention, integration of programmes aimed at assistance and protection, including giving special consideration for women and children (as vulnerable groups), and linking emergency aid and development policies and support. Additionally, where migration is seen as a necessary or inevitable strategy for some groups, assistance in relocation and reinsertion may reduce harmful effects on individuals or communities (Dottridge, 2004). It is possible that new initiatives recently announced by the UN to promote global security, including through the creation of a new Peace Building Commission (UN, 2004, p. 5), will have a bearing on the overall numbers and direction of flow of migrants – at least in the longer term, but meantime, individual states and regions of the Western world take their own decisions about how to operate more selective and restrictive policies, sometimes threatening to draw social professionals into the machinery of regulation and exclusion.

Meanwhile, more general issues associated with migration, including the fact that some Western countries need migrants to counteract falling birth rates and/or labour shortages, tend to be overshadowed by moral panics about people smuggling, particularly as reflected in the emotive area of the trafficking of women and children and the actual or feared corollary of sexual exploitation. The global response to trafficking currently has several limitations, including shortage of resources, and only piecemeal research into its scale. Additionally, there is as yet only partial acknowledgement by some countries of the links between trafficking, poverty, HIV/AIDS, gender and race, leading to a lack of policies and interventions which might address these issues at source, as well as in the destination countries. In the latter, there has been little development yet of programmes to promote recovery of people adversely affected by trafficking, including little attention to the possible advantages of promoting user-participation in research and service development. These shortfalls have resulted in ignorance of the problem by social professionals or the assumption that it is one to be tackled by other agencies.

However, as indicated above, trafficking is only the most recent manifestation of migration and, in many ways, social professionals are well placed to respond to some of the problematic effects of migration, as well as to other concerns expressed by migrant communities themselves. Social professionals' understanding of the effects of loss and marginalization, coupled with values which respect diversity and stress human rights and empowerment, suggests that those engaged in social work and community development have valuable roles to play, not only in addressing the specific needs of individuals and communities but also in advocating for people experiencing the negative effects of migration at local, national and international level.

7 Child Exploitation: Local and Global Protection

Introduction

Pictures of children are often utilized to add gravitas to a variety of international development campaigns. Their effectiveness and persistence lends weight to the notion that children and their welfare matter to us, but it also intimates a perspective in which children are dependant and in need of special protection. The exploitation of children, in its various guises, has been a topical issue since the early 1980s. The subject is complex, drawing in broader concerns of economic development, poverty, loss, globalization, empowerment, self-determination, social justice and human rights. However, the lack of a framework to adequately address international aspects of intervention into global child protection matters has meant that there is a dearth in practice examples (Dominelli, 1999). Additionally, because child labour is often a mechanism of survival (whether selling peanuts on the streets of Lagos, swapping sex for shelter in Montreal, working as a servant in Paris or in a shoe factory in Beijing), children's involvement is often under the radar of social professionals' notice, particularly in countries where child exploitation has not been emphasized.

Childhood represents a time of considerable vulnerability. During this period children can be exploited in a variety of ingenious and horrifying ways, most easily understood as forms of child labour. Sometimes child labour and child exploitation are interlinked with cultural or survival practices, but the severity of effects are difficult to quantify, and issues involved in intervention are complex. Child labour exists on a continuum and in a variety of settings, including within domestic settings (e.g., servants, cooks), sporting and entertainment industries (e.g., camel jockeying and acting), agricultural or manufacturing arenas (e.g., household farms, dynamite factories) and more illicit areas such as benefits fraud, petty crime, panhandling, drug selling/trafficking, child prostitution, child soldiers and organ theft.

While the reality of child exploitation may seem more immediately apparent to social professionals working in the South, social professionals working in AICs still have a significant role to play. Social professionals in AICs may have direct access to child exploitation issues (e.g., when working with child prostitution or abusive domestic work) or indirect access (e.g., working with service users with experience of exploitative environments as children or through broader lobbying work and children's rights movements).

According to Global March (2004), 246 million children are engaged in child labour. This is equal to one in every six children, with many working in hazardous environments or being hidden from view. However, numbers are crude and exploitation varies in its severity and its consequences. Child labour can have a significant impact on children's educational attainment, health care, nutrition, safety, security and leisure time. This is particularly apparent with girls' household work, such as child or parental care and other household duties. The degree of exploitation is the key to understanding the continuum on which child labourers sit. By *exploitation*, we mean the unfair manipulation of, and unjust benefit from, the special vulnerability of children. Children are exploited for their lack of political voice, lack of ability to complain, lack of understanding or education, easy malleability, and their size.

At the outset of this chapter, we will explore some of the ways in which children are exploited globally, particularly through child labour. We will look at several different approaches to understanding child labour that help us to distinguish between survival mechanisms and exploitative practices, with special attention paid to what the ILO has deemed the worst forms of child labour and especially commercial child sexual exploitation. Having outlined these aspects, we will turn our attention to the different ways to approach protection of children, both locally and globally. This will include child protection in families, out of families and most importantly through a promotion of children's rights.

By promoting a better understanding of children's rights and enabling a space for participation and voicing views, exploitation can be curtailed. Lastly, we will look at some of the implications for policy and social professional practice, with specific emphasis on what children are saying and how a movement towards child participation in policy creation is beginning. Before we look at any of these other issues, we must first examine the notion of childhood and family, as these areas are the key concepts on which child labour is predicated. Childhood, we will discover, is by no means a fixed notion. In this chapter, we will focus on exploitative practices that violate children's basic human rights and explore how social professionals can protect them.

Childhood and Child Exploitation

In Chapter 3, we discussed issues of inequality and vulnerability. Children were highlighted as being marginalized and lacking voice, hence in need of protection. In many countries, children (and families) constitute a large focus of the work of social professionals. As evidence of this the World Census of social work education undertaken by the IASSW found that 89 per cent of schools of social work taught some form of children and family work (Barretta-Herman, 2005). So, arguing for the need of social professionals to examine this issue seems unnecessary.

The discussion of child labour is intimately linked to societal norms and understandings of the notion of 'childhood' and this demands a degree of fluidity when examining the issue from a global viewpoint. In fact, the variability of the concept of childhood lies not just in the stages and ages of 'childhood' but also in the underlying conceptualization of childhood. The idea of childhood did not exist as distinct from adulthood until both were understood to have their own distinct versions of work, play and clothing. However, aside from the distinction (from adulthood), there was little consensus about what the special status of childhood meant. Jenks (1996) envisioned two key historical concepts of childhood: the Dionysian conception (children as initially evil and in need of shaping) and today's more dominant definition, the Apollonian conception (innocent, untainted, needing nurturance and protection). Armstrong (1986) (as cited in James *et al.*,

1998, p. 2) argued that there was an exponential rise in the interest in children during the twentieth century because of 'changing patterns of personal, political and moral control in social life more generally', changing both our perceptions of children and our reactions to them. Montgomery (2001, p. 15) sees a contemporary and universal notion of childhood as a time of weakness, powerlessness and ignorance. Similarly, Hoyle (1989) suggests that a western/industrialized concept of childhood assumes children are dependant on adults and lacking political or sexual knowledge. This conception entails the role of adults as protective and nurturing of children and has included a strong emphasis on excluding children from work, while simultaneously encouraging education. In fact the UK-based NGO Plan released a report in 2005 calling for the universal registration of all children born in order to ensure the education of each child. Plan estimates that there could be more than 500 million unregistered children in the world.

The children's rights movement and, to a lesser extent, the women's rights movement have also changed the societal position of children, putting children's issues to the forefront of our collective consciousness. Recently this movement has made some progress towards including child participation in decision-making processes, which will be discussed later. Post (1994) argues that new media has eroded the notion of 'childhood' as distinct, with children sharing clothing and accessing knowledge (through television, books and the Internet) with adults. However, two of the mainstays of our definition of childhood remain: the barring of children from the workplace and an emphasis on (often compulsory) schooling. Post's notion goes a long way to explain some of the dualistic policies and practices, which both see children as vulnerable and in need of protection and, however, give access and in some cases immersion into 'adult domains'. Nieuwenhuys (1994) acknowledges that the notion of childhood is seen differently across cultures, but she also notes that within cultures there is a discrepancy or duplicity, sometimes seeing the same 16-year-old as a child, but, in different circumstances, as an adult. Having said that, this dualism further complicates issues surrounding child labour. For instance, child protection laws, as they exist in AICs such as the UK, the US, Canada and Australia, protect most children from exploitative labour, but the illegality of exploitative labour further entrenches some who do not engage with statutory or voluntary agencies for fear of legal reprisals. This can be seen, for instance, where children are working illegally, for example, in sweatshops, exploitative domestic work, selling sex, or in other illegal areas or 'self-employment' arenas (such as scavenging or window washing). They can be more easily exploited and are less likely to seek help if they lack an adult advocate that they trust, such as a parent or guardian, or if they have unsettled immigration status. This brings us to the role of the family.

The role of the family is central to the welfare policies in many countries, whether formalized or assumed (Lyons, 1999). Primary care of the vulnerable, ill, disabled, infants and the elderly has traditionally been the domain of the family. This has often been based on notions of an idealized nuclear family in industrialized nations and, in non-industrialized nations, of extended family structures. An aspect of modernity and post-modernity has been the break-up of the 'traditional' family. The emergence of a global social work profession over the last century has looked at alternatives to care, by either supporting the family with service provision or finding alternative caring structures. The important point here is that there is still largely the assumption that children will be cared for in the parental home. This is predicated on a supposition that children have parents who are able and willing to support them. Clearly, this is not always the case.

A vague and flexible definition of children and the role of the family can lead to inappropriate and static policies, rendering practitioners ineffective. As an example, family values became a central concern in social work and social policy in the 1990s in Russia. It was felt that families had let society down and a debate ensued around the role of the state in family regulation.[1] This led, over a period of ten years, to 120 new pieces of legislation on previously private affairs, including child protection laws. To put this into context, there were more than half a million homeless children in Russia, with 50,000 in Moscow alone, some of whom had parents.[2] Further, one of the legislative amendments banned NGOs from running orphanages, leaving Moscow with only 250 beds for children (ibid.). Lovtsova[3] called for clarity of policy for practitioners through the creation of a single children and family ministry.

Child Exploitation

With the shifting ideology of what constitutes childhood, we have seen a profound change in society's views of child labour. The twentieth century witnessed a separation of an adult's and a child's access to work with a parallel increased focus on education for minors (Hoyle, 1989). During the nineteenth and twentieth centuries, the declining infant and child mortality rate in Europe meant that more focus was placed on individual children, allowing them to emerge from factories into increasingly organized and appropriate educational facilities (ibid.). That being said, child labour has far from disappeared from Europe. However, it could be argued that it has radically changed, for instance, from full time to part time and from providing survival to supplementary income, rarely hindering school attendance. For example in the UK those under the age of 18 constitute approximately 23 per cent of the population, but according to Global March (no date) great discrepancies exist between agencies on the level of child labour. The ILO forecasted that there would be no economically active children between the ages of 10 and 14 in the UK in the year 2000 (ILO, 1997), but Save the Children and MORI for the Trades Union Congress (TUC) concluded that around 30 per cent of 12-year-olds and about 20 per cent of 11-year-olds were being illegally employed in low paying jobs (stated in Global March, no date). Further research by Child Poverty Action Group and the Save the Children Fund indicated that over a million children worked illegally in the UK (stated in Global March, no date). This clearly shows that child labour is either defined differently by different organizations or that little is known about its existence, indicating significant impediments for social professional intervention.

The picture is quite different in other parts of the world. Today Asia has the highest total number of child labourers, while Africa has the highest percentage, with 40 per cent of 5–14-year-olds involved in economic activities. Comparatively, Asia has 21 per cent child labour participation rate and Latin America has 17 per cent (Kebebew, 1998). One significant reason for the varying rates of child labour is demographics. In many African countries, the percentage of the population under the age of 18 is much higher than in other countries. In Uganda, for example, 56.8

per cent of the population is under the age of 18 and there were 1,162,000 economically active children between the ages of 10 and 14 (1995 figure), representing nearly half of this age group (ILO, 1997). Global March (no date) suggests that children are working in various sectors including casual labour, particularly agriculture and as servants or cooks in private residences. One statistic suggested that children made up 80 per cent of the commercial agricultural industry (ibid.).

Turning to another African nation, Ethiopia has one of the highest rates of child labour in the world. With more than 50 per cent of the population below the age of 14 and a fertility rate of seven children per woman, poorer households have seen children begin to work at an earlier age, sometimes before the age of five (Admassie, 2003). This has been accentuated by insufficient public spending, rapid population growth, economic crisis, poverty, civil war, famine and the HIV/AIDS epidemic, which has left many children orphaned and homeless (ibid.). The vulnerability of HIV/AIDS orphans is an issue experienced more globally according to the tenth annual report *State of the World's Children* (UNICEF, 2005; see also Chapter 8).

Child labour has a great impact on childhood. It can lead to disruption of schooling, with implications for future employment, health and nutrition problems, and exposure to hazardous conditions – but deciding when child labour is acceptable or exploitative is not straightforward. Issues surrounding child labour are intimately tied in with issues of loss and human rights, as discussed in previous chapters.

With regard to rights, in 1924 the League of Nations endorsed the first declaration on the Rights of the Child and in 1948 a second declaration was adopted, as was the Universal Declaration of Human Rights. However, it was in 1989, after a decade of consultation, that the UN Convention on the Rights of the Child was created and ratified by nearly all the world's nations (except Somalia and the US by 2005). The Convention lays out basic human rights afforded to all children in the world with the guiding principles 'of non-discrimination (article 2), best interests of the child (article 3), maximum survival and development (article 6) and participation of children (article 12)'. Finding consensus on the framework for rights for children has been difficult despite the overwhelming consensus for the convention. UN human rights standards, including children's rights, although signed and ratified by many, are largely shaped by euro-centric ethical and moral codes. Many of the rights afforded in the 1989 convention are built on the assumption of a nuclear family, which is not the norm in much of the world. Despite its shortcomings, it is the main international mechanism for promoting children's rights.

Two further important international legal mechanisms relate to child labour: International Labour Organization (ILO) Convention 138 (1973) on the minimum age for employment and ILO Convention 182 on the Worst Forms of Child Labour. The former states that a child cannot work full time before either the age of 15 or before they have reached the minimum age of compulsory education. However, in LDCs, with consultation, a child can be a minimum of 14 years old. The treatise further states that 13- to 15-year-olds may conduct 'light work' only when it does not harm their health or development or interrupt their education. In Convention 138, Article 3.1 states, 'The minimum age for admission to any type of employment or work which by its nature or the circumstances in which it is carried out is likely to jeopardize the health, safety or morals of young persons shall not be less than 18 years.' The former had been ratified by 135 countries and the latter was ratified by 151 countries by early 2005.[4] The worst forms of child labour will be discussed later, but slavery, debt bondage, serfdom, as well as child combatants, prostitution, pornography and the use of children in illegal activities are all banned.

Different Interpretations of Child Labour

Children can be exploited for their lack of political voice, lack of knowledge, lack of consideration of consequences. Children themselves may be vulnerable, but there are sub-groupings that add to vulnerability, for instance girls, migrant workers, asylum seekers or refugees and ethnic minorities, street children and indigenous populations. Larsen (2003) looked at the effects of exploitative child labour on indigenous and tribal children and their double burden of marginalization and discrimination and he argues strongly for a rights-based approach when working with indigenous populations. 'Child labour' is an inadequate term to describe the vast array of children's work (Nieuwenhuys, 1994). To appreciate this, let us turn to the different ways in which child labour has been conceptualized.

Micro and Macro Economic Issues – Causes and Consequences

It is helpful for professionals to understand the underlying factors in local context. In keeping with the economic model of globalization discussed in an earlier chapter, child labour can be seen in the light of supply and demand and O'Gorman's (1992) previously mentioned global division of the 'haves' and the 'have-nots'. According to UNICEF (2005), there are 2.2 billion children in the world, of whom 1 billion live in poverty. For those children who fall into the category of have-nots, they often have little choice but to work, with the survival of poor families depending on children's contribution (Admassie, 2003). Many of the have-nots inhabit the developing world, but let us not forget that in both the UK and the US, two of the strongest economic forces in the world, approximately one-third of children were reported to be living in (relative) poverty up to the turn of this century (Link *et al.*, 2000). (According to British government rhetoric and some policy initiatives there have since been efforts to reduce this proportion in the UK.)

On the demand side of the child-labour equation, globalization has opened the door to many TNCs to exploit lax labour conditions in the developing world, seeking out the cheapest labour supply. Having limited commitment to any country and always looking for the cheapest supply is common. This has left labourers, especially children, in precarious positions, with little leverage to demand fair working conditions and adherence to international labour laws (Hoogvelt, 1997).

Taking a different perspective, Hazan and Berdugo (2002) have looked at child labour as a side effect of the economic developmental process, with early stages of economic development containing high fertility and high child-labour rates. As time passes, the wage differences between adults and children increase and child education becomes a preferred option. They suggest that policies that ban child labour could expedite

economic progress. According to Admassie (2003), a percep-
tion exists that some adult unemployment is due in part to
children's undervalued labour involvement (i.e., they cost less
and 'flood' the labour market). This is intrinsically linked with
the notion that children's labour is inferior, except in specific
circumstances where children's physique is specifically sought
out, such as weaving, where small hands are preferable or
necessary.

In keeping with this economic model, Matz (2003) calcu-
lated the costs and benefits of child labour and child education
and found that the benefits of educating children far outweigh
the costs involved by as much as three times. One of the
roles of social professionals therefore is to support education.
School grant programmes or minimum income schemes such
as provided in Brazil (Lavinas, 2001) offer one social safety
net. These have shown some effectiveness in keeping children
enrolled in school and otherwise avoiding harmful exploitation. However, it is crucial that the correct balance is found.
Rammohan (2000) found in his study of various countries that a
rise in children's wages, particularly education allowances, actually increased fertility rates and decreased education spending
overall.

But looking solely at one dimension of social phenomena can
be misleading, counterproductive and can lead to inappropriate
actions. For example, in Nepal, energetic national and international campaigns to end child labour in the carpet industry led to
intervention by state, the industry and NGOs. They were unable
to end this labour, but international press adversely affected the
demand, which led to a massive decrease in wages of all workers,
further entrenching people in poverty and tying their children to
labour (O'Neill, 2003). In Pakistan, child labour is endemic and
according to a CRIN report, children in Peshwar are working, for
instance, in auto workshops, furniture factories, shoe factories,
brick kilns, carpet-weaving centres and tyre-repair centres, as
well as in hotels, restaurants, shops and street vending. As evidence of the interweaving of macro and micro perceptions of
child labour, local NGOs and social professionals are intervening
where they can, but they are finding that without government
policy backing and societal change their effectiveness is severely
hampered.[5]

Child Labour as an Educational or Empowering Tool

Education for all by 2015 was agreed by 155 governments, yet by 2004 more than 115 million children were not in school and more than 211 million children between the ages of 5 and 14 were working (Global March, 2004). Information from UNICEF's *Voicing our Views* (2004a) suggests that when children are asked, they believe that employment can, when separated from exploitative practices, be educative and help with career planning. Some authors have looked at the role of employment in the formation of responsible adults. For instance, Bey (2003) found that seasonal migrant populations in Mexico believed that work provided necessary socialization and parents were torn by the pressure to send children to school. They saw work and education as two diametrically opposed options, but perhaps a social professional could have acted as a mediator finding a balance between socialization of work and education. From a practice perspective, one Mexican NGO has attempted to address this imbalance. El Caracol provides (job) training for street kids, as an alternative to formal education or a street-based lifestyle (Goulet, 2001).

Child Labour as a Survival Mechanism

According to Nieuwenhuys (1994), children's work has been clouded by moral considerations. Political will to change child labour policies has often come with little understanding of reality. For instance, as mentioned previously, demographics in some countries show a much higher percentage of the population below the age of 18, by as much as half. In these countries, the practice of narrowing the age range of those who can work is unsustainable.

Ravlolomanga and Schlemmer (2000) emphasized, from the case example of Madagascar, the need to understand child labour in relation to adult labour. Their study found that child labour in Madagascar developed as a necessary coping strategy for the harsh economic conditions facing the country, but they noted that what was important in that context was that children were not specifically exploited nor treated differently from adults because of their inherent childlike qualities. Social professionals can benefit from understanding that in certain circumstances child labour is a survival mechanism for the child, the family and sometimes the community. Conversely, in 1997, in post-genocide Rwanda,

200,000–400,000 children lived with families other than their own. They were often obliged to work as housemaids, and in this context many were likely to be exploited (UNICEF, 1997).

Unremunerated or Hidden Child Labour

Possibly the best way to visualize unremunerated child labour is to separate labour carried out within the family unit and labour carried out in the open market. Nieuwenhuys (1994) stated that many of the activities of the rural poor, including the children's, are rarely remunerated, but are central to survival. This is particularly so for agricultural and household work. According to Nieuwenhuys, this was exposed after the increasingly developed birth control debates illustrated the need in poor rural families for children to act not only as social security in old age, but also as household labour. The ILO (2001) illustrated several cases of good practice in relation to child labour, for instance with the provision of non-formal, peripatetic education for children scavenging rubbish heaps in Philippines. In the case of domestic labour, the ILO highlighted the importance of awareness raising and advocacy on behalf of individual children, as well as the prevention of further recruitment. Goulet (2001) provides another example of good practice in Bolivia. The NGO Centre for Research, Education and Services in La Paz provides one-to-one interactives and small group work with young people vulnerable to sexual exploitation, including children working as domestic labourers.

Child Labour versus Academic Achievement

Child labour is often discussed in opposition to academic achievement. This, incidentally, is seen through campaigns like Education for All (signed up to by many nations at the World Education Forum in Senegal in 2000) as the main tool in tackling global poverty. However, in terms of choosing education or employment, what parents and communities must consider is the quality of the education received. But is that all they must consider? Canagarajah and Skyt Nielsen. (1999) examined child labour and school attendance in Côte d'Ivoire, Ghana and Zambia. They found that transportation costs were a key factor in the decision to send children to school. Ravallion and Wodon (2000) found that in Bangladesh subsidies for school attendance increased school attendance, but less so for girls. Understanding the barriers to school attendance are crucial. For instance, an extreme example of dividing school attendance from child labour is evidenced in India where a national programme has rigidly defined child labour as any work that impedes a child up to the age of 14 from attending school. Another tactic is illustrated in a recently launched campaign in Morocco that intends to set up 'vigilance cells' within schools to report working children, particularly girls working as servants.[6]

'(C)hild labour is a dis-investment in human capital formation and has detrimental effects on the subsequent private and social returns from it' (Admassie, 2003, p. 168). Assaad *et al.* (2001) suggest that in Egypt, child labour affects school attendance (more so for girls), both with a narrow and broad definition of work, that is, work in the household and out of the household. As is mentioned in Chapter 8, girl children often leave school to care for parents who are ill with HIV/AIDS or other diseases. Similarly, Binder and Scrogin (1999) found a directly negative correlation between hours spent in work and academic performance in Mexico. Heady (2000) likewise studied the effects of work on children's academic achievement and identified negative effects. In Peru, Ilahi (2001) also found negative effects of work on education and again found that girls were disproportionately affected. Ilahi suggested the implementation of safety nets and childcare provisions to counter the problem.

Worst Forms of Child Labour

The ILO convention 182 Worst Forms of Child Labour (1999) sets out the following:

(a) all forms of slavery or practices similar to slavery, such as the sale and trafficking of children, debt bondage and serfdom and forced or compulsory labour, including forced or compulsory recruitment of children for use in armed conflict;

(b) the use, procuring or offering of a child for prostitution, for the production of pornography or for pornographic performances;

(c)   the use, procuring or offering of a child for illicit activities, in particular for the production and trafficking of drugs as defined in the relevant international treaties;

(d)   work, which, by its nature or the circumstances in which it is carried out, is likely to harm the health, safety or morals of children.

Further in article 7, prostitution and pornography, armed conflict, slavery or bondage are clearly stated as areas of worst forms of child labour and further special vulnerability is attributed to girls. We included some discussion of child soldiers in Chapter 5, so here we focus primarily on child criminal labour, voluntary or forced labour and commercial sexual exploitation of children.

Child Criminal Labour

Most children involved in criminal labour are concerned with petty crime. However, a minority are mixed up in more dangerous areas of the criminal world. De Souza and Urani (2002) investigated the role children play in drug trafficking in the 'favelas' of Rio de Janeiro. They found that children use trafficking to gain power, having usually had low levels of education and coming from extremely poor backgrounds. As for imprisoned children in Uganda, 1 per cent of the total prison population is made up of juveniles (UNDP, 1999), with 34 cases of murder in 1999, 189 cases of serious assault, 119 cases of all types of theft and ten cases of robbery and violent theft (INTERPOL, International Crime Statistics for 1998). Further, in Uganda in 1998, 25 boys were charged with treason and received death sentences (CSUCS, 1999a). In Rwanda, the ICRC reported that in 1999 there were approximately 570 children under the age of 14 in prison on previous genocide-related charges and a further 25 were incarcerated that year (CSUCS, 2001).

An unnamed programme, listed by the ILO's good practices report (2001), works to release and re-integrate children caught smuggling goods across the borders. This is done with the help of skills training, re-integration of children into mainstream education and family work. Other social interventions with young offenders include restorative justice or other diversion programmes, as discussed in Chapter 3, and as in evidence in various countries, including New Zealand, Australia and Canada.

Although child soldiers were discussed in detail in Chapter 5, it is worth noting here that there is evidence in Uganda that in addition to survival labour and voluntary labour, many children have been kidnapped or forcibly taken as sexual slaves, 'wives' of military personnel, guards or smugglers, including by the Lord's Resistance Army and the Allied Democratic Forces. Another report suggested that children were sold as labour to Sudan, with those intended for sexual slavery or prostitution coming from slum areas (Global March, no date). Here again, social professionals have a role to play as advocates (for individual concerns and for national and international policy reform), and in prevention and reintegration progammes.

Child Sexual Exploitation

Of the various forms of child exploitation, perhaps one of the most pervasive and prolific, both in terms of the severity of affects and the areas in which it exists, is child sexual exploitation. It is also perhaps the area where social professionals are most involved. Castells (1998) called it the worst form of child labour. Although commercial exploitation is more common in cities, elements of non-commercial exploitation can be found in most places around the world, from mega-cities like Cairo, Mexico, London, Tokyo, Lagos and São Paulo to small communities in remote areas of northern Greenland or atolls in the South Pacific (personal communications). According to ECPAT (End Child Prostitution, Pornography and Trafficking), international commercial sexual exploitation of children exists in all regions and countries (ECPAT, 2002). In recognition of this growing issue in 1996, the first World Congress Against Commercial Sexual Exploitation of Children in Stockholm, Sweden, brought together international actors interested in understanding and eradicating the international sex trade of children (UNICEF, 1996). A second Congress in Yokohama, Japan, followed this in 2001. The Declaration for Action of the first Congress (1996) defines commercial sexual exploitation of children as the fundamental violation of children's rights. It comprises sexual abuse by the adult and remuneration in cash or kind to the child or the third person or persons. The child is treated as a sexual object and as a commercial object. The commercial sexual exploitation of children constitutes a form of coercion and violence against children, and amounts to forced labour and a contemporary form of slavery.

The commercial sexual exploitation of children is riddled with paradox. If understood as child labour, it can be analysed as an economic issue, for example as a family survival strategy, as unremunerated or hidden child labour, as oppositional to academic achievement, and most commonly as exploitative. Much of the research reflects a discrepancy between the user and the used, the child and the adult, the participant and the non-participant. It has been only recently that child or youth prostitution has been disaggregated from adult prostitution and labelled a distinct form of sexual exploitation (Gorkoff and Runner, 2003) and/or slavery (Bramley *et al.*, 1998). Recognition of commercial sexual exploitation of children has only come into being after the recognition of the broader phenomenon of child abuse and more specifically child sexual abuse (Manion, 2004). Additionally, it has only been relatively recently that the children involved in the sex industry have been seen as victims of exploitation and not instigators of criminal activity. However, while this change has happened at policy level, it has not always translated into practice.

Accurately quantifying the numbers of children involved is problematic, not least because international research addressing the extent of commercial sexual exploitation of children has been variable in both extent and accuracy. In addition, despite the definition above, it is difficult to delineate which cases constitute commercial sexual exploitation for a variety of reasons (particularly in relation to the definition of 'commercial'). However, Ward and Roby citing UNICEF data suggested that an estimated 30 million children 'are being vicitmised by CSEC related practices' (p. 17) and that the total number of such victims is highest in Asia and Central and South America. But looking at such large numbers also detracts from the individuals who have experienced the abuse. However, the extent and widespread nature of child sexual exploitation is basis enough to recognize and address both its causes and effects.

Prostitution itself embodies a great diversity of activities, although most research has focused on streetwalkers. At its core, prostitution exhibits a great power differential and is, as O'Connell-Davidson (1998) describes, the commodification of personhood or the selling of an hour to do whatever the buyer wishes. Flowers (1998) states that the only difference between child prostitution and statutory rape is the exchange of money. However, little focus or research has gone into the role of choice for children in sexual relationships (Montgomery, 2001). Although adults, unlike children, can consent to sexual contracts, their ability to do so is still shaped by their gender, race, ethnicity and surrounding cultural values (Lowman, 2000), as well as age, occupation, geography, personal history, educational attainment and addiction to substances.

The child sex trade is a multi-billion dollar global industry. The global picture is complex and both culturally and geographically specific, making it difficult to conceptualize who is involved (O'Connell-Davidson, 1998). The media, in recent years, has exploitatively focused on specific cases, largely in developing countries, that involve Western men and extremely young children. Although there is no denying this as a problem, it represents only a small segment of an enormous industry, which includes children of all ages. It includes a continuum of what Gorkoff and Runner (2003) conceptualized as sexual slavery to survival sex to more 'bourgeois' forms of the sex trade. This continuum moves from complete entrenchment to loose affiliation with the sex trade and from no choice to some choice. Context is crucial. Schlemmer (2000), for instance, questions how exploitative both social policy and social workers are when dealing with sexually exploited children because they do not tend to differentiate between survival work and survival sex (i.e., selling sexual services for money or swapping sexual services for basic needs, like food).

Muntarbhorn (1996, p. 20) suggests that 'the catalysts in the process are multifarious: governments, non-government, community and individual, parent and child'. A broad conceptualization encapsulates a greater diversity of actors involved, engaged in supply, demand and facilitator roles, who ensure that the transaction happens (Manion, 2004). Understanding the local context and the actors is important for social professionals to construct appropriate interventions.

The supply side includes a disparate grouping of children and young people. Ennew (UK) (1986) characterized most sexually exploited children as 'runaways, walkaways and throwaways', that is, children who ran away from home because of intolerable situations; children who have loose relationships with home and freely come and go; and children who are not wanted in their home environments or have lost parents or guardians. Recruitment, according to MacInnes (Canada) (1998), occurs through seduction, coercion and kidnapping. De Oliveira (2000) further discusses the special vulnerability to sexual exploitation of street children in Latin America. One organization of note working with street children in Latin America, specifically Honduras, Guatemala and Nicaragua, is Casa Alianza (www.casa-alianza.org). They conduct various programmes including street-based outreach and drop-in facilities, training, housing, education, psycho-social support, advocacy and lobbying, with young people, with families and with communities.

Most intervention concerning commercially sexually exploited children happens with children and not with others involved in the supply and demand chain. Response comes at various levels. With a push from national and international campaigns, policy level response can strengthen the legal framework and provide (political and economic) support for programmes. At the community level most intervention is prevention based, for instance, awareness programmes in schools and community centres. At the individual level the intervention is the most intense, with some programmes focused on health care or specifically sexual health or substance misuse issues, harm reduction strategies; on education or vocational training and re-integration into mainstream schooling; and on provision of basic needs. This can take place in residential programmes, outreach and drop-in facilities, or via support groups which can include family work or counselling (Manion, 2004). Kingsley and Mark (2000) in Canada found that when asked about service provision, most of their respondents, again girls working in prostitution, wanted someone to talk to, particularly someone who had been in the same circumstance. In Philippines, Ward and Roby found that many of the girls living in a girls shelter in Manila displayed symptoms of post-traumatic stress disorder. However, staff at the centre were unable to offer therapeutic interventions, but aimed to provide a safe and stable environment in which the girls could gain sufficient respite and opportunity for recovery before re-entering society. The authors also suggested that government policies are generally supportive of efforts to address CSEC and that there is a powerful youth-led movement to eradicate it.

The demand side comprises a category of people that has been little researched (O'Connell-Davidson, 2001). It generally, though not exclusively, involves males of various ages (O'Connell-Davidson, 2001). Anderson and O'Connell-Davidson (2003) conducted a study on demand in five countries and could find little consensus on whether 'punters'[7] decide whether prostitutes were able to consent. The demand for child sexual exploitation has a strong link with the cultural tolerance of prostitution and commercial sexual exploitation of children (O'Connell-Davidson, 2001) and recent studies have suggested a direct link between the use of pornography and commercial sexual exploitation of children (e.g., Itzin, 2001). Specific groups that have been involved in prostitution include the police, the military, seafarers, truckers, travelling businessmen and other groups of men who live for long periods of time in isolation from home and family (O'Connell-Davidson, 2001). Demand also comes from a separate group of 'benefactors' or 'sugar daddies' (O'Connell-Davidson, 2001). The demand in many places is ingrained in a machismo culture (Mänsson, 2001), where a sexual double standard persists, that is, where men are expected to have far more sexual licence and experience than women. However, demand is further facilitated by an increased market in sexual tourism, the proliferation of sexual migrants (forced or otherwise) and the Internet. Although, as already mentioned, most social intervention is with the young person, there are some programmes that focus on the supply side, particularly in terms of prevention, for instance in public awareness campaigns; school workshops based on respecting the opposite sex; and 'John Programmes' or education diversion programmes (Kennedy *et al.*, 2004). The last is aimed at rehabilitating punters and programmes are usually undertaken by multi-agency teams, including, for instance, police and social workers, as well as exited sex workers.

The most diverse group of actors involved in commercial sexual exploitation of children are the facilitators (or the abusing adults). It is also the group least addressed, in terms of intervention. Traditionally, we associate this group with 'the pimp'. However, the group of facilitators is much broader and can include individuals or groups who do not necessarily intend to facilitate supply and demand. For instance, there are increasing numbers of groups and individuals who in good faith buy girls from debt bondage, thereby helping the individual, but reinforcing the networks that put her into the situation in the first place (e.g., in Cambodia). The facilitators also include the families that pass their profession on to their children (Fredrick and Kelly, 2000); family members or friends who introduce sex work (Estes, 2001); and families that allow children to be passed on to traffickers or pimps (for money or otherwise). Facilitators include traffickers, organized crime rings and a myriad of people involved in businesses surrounding the sex trade, including managers of exotic dance clubs, brothels, massage parlours, taxi drivers (who often have knowledge about the local sex trade and pass it on to clients), travel agents and hotels. Social professionals have been little involved with this group, but could be more involved in researching the issue and tackling issues not only with exploited children, but also with the exploiters, the families and the communities, through both preventative and reactive services.

Children's Rights Movement

The children's rights movement has seen the evolution of new child-centred programmes and policies, a movement in research to meaningfully including children's participation and a growing number of child-focused agencies, which are including young people on staff to represent children. As evidence of this growing trend, the first Children's World Congress on Child Labour was held in Florence, Italy in May 2004. Unfortunately, a problem with visas meant that many delegates could not attend, but the congress put children at the heart of advocating for the abolition of exploitative child labour and national implementation of children's rights.

Even so, few studies to date have examined the point of view of the children involved in child labour. Leonard (2004) interviewed 245 children aged 15 years in Northern Ireland and asked them their opinion of child labour and found that they highlighted their right to work. The uniqueness of this argument was that child protection legislation has traditionally excluded young people from the employment sector, but suggests that, given children's viewpoints, empowering children within the employment field may present a more effective legislative framework. Similarly, in 1997 UNICEF (2004b) launched an international, Web-based discussion board aimed at gathering and posting the opinions of young people on a variety of topics. The *Children and Work* discussion board became the most active, with 2500 messages from over 100 countries by 2004. Much of the discussion revolved around why child labour exists and what the 'causes' were, including poverty, lack of effective laws and enforcement, low wages for parents and caregivers, self-interest among employers and Southern debt. All participants agreed that exploitative child labour contributes significantly to the vicious cycle of poverty, denies the right to an education, as well as to being a child, but many also discussed the potential benefits of working in a safe and supportive environment, reminding us that the opportunity to work can be an empowering and confidence-building experience. Participants suggested actions that directly addressed child labour, such as enforcing laws that protect children and punish employers, as well as steps to improve overall quality of life and opportunities, such as employment opportunities for parents and ensuring access to quality education for all. Young people called on their leaders, their parents and their peers to end exploitative and harmful child-labour practices.

Returning to the example of commercial sexual exploitation of children, in a study on models of good practice with sexually exploited children, Manion (2004) found that respondents stressed the crucial importance of child participation in both the design and implementation of services targeting them. This was evident from programmes in countries as diverse as Moldova, Canada, Cambodia and Lebanon. Child participation acted both as a means of strengthening the focus of the services and as a way of empowering the child. Goulet (2001) advocates the work of the Canadian-based NGO PEERS, which helps young people involved in prostitution (in Victoria and Vancouver) to exit. The majority of its staff have themselves had experience of the sex industry and are therefore specially placed to provide expert advice. As mentioned above, there is also evidence of a youth-led movement to eradicate CSEC in the Philippines (Ward and Roby, 2004).

Focusing on children's rights and children's involvement in society has led to the rethinking of some mainstream programmes. For instance, an education programme in Indonesia (Suanda, 2003) has seen the complete overhaul of the way secondary school education functions. Rather than an emphasis on rote learning, students enjoy a combination of in-school, formal classes and community-based, less formal classes. The school emphasises democracy and active citizenship and encourages attendance of disadvantaged youth and former child workers. This has helped to convince family and community members that education can have a more relevant role in the lives of its younger members and that it can provide a beneficial alternative to work.

Conclusion

Social professionals have a crucial role in both the policy making and implementation of policies in relation to child labour, with important roles to play in grass-roots voluntary sector agencies, statutory services and INGOs. McIntyre (2005) suggested that the failure of social services to provide early intervention in child sexual abuse and child sexual exploitation equated to a form of state-supported sexual abuse. A multi-pronged approach is necessary to tackle child exploitation and therefore there is a strong call for multi-agency work, for instance requiring social professionals to work in collaboration with police, trade unions or labour rights organizations, government, teachers and health-care professionals. This point has particular significance as children may be exploited beyond social professionals' notice in numerous countries and settings. Further, most contemporary social work texts have largely ignored this area and Dominelli (1999) suggested that social workers lacked the training to deal with international child welfare issues. Better understanding of the issues by social professionals could support more sustainable interventions.

Many authors suggest a gradual decrease in child labour, through an increased focus on education, including non-formal or locality-specific education. While this may be the best possible solution, child labour needs to be understood in the context in which it is taking place, the extent of exploitation involved and what options actually exist for its eradication. For example, in agricultural areas, classes could be organized outside of harvest seasons to allow children the maximum opportunity to attend school and perform household duties. Admassie (2003) made suggestions for interim policies in Ethiopia to encourage maximum educational attainment by understanding that most children have household responsibilities and ensuring programmes take this into consideration. Similarly, ILO and UNICEF have been involved with several initiatives that focus on early childhood programmes, distance learning, bilingual education and flexible scheduling of classes in order to improve the enrolment and retention of children in school. However, for victims of the worst forms of child labour, education is only one component of what is likely to be a more complex set of needs.

Social professionals need to understand the influences of globalization and the effects of international legal and ethical standards, and also need to be familiar with human rights as specifically related to children, and appreciate the tools that such standards and conventions present. We are likely to see the continued encouragement of child participation, child-centred policy, partnership, and ownership. Influencing consensus-building on the role of children in the community and family, their right to education and the effect that this has on future employment opportunities is also important. Ensuring access for open dialogue between policy makers, social professionals and children at the global and local level seems the least we can do.

8 Spreading Disease: Global Pandemics with Local Impact and Responses

Introduction

Infectious diseases have been present throughout human history. Epidemics have been documented since recording of such data began, and the World Health Organization (WHO) has tracked numerous diseases since its inception. With few exceptions (for instance, tuberculosis, influenza, plague), infectious diseases have been primarily local phenomena. In the past 20 years, an unusually high number of previously unknown infectious agents, roughly 30, have been identified – for example HIV, rotavirus, and Ebola. Others previously thought by the world community to be defeated have re-emerged, for example plague, cholera, yellow fever and diphtheria. Many of these are more virulent and some are becoming resistant to drug treatments (Lague and Saywell, 2003, p. 19).

Over 14 million people die each year from infectious and parasitic diseases (one in three deaths in some developing countries). Most deaths occur in nations where one-third of the population lives on incomes of less than US$1 per day – altogether 1200 million people. Poor people, women, children and the elderly are the most vulnerable. Infectious diseases continue to be the world's leading killer of young adults and children. Heymann (in Kindhauser, 2004) has provided three categories of diseases. The first category, major infectious diseases, includes AIDS, tuberculosis and malaria, which together account for approximately 39 per cent of deaths attributed to infectious diseases (p. 6). A second category of infectious disease, the so-called 'neglected diseases', creates an additional toll of severe and permanent disabilities. While mortality associated with many of these neglected diseases is not high, lifelong disability and chronic social and economic consequences may be dramatic. Examples include meningitis survivors with mental impairment, people with blindness caused by onchocerciasis, and children with impaired cognitive development associated with schistosomiasis. A third category of infectious diseases is the emerging, epidemic-prone diseases (e.g., influenza, cholera, Ebola virus, haemorrhagic fever). These tend to be more localized, but with the post-9/11 threat of biological terrorism, they can threaten global health security because they frequently and unexpectedly challenge national health services and disrupt routine control programmes, diverting international attention and funds.

Infectious diseases cause death, disability and disruption worldwide. Their increasing spread and devastating impact can be related to the many processes of globalization, including human migration across national borders.

> Outbreaks and epidemics do not recognize national boundaries and, if not contained, can rapidly spread internationally. Unverified and inaccurate information on disease outbreaks often results in excessive reactions by both the media and politicians, leading to panic and inappropriate responses, which in turn may result in significant interruptions of trade, travel, and routine, thereby placing further economic burden on affected countries. (WHO, 2003, p. 10)

WHO states, 'these diseases attract little medical and donor attention, but they must be tackled' (WHO, 2003, p. 12). The bulk of the literature that is available on emerging diseases is in public health and medical literature and focuses on HIV/AIDS. Some are now arguing that the effects of chronic diseases (e.g., heart disease, cancer, diabetes), as well as acute diseases, must command international attention.[1] Social work as an international profession has not given adequate attention to these trends. The overall purpose of this text is to enhance the international perspective of social professionals and this chapter introduces the spread of global disease and its relationship to globalization, with primary attention paid to acute diseases such as HIV/AIDS. It describes a sampling of the multidimensional social effects of spreading disease. It includes global and local responses to disease, and discusses implications for social work education, prevention, direct care practice, policy and research.

The Global Spread of Old and New Diseases

It is not difficult to find evidence that global diseases are increasing in number and spreading to disparate populations. Diseases have unprecedented opportunities to spread throughout populations and across international borders. Two million people cross international borders every day, compared to about 69,000 fifty years ago (Lague and Saywell, 2003, p. 19). As mentioned in Chapter 5, the UN World Food Programme says war puts millions of Africans at risk of the spread of HIV because of displacement. Modes of disease transmission include air (e.g., tuberculosis), food (e.g., bird flu) or body fluids – blood, semen, vaginal fluid or breast milk (e.g., HIV and Rift Valley Fever). Heymann (in Kindhauser [2004, p. 7]) summarized the major causes of mortality from infectious diseases in 2001 as AIDS (2.9 million), diarrhoeal diseases (1.9 million), tuberculosis (1.6 million), and malaria (1.1 million).

Recent emerging diseases with an international impact include avian influenza ('bird flu'), bovine spongiform encephalopathy (BSE or mad cow disease), Rift Valley fever; Nipah virus, plague, and polio. Avian influenza spreads among chickens and can spread to humans who are in close contact with the infected animals (and rarely from human to human). Fear about chickens being sold in markets has affected the economy in many Asian countries.[2] BSE on the other hand depends on food for transmission, and has affected travel between Britain and other countries. It also has prevented Canadian and American citizens from donating blood if they have lived in the UK since the outbreak of BSE in 1980 (Centres for Disease Control, 2004).

Rift Valley Fever was first isolated in 1930 in sheep in the Rift Valley of Kenya. It has now been found in sub-Saharan and North Africa. In 2000, the first non-African outbreak occurred in Saudi Arabia and Yemen. It can cause severe disease in animals and humans, as well as severe economic losses. Meanwhile, Nipah virus was first identified in 1999 when it caused an outbreak of neurological and respiratory disease on pig farms in peninsular Malaysia, resulting in 105 human deaths and the culling of 1 million pigs. An outbreak (confirmed in April 2004) in the Faridpur district of Bangladesh, affecting 30 people and resulting in 18 deaths, may have involved person-to-person transmission, an event not previously observed.[3] Lastly, plague is transmitted through infected rodent bites or direct contact with infected animal tissue. In areas where humans live in close quarters and sanitation is poor, the presence of infected rodents can increase the spread, although vaccinations and surveillance have reduced the incidence of plague sharply in recent years. In 1999, 14 countries reported cases of plague (WHO, 2002). Mortality rates are high if untreated, though nearly all can be cured if diagnosed and treated with antibiotics in time.

Several diseases were thought to have been eradicated or nearly eradicated, including polio and smallpox (Seipel, 2005). Polio constitutes a relatively bright spot in the discussion of global disease. The UN had hoped to eradicate polio by 2005. In India, this is nearly accomplished, with only 29 cases reported in 2004 (after 260 in 2003 and 1556 in 2002).[4] However, policy makers and health workers are running into challenges in some parts of the world. Some people in the slums of Gaya in Bihar, are refusing to take the anti-polio drops, believing they contain anti-fertility or impotency-producing drugs to curb the population.[5] Similarly, in the Kano area of Nigeria in 2003, some religious leaders alleged that foreign powers were spreading AIDS and infertility among Muslims through the polio vaccine.[6] And the first four cases of polio in the US, in five years, are in Minnesota's Amish community.[7] (WHO recently announced the disease is still endemic in Nigeria, India, Pakistan, Afghanistan and Egypt, so it will fail to meet its 2005 eradicating target.)[8]

Three diseases with global impact at the time of writing are severe acute respiratory Syndrome (SARS), avian flu and HIV/AIDS. SARS has potential for rapid spread due to interconnectedness of humanity. High-rise apartments in Hong Kong, for example, provided easy opportunity for the virus to spread and airline passengers have helped to spread SARS faster than any new disease in history (Lague and Saywell, 2003, p. 20). In the words of Wildlife Trust President Dr Mary Pearl, the re-appearance of SARS in China and the identification of Nipah virus in Bangladesh . . . are serious warnings. The current state of understanding of lethal disease agents that move from one species to another, and then to humans in crowded landscapes, is woefully inadequate. People must recognize that disease emergence is yet another potential consequence of ecosystem disruptions'.[9]

Given the particular association of SARS with the Asian region, the *Asia Pacific Journal of Social Work* produced a special issue on social work responses to this disease in 2004 (Vol. 14, No. 1).

While avian (bird) flu is spreading westward from Asia along migratory routes, and WHO advises people to exercise caution when handling poultry, the agency has kept its level of pandemic alert at phase 3. This means that this virus causing infections in humans is not new, but does not spread easily from one person to another. Countries worldwide are discussing ways to prevent the spread of this flu and are gearing up systems to respond should it reach pandemic proportions.

An estimated 34–46 million people live with HIV/AIDS worldwide, and more than 20 million have died. The most explosive growth of HIV infection occurred in the mid-1990s especially in Africa. Sub-Saharan Africa has 10 per cent of world population, but two-thirds of those with HIV (WHO, 2004a). While 1 in 12 African adults live with HIV/AIDS, a further one-fifth of people globally living with HIV/AIDS are in Asia (ibid., p. 1) and Asia is one of two regions with the fastest growing AIDS epidemic in the world (the other being Eastern Europe). Young people (age 15–24) account for nearly half of all new HIV infections worldwide (UNAIDS, 2004b) and women now account for about 50 per cent of total infections. In 2003 almost five million people became infected with HIV, the greatest number in one year since the beginning of the epidemic (WHO, 2004a).

Causes of HIV spread are complex. WHO (2000a) suggested that unequal gender (social, economic, power) relations are driving the epidemic. Further, the UNHCR suggests that in refugee camps, local traditions and gender inequalities exacerbate the HIV/AIDS problem.[10] In war-torn countries such as Rwanda, rape as an act of war has left many women HIV-infected, in a country with few resources to treat them.[11] HIV may be spreading undetected among several groupings because of local condemnation, including amongst injecting drug users, sex workers and men who have sex with men (UNAIDS, 2004b), although in the last case, men who have sex with men now accounts for only 5–10 per cent of global cases (UNAIDS, 2004a). This group is highly stigmatized – in 2002, 84 countries had legal prohibitions against sex between men, and this hampers prevention efforts. Specific causes of HIV spread are being debated, for instance, arguments over the role of circumcision in the spread of HIV in Botswana (Kebaabetswe *et al.*, 2003; Hill and Denniston, 2003) and traditional sexual practices in Tanzania (Carlsen, 2005b).

Globalization and Disease

If globalization is defined narrowly as the development of a global economic system, then direct cause and effect with disease spread is difficult. However, taking into account our broader definition of globalization that includes the internationalization of markets and information, global technology, and the movement of people and goods across international borders, the relationship between disease spread and globalization is evident. The trend in many countries towards privatization and away from a centralized economy is a direct indicator of globalization. Disease spread is more difficult to measure and control when government resources are reduced or when populations within a country or between countries have widely disparate states of well-being. As government budgets for infrastructure shrink in many developed nations and as in other countries the structural adjustment programmes of the World Bank require reduction of such funds, poverty remains a serious concern.

For instance, MacDonald (2005) has written critically about the way present systems are used to mediate the globalization of finance, suggesting that the policies of international financial institutions (the World Bank, IMF and WTO) make it increasingly difficult for developing nations to operate health (and education) programmes effectively, compounding rather than contributing to the alleviation of poverty. The spread of TB and HIV/AIDS results from their 'feeding on each other, each sustained by poverty' due to the 'decaying infrastructure of the world's metropolitan inner cities.'[12] Christian AID, while it supports the WHO '3x5' initiative (to get 3 million people on antiretroviral [ARV] medications by 2005), has concerns that prevention will be increasingly ignored. As Dr Rachel Baggaley states, '(p)overty is one of the key drivers of this epidemic. Unless we tackle issues of trade, debt and the lack of trained health workers, we cannot begin to win the battle'.[13]

A number of local examples can be given to illustrate these concerns. In Zimbabwe, 'wages plummeted and employment became scarcer in cities during World Bank and IMF economic structural adjustment programmes of the 1990s. Many women turned to commercial sex as a source of income, putting them at greater risk of HIV and other sexually transmitted diseases (STDs), (Kawewe, 2001, p. 477). A significant problem with STDs emerged in the Czech Republic as a result of geopolitical, social and economic changes in the state. A study by Resl *et al.* (2003) demonstrated that prostitution (concentrated around border areas with Austria and Germany) contributed to the increase in STDs. The majority of prostitutes were foreigners, mostly Ukrainians and Russians. Msimang (2003) documents the 'recipe for creating an AIDS epidemic in South Africa', which has relevance for many parts of the world. He blames globalization, '. . . the drive towards an economic system dominated by supranational trade and banking institutions that are not accountable to democratic processes or national government . . . characterized by an increase in cross-border economic, social, and technological exchange under conditions of (extreme) capitalism' (p. 109) as a cause of disease spread.

The UNAIDS 2004 Report (UNAIDS, 2004b, p. 9) states that the HIV 'epidemic has created a need for robust, flexible health systems at a time when many affected countries have been reducing public services spending to repay debt and conform to international finance institutions' requirements. In African countries, studies estimate that between 19 and 53 per cent of all government health employees' deaths are caused by AIDS. The epidemic is quickly outstripping growth in the supply of health sector workers' (UNAIDS, 2004a, p. 9). Governmental services are curtailed at the same time as there is a growth in populations vulnerable to disease spread. (The possibility that the shortfall in social, as well as healthcare, professionals working in this field is also in part due to individual decisions to migrate to wealthier nations is discussed further in Chapter 9.)

In some countries, the increase in vulnerable populations (the poor, the aged, women and children) contributes to the incidence and spread of diseases. The World Health Report (WHO, 2000b, p. 2) states '(i)n some countries rapid growth of the size of the vulnerable population – as a result of civil unrest, a rise in poverty or other social and economic factors – triggers epidemic growth and wider spread of the [HIV] virus'. For example, in Ugandan society women have less power and experience more poverty than men. Some turn to sex work (one survey found that 86 per cent of sex workers started because of financial problems), putting them at greater risk of HIV and other diseases. The long-term strategy there must be to improve economic position of women vis-à-vis men (Gysels *et al.*, 2002). Similarly, in Kenya, women sell sex to supplement their small income (Hawken *et al.*, 2002).

As mentioned, disease spread can also be a result of population mobility, whether within a country or trans-nationally. For instance, the spread of infectious disease into rural areas in Cambodia has been facilitated by the movement of older female sex workers (who have a high rate of HIV and syphilis) out of cities into rural and less competitive but also less sophisticated markets. Their mobility may thus contribute to the expansion of the HIV epidemic into rural areas where populations have previously been at less risk (Sopheab *et al.*, 2003). Two Western examples (local to one of the authors) of disease spread are related to trans-national population mobility. Of the new HIV infections diagnosed in Minnesota, US, in 2004, 20 per cent were among the recent African immigrant populations; most of them are people displaced by wars in Sudan, Somalia and Liberia (Minnesota AIDS Project, 2004). Also in Minnesota, a programme of resettlement of Hmong refugees from camps in Thailand stalled in 2005 due to an outbreak of TB in that population.[14]

Malnutrition caused by poverty can put people, especially the young, at greater risk of life-threatening and disabling infections such as diphtheria, yellow fever and cholera (Seipel, 1999, p. 35). Often those who are vulnerable try to migrate across borders to obtain work or care. So, for instance, in addition to the examples above, the movement of HIV and other STIs across borders has been demonstrated in several studies. HIV is now well established in the Caribbean, and the inward migration from the Caribbean to Britain together with a high incidence of some bacterial STIs among Britain's black Caribbean communities suggests a considerable potential for HIV spread (Hickson *et al.*, 2004). In addition, in the last 10 years, many south European countries have experienced considerable immigration of people from economically disadvantaged countries. Spain has rapidly changed from a country of emigration to one of immigration and many migrants in Spain, especially the undocumented workers, have problems accessing health services, particularly HIV testing (Castilla *et al.*, 2002). Trafficking of women and girls increases the spread of HIV, as well, in both Europe and Asia. For example, Beyrer (2001, p. 543) documented that women victims of the civil conflict in Myanmar have become part of the Southeast Asian sex industry.

Whether people move across borders permanently or temporarily, the risk of disease spread increases with such movement (see Chapter 6). People move in search of increased opportunities or safety and bring with them dreams, aspirations, and sometimes HIV or other diseases. Only 7 per cent of people needing ARV treatment in developing countries have access to it (UNAIDS, 2004b), so sometimes people come seeking treatment for disease – although, in other cases, they meet disease at their destinations. For instance, in Tunisia, half the people officially reported to have HIV have apparently come from Libya to obtain antiviral treatment and/or undergo drug rehabilitation, as Tunisia has been providing free and universal antiviral treatment since the turn of the century.[15] Conversely, in relation to the latter possibility, there is anecdotal evidence in the UK to suggest that some asylum-seeking women become infected with HIV following liaisons with men from their own national communities (personal communication).

The opening of global markets for food and other goods can also assist disease spread. The World Bank has recognized the impact of HIV spread throughout Africa, and has targeted a busy trade corridor that crosses five countries from Ivory Coast to Nigeria; US$16.6 million are being spent to reduce its spread among transport workers, migrants, commercial sex workers and local residents.[16] As mentioned, bird flu spread in Asia through the sale of infected chickens in markets across borders of ten Asian countries in 2004. Other countries watched carefully the efforts of local governments and WHO to track the disease and limit its spread. Western countries were relieved when a German tourist, returning from Thailand, was declared not to be suffering from this disease,[17] but the fear of its spread and indeed of a pandemic – has been ongoing, with a new outbreak in late 2005.

People are increasingly aware of the global spread of disease. One study (Joffe and Harhoff, 2002) reviewed how the representation of Ebola in the British news media affected the thinking about this disease of people in The UK. They concluded that most 'lay thinkers still feel detached from it, and draw an analogy between Ebola and science fiction. This is discussed as a method of symbolic coping on the part of the readers as a way to take away the potential of Ebola to globalize.' Perhaps it is more difficult with mass communication and instant availability of information for some more closed countries to continue their pattern of denial about epidemics, especially HIV in parts of the Middle East and North Africa, for instance.[18] As information is more readily available, some countries in the region are beginning to develop more prevention programmes (e.g., Algeria, Iran, Lebanon, Morocco), even paying attention to injecting drug users in Iran and Libya.

It is clear from this discussion that some disease spread is related to globalization processes. The growing reality and social impact of these diseases is part of the knowledge required by social professionals worldwide.

Impact of Diseases on Countries, Communities and Particular Populations

Many studies document the demographic, economic, political and even environmental impacts of the global spread of disease. For instance, the greatest mortality impact globally for HIV is for people aged 20–40. The pandemic reverses gains made in the 1960s and 1970s on life expectancy in sub-Saharan Africa (WHO, 2004a, p. 2). AIDS has left 14 million orphans (one or both parents lost to AIDS) in 2004, most in Africa, and by 2010, estimates suggest there will be up to 25 million. The enormous social impact of HIV and other diseases has received less attention than the economic effects. Loss, grief, disability and changes in cultural patterns are all manifestations of this disease spread. This section examines the social effects of disease on certain sectors of countries and communities, with special attention to vulnerable populations within them: girls, women, the poor, and men who have sex with men.

People with HIV-related conditions exacerbated by TB or other diseases can take a toll on already overburdened health care systems. In countries in sub-Saharan Africa, the occupation of hospital beds by AIDS patients often exceeds 50 per cent (WHO, 2004b, p. 11). Civil rights violations, including denial of treatment, violations of privacy, deprivation of parental rights, workplace discrimination and refusal of admittance to nursing homes and residential facilities for people with HIV/AIDS have also been reported in the US.[19] In Latin America and the Caribbean, homophobia is a major factor in HIV/AIDS discrimination in health care.[20] As mentioned, many African countries face a crisis in the delivery of vital public services that are crucial to the AIDS response. Reasons range from migration of key people from public- to private-sector work or migration abroad, to the deadly impact of the virus itself (UNAIDS, 2004b).

The education system in some African countries is at fundamental risk as more teachers are dying than are being trained. Children (especially girls) are not as likely to go to school in poor countries when a parent is ill or dead due to care-giving responsibilities or the inability to afford school fees. Both this reality and the tragedy of too few teachers are compromising one of the Millennium Goals to enrol all children in school by 2015 (WHO, 2004b, p. 10).

The agricultural sector is also at risk; there are intensifying chronic food shortages in countries where people are already undernourished, and estimates are that AIDS will have claimed one-fifth or more of agricultural workers in southern Africa by 2020 (ibid., p. 50). The effects of HIV include rising household debt levels and changing farming techniques and diets.[21] Clearly, epidemics of disease have impact on the organizations and local resources that sustain communities.

Whole communities can see the effects of widespread disease. For instance, South Africa has the highest HIV caseload in the world, estimated at 5.3 million, more than 12 per cent of population.[22] Increasing age dependency ratios – the relationship of working adults on whom children and elderly depend to those who are dependent – are common. The processes of accumulating human capital and transmitting it across generations by passing on knowledge, skills, experience and values is interrupted or ended in some communities. For example, with extended families no longer able to provide care for all orphans, many end up on the streets (WHO, 2004b, p. 3) or in orphanages (Tucker, 2005). As described in Chapter 4, the effects of such community-wide loss can be devastating.

The HIV/AIDS epidemic has given rise to major demographic changes including an alarming number of orphans in sub-Saharan Africa. One study describes a rural community in western Kenya in which one in three children below 18 years of age had lost at least one biological parent – and one in nine had lost both. The findings clearly summarize the impact:

> The main problems these children faced were lack of school fees, food and access to medical care. The high number of orphans has overwhelmed the traditional mechanisms for orphan care, which were based on patrilineal kinship ties. Thus, 28 per cent of the orphans were looked after by culturally 'inappropriate' categories such as matrilineal kin or strangers. Furthermore, many of the caretakers were themselves not capable due to ill health or old age. Factors such as poverty, negative attitudes, and traditional funeral customs made the orphans' situation even worse. (Nyambedha *et al.*, 2003, p. 301)

Children can suffer from discrimination, stigma and social exclusion. In a stunning example, two children in Kerala, India, who were orphaned by AIDS were banished from their school due to their HIV status. After a hunger strike by them and their grandfather, the Chief Minister ordered a state school to admit them. The school's students boycotted, and bowing to pressure, the government ordered the children schooled at home. The President of India, the Health Minister, local AIDS authorities and activists have tried to work with the community to appeal to them on behalf of these children and to fight the fears and misconceptions about HIV. Yet at the end of 2003 the children were still being kept from school.[23]

Diseases disproportionately affect women. In the African region, women comprise 58 per cent of those infected with HIV/AIDS. Infected 6 to 8 years earlier than men, many women die faster. Unequal distribution of infection rates in the future is a concern, as many men then turn to ever-younger sexual partners (WHO, 2004b, p. 3). The HIV epidemic is overwhelmingly heterosexual, nearly exclusively so in Africa and South and Southeast Asia. Women are more vulnerable to infection than men for several reasons, including biological, economic, social and cultural factors.

Women's material dependence on men can mean women cannot control when, with whom and in what circumstance they have sex. Many have to exchange sex for material favours, for daily survival. They are biologically more vulnerable to virus in sperm and to risk of micro-lesions in cases of coerced sex or rape (see Chapter 5). Also,

> for women who have lost a husband to the [HIV] disease, it can mean losing everything else as well – property or assets, such as land, farm equipment or livestock – effectively undermining their capacity to earn an income and grow food to feed themselves, their children and the orphans they are often caring for.[24]

In addition, older women often care for ailing adult children and later the grandchildren, at a time of their lives when they assumed they would be receiving family care (WHO, 2000a). Socially and culturally, women in many societies are not expected to discuss or make decisions about sexuality, they cannot request, let alone insist on using, a condom or any form of protection. If they refuse sex or ask for a condom, they may risk abuse or there is a suspicion of infidelity. In many contexts, women are seen as 'vectors' (Msimang, 2003). Meanwhile, it is culturally acceptable for men to have multiple partners, and ever younger partners (WHO, 2000a).

Girls are at special risk of social ill effects due to HIV and other diseases. In many countries, girls drop out of school to care for sick parents or for younger siblings (WHO, 2000a). In Tanzania, children, especially girls, are at risk due to rape, sodomy and other forms of sexual violence in the family. Myths 'perpetuated by traditional healers or witchdoctors' (Nyaywa, 2003, p. 2) hold that sex with a daughter or a child can cure HIV/AIDS and help people become rich, or rejuvenate and strengthen aging men.

Families can become poor or poorer because of HIV and other diseases. Assets and skills are not passed on by parents who die young. Loss of income and diversion to health care costs can result in migration, child labour, the sale of assets and spending of savings (WHO, 2004a). Short-term costs of care and funeral; and long-term costs of reduced productivity can decimate the financial resources of a family and whole communities. On average, AIDS-related care can absorb one-third of a household's monthly income (UNAIDS, 2004a, p. 9). Families are not always assured of support from their extended family or community, due to the stigma of AIDS or a high rate of infection among friends and family.

Men and women who live with TB and/or HIV/AIDS often suffer social stigma and loss of wages because of time taken off to seek medical assistance. Job losses and threats to confidentiality can be severe (Fornbad, 2001, p. 648). Individuals who are members of certain groups may suffer particular discrimination as a result of certain diseases. Homophobia and discrimination by families, communities and health-care workers towards gay men in Latin American countries have been documented.[25] Certain diseases can also disrupt community rituals of mourning (see Chapter 4). SARS, by depriving its victims of human contact, is hard on traditionally minded Chinese families, who are no longer able to practise key rituals during mourning that can normally be relied on to offer some measure of solace (Fowler, 2003).

Some International and Institutional Responses to Health-Related Concerns

Some communities have demonstrated creative responses to disease epidemics. Tribal chiefs in Zambia[26] model by being tested for HIV. Volkswagen in Brazil has led by example with HIV information and treatment.[27] AIDS Initiative works with communities to return street children to the communities from which they came. In Hong Kong, hospitals that previously banned telephones have not only allowed those with SARS to use mobile phones, but have introduced teleconferencing to link patients and families (Fowler, 2003, p. 49). Some Spanish clinics offer open, free and confidential HIV counselling and testing including to migrants and require no identification documents for testing. Before and after HIV testing, trained professionals offer counselling in Spanish (Castilla *et al.*, 2002). Ethiopia, Mozambique and Malawi are among many poor countries that are training paraprofessionals to do important health work,[28] but more remains to be done and in many countries, and social professionals have a role in the prevention and amelioration of diseases and their social impacts.

Implications for Social Professionals

In the face of the tremendous social impact of diseases on human lives, it is tempting to allow the enormity to overwhelm efforts to address these global concerns. However, social workers have much to offer in local, national, and international efforts to prevent, and ameliorate the effects of, such diseases. Indeed, the IFSW policy on globalization exhorts social workers to work at all three levels. Social professionals can make a difference in prevention, education and culturally competent direct practice with individuals, families, groups and communities, as well as through policy and programme development and research. The IFSW Policy on HIV/AIDS (1990, p. 6) provides strong guidance for global practice, including the exhortation to 'confront and deal with fears, attitudes and prejudices towards AIDS, both amongst social workers and the general public', it urges 'examination of biases towards sexual orientation' and acceptance of 'the variety of sexual practices and activities in which people may engage', and as well as collaborative work with other personnel with experience in this area of work. Guidelines on infection control can be obtained from country-specific agencies or from WHO. Such policies and guidelines can be used for other diseases as well; and examples from various countries of work in the field of social responses to disease (primarily but not exclusively in relation to

HIV/AIDS) can illustrate existing and potential roles for social professionals.

Education for information and prevention can make a difference. The IFSW (1990, p. 6) Policy on HIV/AIDS directs social workers to 'undertake educational programmes which inform all sections of the community about HIV/AIDS' and to help others to access important sites for information. For example, the website www.aidsmap.com has comprehensive HIV information for patients and professionals. All efforts to reduce transmission and provide care must be culturally sensitive and address factors such as gender inequality and level of social and economic development (WHO, 2004a, p. 13), as well as being tailored to the needs of specific groups (e.g., injecting drug users). For example, culturally adapted interventions at clinics that serve immigrants can address specific concerns (Castilla *et al.*, 2002).

There are a number of country-specific examples of social workers using creative means for education and prevention about HIV and other diseases. In Russia, police officers work together with other professionals on harm-reduction strategies for HIV (Jackson, 2004). In India, counsellors work to counter concerns about the polio vaccine,[29] and social workers develop innovative programmes in relation to hard-to-reach populations (such as sex workers) through training programmes in peer education (Dr Ravi Raj William, personal communication). In the West Bohemian Region of the Czech Republic social professionals do street work with prostitutes working in nightclubs, streets and roads of three districts (Resl *et al.*, 2003). In South Africa social workers in the schools help teachers build on students' strengths, for example in helping them gain self-confidence to say no to those who want to have sex with them (Bak, 2004).

Social professionals can follow WHO priorities to make condoms accessible, affordable, and understandable through free distribution, subsidies, or social marketing (WHO, 2000a). In addition, it is crucial to retain adolescent sexual health as a top priority globally if any impact is to be made on unwanted pregnancies and the rising prevalence of HIV and STIs (Castilla *et al.*, 2002). And at the other end of life, social workers can provide information on personal care and infection control and in the last stages of the disease address the palliative-care needs of the person with HIV/AIDS (IFSW, 1990, p. 7).

Programme Development

Social professionals are skilled at assessing the need for services and then working within and among organizations to provide them. IFSW (1990) policy suggests social workers 'mobilize existing organizations' (p. 8) and '. . . train and empower others to provide adequate services' (p. 6). A number of examples can be cited from the US. In Minneapolis, Minnesota, US, an advocate at the Minnesota AIDS Project collaborates with the Department of Human Services, the Department of Health, the African American AIDS task force and the International Institute of Minnesota.[30] They host wellness gatherings for African women immigrants with HIV to meet for support and help in navigating health and social systems[31] 'Sisters for Life' (based in Washington DC) organizes volunteers for extended stays in African communities to support women, assist in care for orphans and work on projects (Global Initiative on AIDS, see Appendix for website). African and African-American grass-roots organizations partner to deliver community-based services through the assistance of the Global Initiative on AIDS. Palliative-care programmes hire, or use as volunteers, refugees who are trained health professionals in their home countries.[32] The US government Emergency Plan for AIDS Relief has committed 35 million rand (South African) for care in South African hospices, and the development of palliative-care services through non-governmental, community and faith-based organizations.[33] Elsewhere, in Botswana, Ethiopia, Tanzania, Uganda and Zimbabwe, a project to initiate a community-based palliative-care approach is aiding those suffering all the losses from HIV, cancer and other terminal diseases (Sepulveda *et al.*, 2003).

Direct practice/social care that is culturally competent is the hallmark of global social work. Social professionals can work to strengthen families and communities and increase access to resources, develop human capacity, adopt a 'clinical activist model' as advocates on behalf of those exploited or harmed by the socio-political and economic systems (Noyoo, 2004, p. 463). In Hawaii, social workers and other care providers learn from Native Hawaiian initiatives that emphasize the fundamental differences between the traditional Hawaiian view of health as holistic and that of the biomedical paradigm reflected in conventional Western healthcare systems. The issues raised by native researchers and providers about cultural values and practices in human behaviour and the need to develop interventions with an ecological view of health and build on cultural strengths have implications for practice in many communities worldwide (Ka'opua and Mueller, 2004). In Botswana, the crisis of confidentiality in the control of the HIV/AIDS pandemic is being addressed by social workers who are adopting a code of ethics, which helps to assure people that getting medical care for HIV will not automatically place them at risk of discrimination (Fornbad, 2001).

The IFSW policy on HIV/AIDS (1990) exhorts social workers to 'provide *counselling and personal support service* to persons with HIV/AIDS, their families, partners and significant others, which maintains confidentiality'. This includes counselling individuals before testing by providing information and assessment to individuals, and counselling individuals after testing whether the result is negative or positive. This support should include the provision of information on safe sexual behaviour and practice, and available resources, and in the event of a positive test result, how to cope with a range of reactions (including lack of understanding or total non-comprehension; cultural interpretations; shock, denial, grief, fear and despair). Additionally, social workers can counsel families, partners, friends and employers.

We should not overlook the possible role of ICT in provision of direct services by social professionals in relation to disease and pandemics. This may be a particularly useful means of offering some response in situations where there is a realistic fear of contagion, as was the case with the SARS outbreak in 2003. For instance, an imaginative initiative was taken in Hong Kong, whereby 20 telephone hotlines were open 12 hours a day, 7 days a week, to provide telephone counselling to those affected, whether directly or indirectly. This was staffed in shifts by students and staff from the social work and nursing courses at one of the island's universities in conjunction with a local hospital (Hui and Tsui, 2004). Similarly, Rowlands (2004) records how hospital social workers in Singapore set up a telephone hotline (for use by patients and other hospital staff) as part of their wider response to the SARS outbreak there. This included establishing a buddy scheme, with training for the volunteers running it (who were themselves mainly hospital staff); as well as undertaking direct counselling with families of patients who died;

and running debriefing sessions for health-care staff. One social worker worked directly with the 'index patient' (who had been identified as bringing the disease from Hong Kong to Singapore), who survived but had to face the death of a number of family members as well as public disclosure. Rowlands' account also illustrates the limitations placed on normal interactions with SARS patients (since social workers seeing them had to wear full personal protection equipment – goggles, masks, gowns and gloves); and the pressures from family members faced by the hospital social workers, on account of fears about the virulence of the disease.

Returning to responses to HIV/AIDS, more particularly, social professionals can work to *strengthen the coping capacity* of families affected by providing direct financial assistance, home visits, food and nutritional support, and waiving of school fees (WHO, 2004a, p. 10). A study from Columbia University in New York showed that stable housing can decrease risk behaviours associated with spread of HIV in the US; and rates of needle use and sex exchange for money are also reduced.[34] Whole Life Children's Villages, started in Swaziland in July 2004, aims to develop villages with a full range of support for orphans' care, education and development.[35] They will include places for parents to come and stay as they are dying, in order to see where their children will be cared for after they die. Social workers at Kiwakkuki in Moshi, Tanzania work to empower women in communities to care for orphans in their own homes so they need not move out of their communities to orphanages (www.enda.sn/africaso.org/womenkili.html). Finally, social workers can encourage local caregivers to join support networks. For example, in Nigeria the West African Health Care Professional Network (WAHCPN) is an online, virtual community for patients, nurses, social workers, counsellors and volunteers to share information online about palliative care.[36]

Social professionals can *advocate for policy changes* at local, national and international levels on behalf of people affected by disease. There are many examples of possible strategies in policy work. For example, social professionals can fight discrimination towards people who are disabled by disease (Seipel, 1994, 2005), especially through legislation to protect people with HIV (only about 50 per cent of sub-Saharan African countries have such legislation [WHO, 2004b, p. 18]). The IFSW (1990, p. 7) suggests that social workers 'lobby for the rights of people with HIV/AIDS and guarantee that the special needs of minorities and stigmatized groups in the community are met'. Social professionals can encourage governments to recognize the savings in universal coverage for ARV (Argentina, Barbados, Chile, Costa Rica, Cuba, Mexico, Uruguay (WHO, 2004b, p. 13) and pressure companies with a stake in controlling disease to work on prevention.[37] It is possible to encourage public officials and well-known people to speak out. In Lesoto in March of 2004, Prime Minister, Pakalitha Mosisili and more than 80 senior civil servants were publicly tested for HIV, in an attempt to break the stigma that discourages testing (WHO, 2004b, p. 17). Social professionals can work to assure that equity remains foremost as policies are developed, keeping in mind the needs of women, children, drug users and sex workers, among others (IFSW, 1990, p. 7). This suggests the need for advocacy and pressure on national governments to instigate access to palliative care (for example, in Belarus, where opiates are limited and adults and children suffer);[38] or on governments in Western countries to support palliative care in Africa[39] (for instance, in the US through Bush's Emergency plan for AIDS Relief). Stephen Lewis, UN Special Envoy for AIDS in Africa, warns that pledges by the G8 leaders to double aid to Africa will not be enough: advocacy must include pressure on individual governments.[40]

Social workers can also use positive reinforcement. It can be effective to congratulate and then monitor governments who make useful contributions, such as the European Commission decision to pay an additional 42 million euros to the Global Fund to fight AIDS, TB and Malaria in July of 2004;[41] Philippines' HIV/AIDS Control and Prevention Act; and Venezuela's Accion Cuidaadana Contra el Sida.[42] Many countries have national AIDS plans which incorporate ARV treatments' coverage targets. Some have allocated funds from national debts and debt relief to support treatment service (WHO, 2004b, p. 13).

Taking into account the devastating effects of HIV and other diseases on women, social professionals can work to strengthen micro credit and income-generation schemes, school support and food assistance programmes (WHO, 2004, p. 10). Msimang (2003, p. 112) suggests that it is important to connect feminists from the North and South and to see HIV/AIDS as a feminist issue of political, social and economic power in addition to having race, class and gender dimensions. And the WHO boldly proclaims that advocates should

> (c)ondemn all forms of coerced sex, from violent rape to cultural/economic obligations to have sex when it is not really wanted . . . Condemn harmful cultural practices from genital mutilation to practices such as 'dry' sex, to having sex with ever younger girls in order to avoid infection or be 'cured' . . . Respect confidentiality and address inequalities in partner notification and disclosure of status, recognizing that women are often stigmatized as vectors' when they were only infected by their partner or husband . . . [push for the] Right to informed consent to testing for HIV during pregnancy, to intervention with antivirals to prevent spread to the foetus, to option of terminating the pregnancy . . . [and the] right to family planning services, protection of confidentiality, information about retrovirals. (WHO, 2000b)

Advocacy by people living with AIDS and world leaders has helped bring down the price of ARV to US$300 a year from $10,000–12,000 on world markets (WHO, 2004a, p. 14). The price of many drugs has fallen dramatically in sub-Saharan Africa in recent years as a result of the development of a large generic drug industry in developing countries, such as India and China, and a vigorous campaign by WHO and NGOs, such as Médecins Sans Frontières, for better accessibility to essential drugs. The previous financial obstacles to rapid and effective treatment of sexually transmitted infections in developing countries have largely been addressed because the interests of the public health sector coincided with those of the profit-oriented generic drug industry, and market forces were not hampered by protectionist regulations. We hope that current negotiations under the aegis of the World Trade Organization will not prevent further progress being made towards providing affordable solutions to health priorities identified by WHO (for further discussion see Manion, 2005). Certainly the right hand must be aware of what the left hand is doing in relation to drug availability and health-care programmes (Pepin and Mabey, 2003).

Finally, social professionals can be more active in *research projects* related to social implications of disease. Small-scale examples include opportunities in the US for post-graduate fellowships in palliative care, programme development, and research through the Open Society Institute Project on Death in America; and the collaboration between Ke Ola o Hawaii, the Life Foundation, the Maui AIDS Foundation, Papa Ola Lokahi/the Native Hawaiian Health Care System, and the Queen Lili'uokalani Children's Centre to fund a social work graduate student doing research with Native Hawaiians (Ka'opua and Mueller, 2004).

Mupedziswa (2001) suggests that social workers should focus research on issues for marginalized populations, especially AIDS home care, social impact of structural adjustment programmes and social security for the rural poor. It is also important to study the socio-economic impact of HIV because 'more than 40 per cent of countries with generalized HIV epidemics have yet to evaluate this impact' (WHO, 2004b, p. 10) and social professionals can frame culturally appropriate research questions. It is critical that social workers in the West/North support research funds going to African researchers, as well as those outside the African continent (see www.aidsinafrica.com).

Social workers can support governmental efforts to cooperate with other governments, for example the European Centre for Disease Prevention and Control, which began in September 2004. Its purpose is to monitor Europe's health knowledge to enable better preparation for, and response to, future epidemics (see www.europa.eu.int). Experience shows that the public and private sectors and networks of researchers can, through appropriate mechanisms, work together to design and improve tools and approaches for disease control (WHO, 2003, p. 14).

Conclusions

This chapter's aim was to provide an introduction to the global spread of diseases and the impact these diseases can have on individuals, families and communities, locally. It explored the great impact of disease on vulnerable populations, particularly women and children worldwide. With the pandemic of

HIV/AIDS and outbreaks of other diseases, social professionals must enhance their knowledge of the effects of diseases in their own communities, while at the same time maintaining awareness of the potential for disease spread through processes connected to globalization. Travel across borders, whether legally for business or holidays, or illegally, as in the trafficking of people for sexual purposes, can all result in the spread of diseases.

It is crucial for social workers in the West to keep in mind the global inequities evident in disease impact and in efforts to prevent and ameliorate disease. Spending per person for HIV in the US, for instance is 35 times that in Latin America and 1000 times that in Africa (WHO, 2004a, p. 15). Such inequities must be named and addressed through political and educational means. We also need to view vaccines and microbiocides as 'global public goods' that benefit others beyond those who use them directly: each prevented infection cuts off a potential chain of infections resulting form the primary infection (WHO, 2004a, p. 15).

In addition to the suggestions for social professionals expressed earlier, social workers can advocate for discussion of HIV and other diseases in human rights terms, including that women have a right to sexuality that does not endanger their lives. A human rights framework for social work practice is gaining in credibility and importance, and is included in a number of useful texts (including through the Centre for Human Rights; Reichert, 2003). WHO suggests that strategies to protect women from sexually transmitted infections should include an increase in women's control over their sexuality and sexual relationships and increased resources in families for women's health, as well as for men (WHO, 2000b). Seipel (1999) proposes that social workers should promote principles of human rights in their efforts to address the impact of malnutrition and diseases on peoples' lives. He particularly emphasizes that social work practice should oppose harmful practices against women and should enhance community participation by those affected directly by disease.

Social workers can support the work of IASSW and IFSW with the UN committees on aging; family; environment; immigrants and refugees; mental health; human rights; and education; as well as the work on global disease of the Commission on the Status of Women and UNICEF. One of the UN Millennium Development Goals is to halt and begin to reverse the spread of HIV/AIDS and the rise in the incidence of malaria and other major diseases. Health and HIV/AIDS were among the topics included in the agenda for an IASSW/IFSW annual Social Work Day at the UN in 2005 (including also immigrants and refugees, the girl child, social and economic development, and poverty). As one of the IASSW representatives at the UN (Janice Wood Wetzel) (JWW) has suggested, social workers (who tackle these issues on a regular basis) and social work educators (who study them) can provide knowledge needed to address problems at the grass roots.

If social professionals recognize that local practice in prevention, education, care, policy and research on social effects of diseases has global dimensions, then local practice is enhanced. If as global professionals we work through the already established mechanisms and organizations that advocate on behalf of those whose lives are so disrupted by disease, the profession cannot help but have a global impact. While 'HIV/AIDS is predominantly a global problem, requiring a global collaborative response, in prevention, and the provision of a wide range of economic and social resources' (IFSW, 1990, p. 4), the example of HIV can also assist social work efforts to prevent and ameliorate the local issues caused by the global spread of disease.

9 New Directions for Social Work in Conditions of Globalization

Introduction

We have argued in this book that it is increasingly important for social professionals – whether involved in international or local activity (within an apparently national context) – to equip themselves with knowledge of global events and processes and cross-cultural issues. The world is now a complex and interconnected place, with implications for the genesis and manifestation of both 'old' and new social problems. As Gane (2004) has noted, '. . . globalization marks not the death of the social, but rather the birth of a new era of rights and citizenship, or what might be termed the hyper-social' (p. 8). Caragata and Sanchez (2004, p. 244) have argued,

> Accompanying our new global economic interdependence is a related political and social interdependence. Problems such as AIDS, refugee settlement, immigration and most environmental issues require an international perspective and response. While individual communities and even nation-states can and should formulate their own local response to these and other global issues, these alone will be insufficient.

Those who work within the social welfare field therefore need to be knowledgeable about globalization and related socio-economic and cultural phenomena. At the local level, wider understanding is needed for 'front-line' practitioners, managers and others concerned with service and community developments to respond to 'new' social problems. However, it can be argued that it is also important for social workers themselves to collaborate at international levels and to be involved in the work of international organizations, such as the UN and IFSW, to tackle problems that are increasingly recognized as trans-national in character; for instance, the growth of people smuggling or the spread of disease.

The impetus for 'international developments' in social work has often been apparent at a regional rather than international level, for instance the formation of European networks of schools of social work supported by European funding, but Pugh and Gould (2000) have suggested that globalization is challenging the tenets upon which 'European social work' is based and question whether we need to analyze the existing education of social workers to see if it is still relevant. Others have raised questions about the influence of 'Western' ideas on social work (its practice and educational forms) and emphasized the need for indigenous developments (Midgley, 1995). Globally, we continue to see the after-effects of colonization and other forms of power imbalance, in the relationships both within countries and between countries, and it is important to promote policies, practices and curricula in the social and educational fields that do not re-create or perpetuate forms of dominance and dependence. New developments need to facilitate cross-national relationships and reciprocal learning, as well as research, to underpin internationally informed analysis and action.

It is important to consider the 'psycho-social' aspects of the wider context within which social work is operating. The rise of individualism in many parts of the Western world has been analysed by Rose, who has argued that this has left individuals responsible for their own self-determination, without the support of collective agency (cited in Gane, 2004, p. 10). 'Contemporary individuals are incited to live as if making a project of themselves' (Rose, 1992, p. 149) and it seems as if we now need experts to help us understand that project, or, failing that, we have the burgeoning industry of self-help. Rose's thesis, about the growth of 'psy-cultures', suggests that professions such as social work are part of the post-modern concern about 'making things better' (Rose, 1992). Correspondingly, Phillips and Berman (2001, p. 18) have discussed the notion of *social quality* (a term coined at a European Union meeting in 1997) as referring to how citizens participate socially and economically within their communities. This term encapsulates four dimensions: socio-economic security/insecurity, social inclusion/exclusion, social cohesion/anomie and empowerment/disempowerment – all highly relevant to how social professionals exercise and develop their roles.

Meanwhile, in large swathes of Asia, Africa and South America self-help takes place in the context of societies in which the extended family, local community and voluntary agencies, including religious bodies, still have a significant role in providing care and protection, as well as being the main focus and engines of development. Many such communities have traditionally been the 'recipients' of 'aid' and other forms of external intervention. However, in the face of heightened fears about security threats, it has been suggested that international donors now assess their priorities according to their own security interests and the 'war on terror' (Reality of Aid Network, 2004), paradoxically potentially increasing the pressures on people to emigrate from poverty stricken and/or war-torn areas while Western countries are also tightening their borders.

We have addressed a range of themes in this text, sometimes separating them in what may seem like arbitrary ways. However, it seems evident that a key word in the current conditions of globalization is 'interdependence'. We have already made reference to the way in which the inter-relationships between states and within and between societies are to some extent based on economic, corporate, institutional and structural factors, as well as issues related to the physical environment – and we will be giving further consideration to the last factor in this chapter. But it is also apparent that there is a considerable inter-relationship between the international problems which have previously been selected for discreet consideration in this text as being of concern to social professionals. For instance, it is hard to separate out issues related to health-care needs from those of poverty or from migration or from conflict. Additionally, a process such as migration has implications for both sending and receiving countries as well as the individuals and families involved. It is therefore important to engage in multi-factor analysis of social problems, as well as working co-operatively with other professionals to develop relevant services and programmes which connect personal problems with structural and political aspects.

As also mentioned at various points, social professionals need to form alliances at local, regional and international levels to promote policies as well as practices that address fundamental inequalities and injustices within and between societies. New conditions require us to review the knowledge and skills which are needed and the approaches which are relevant to local and international practices, and to appreciate anew the experiential knowledge which resides within social professionals themselves. For instance, there have always been periods when social workers have been willing or unwilling migrants and it can be speculated that we are likely to see greater mobility within the worldwide workforce. This phenomenon requires us to consider the implications for the education of social professionals and how we might ensure 'comparability'. We therefore consider further in this chapter some aspects of social work: labour mobility, arguments for and means of 'internationalizing' social work education, and the setting of global standards.

(Re)engaging with Environmental Issues and Responding to Disasters

The need to adopt a wider understanding of the environment has begun to come onto the agenda of professional concerns (Hoff, 1997; Lyons, 1999). Healy (2001, p. 106), in a chapter on global inter-relatedness, identified environment as one of three main areas of interdependence (the others being cultural and economic). She also suggested a fourth area, 'security', and, from a professional perspective, welfare interdependence. Healy identified two main areas of environmental concern – pollution and resource depletion. The latter includes minerals, forests (with implications for soil erosion and climate change), water, soil (desertification) and, to which could be added more explicitly, fossil fuels. We must agree with Healy's overall thesis that the health, security and well-being of whole populations are directly affected by a range of interdependencies, including in relation to the environment. As previously discussed (Lyons, 1999), air and water are not contained by political borders and both have been the source or the carrier of major disasters with local and international repercussions (as well as sometimes being the carriers of disease as described in this text).

Prigoff (1999) has made reference to the limited ways in which we value, measure and protect different aspects of the natural environment unless it has become a commodity, in which case corporate and financial interests (and, we suggest, also sometimes governments) favour exploitation, not conservation. Globalization has opened up new areas to environmentally abusive economic development, in which corporate rights – based on international trade agreements – supersede the rights of human communities. One example of this is through trade-related intellectual property rights (TRIPS, see Manion, 2004), under which the environment and knowledge of indigenous people can be plundered by pharmaceutical companies. While such issues are usually seen as 'outside' the concerns of Western social workers, they are sometimes actively being addressed by social professionals in developing countries and, as stated, have implications for human welfare, globally.

The early twenty-first century is an opportune point for social professionals to re-evaluate their engagement with environmental matters. In 2000, environmental sustainability was one of several Millennium Development Goals agreed by political leaders representing 189 countries (the others being to reduce poverty and hunger, promote gender equality, reduce child mortality, improve maternal health, and combat major diseases). One target is to reduce by 50 per cent the number of people without access to safe water and basic sanitation by 2015 (Rees, 2004), and 2005 marked the start of the UN International Decade on Water for Life, in the face of a projection suggesting that nearly 2 billion people will face water shortage by 2050 (double the current number). This is the third major hydrological initiative since the 1960s, yet there are still 30,000 deaths a year from water-related diseases and increasing numbers of people suffer the effects of floods, droughts and increasing degradation of water eco-systems (Rees, 2004). Water has become a commodity subject to poor management, corruption and even conflict, and increased efforts aimed at its conservation and equitable use (in both developed and developing countries) is fundamental to effective development strategies, and indeed survival.

Notwithstanding previous references, and despite its (obvious) relevance to human well-being, the relative lack of literature in this field suggests that interventions with an environmental element have received little attention by social professionals, a view supported by Marlow and Van Rooyen (2001). In a cross-national study of environmental issues in social work, they found that the majority of 113 respondents to a mailed questionnaire thought that professional interventions *should* address environmental concerns, though different issues and approaches were identified by respondents in New Mexico (US) and KwaZulu Natal (South Africa). They suggest that an understandable focus on people's social and cultural environments has led to a neglect of the physical and biological environment. But, as indicated, environmental damage and change do not only impact on those likely to be the focus of social professional concern, which may account for the wider attention being given to this issue, globally.

At a political level, the international community had paid little heed to environmental issues since a G8 meeting in Rio (1992, the 'Earth Summit') and the drafting of a supplementary protocol (to cut 'greenhouse gases') in Kyoto in 1997 (which came into force in 2005). Efforts to address issues related to climate change and bio-diversity are now supported by 38 industrial nations including Japan and most European countries (including Russia), but at the time of writing, the US (responsible for 36 per cent of greenhouse gas emissions)[1] is not a signatory. Bayne *et al.* (2004) suggested that US producers' and business interests in energy, agriculture and pharmaceuticals play an important role in influencing the policy position of the US government and that one of the tasks of the G8 meeting in Gleneagles (Scotland) in 2005 was to address the US position in an agenda in which Africa and the global environment have pole positions. The latter focuses specifically on climate change: this began to be targeted in the 2004 summit with the setting of the 3R Action Plan (to reduce, reuse and recycle products).

Bayne *et al.* (2004) also suggested that another challenge facing world leaders is how G8 members might engage with civil society, since it is clear that consumer and civil movements are playing an increasing role in environmental activities, with rising concerns about toxic waste disposal, deforestation, acid rain, pesticides in food, and the related issue of climate change. Environmental measures are clearly a significant dimension of efforts to address poverty in Africa, where two of the biggest threats to development are disease and conflict, and where

190

environmental degradation is one factor leading to food insecurity and lack of potable water affecting millions (see Ethiopian example later). Such efforts were partly foreshadowed in the Africa Action Plan linked to the New Partnership for Africa's Development (NEPAD) following the G8 meeting in 2002 (see Sewpaul, 2004).

NEPAD is also concerned with peacekeeping, standards of governance and economic development; and initiatives by the G8 (to increase aid and reduce the burden of debt) need to be matched by improved market access and trade opportunities. However, there are already concerns that new debt relief proposals (in 2005) may cut aid to Africa in the longer term (Mathiason, 2005), while there are also reports from INGOs that the generosity of governments and the public in responding to the effects of the Indian Ocean tsunami (in December 2004) have reduced aid to Africa, at least in the short term.

Mention of the tsunami also reminds us that some aspects of the natural environment (including earthquakes, hurricanes, volcanoes) cannot be controlled (although in the tsunami case, investment in early warning systems could probably have saved thousands of lives, if not preventing damage to seashore property and livelihoods); and also that such disasters may well have international repercussions. Other 'environmental' disasters, such as floods and famine resulting partly from drought, are perhaps more appropriately seen as having a human agency dimension (Lyons, 1999) and are thus potentially more amenable to prevention or alleviation by economic means, if backed by political will and implementation of well-managed schemes and programmes (often requiring international as well as local collaboration). The relevance of social work knowledge and skills in the aftermath of environmental (and other) disasters, both in responses to traumatized individuals and families and in utilizing a strength-based approach to assist in the rebuilding of communities, has been recognized (Lyons, 1999) but given surprisingly little attention in professional education and the wider literature (although it can be noted that a special issue of the journal *International Social Work* focusing on responses to disasters, is planned for 2007).

Lack of education and training has been cited as one reason for non-involvement of social workers in relation to incorporation of environmental concerns into policy and practice developments.

However, Marlow and Van Rooyen (2001) suggest that if we extend our ideas about what constitutes the environment, inclusion of this area of work sits comfortably within an ecological approach, in which social professionals adopt a community focus and engage in partnerships with other professionals (including in the public health sector) and, we suggest, with broader movements in civil society. In their New Mexico–KwaZulu Natal study they found that practices among those already claiming to take environment into account could be grouped into five areas: philosophical interpretations; voluntarism; political action/ lobbying; therapeutic contact with nature; actions to clean up the environment (including recycling); and education for increased awareness.

Central to the efforts to address current or potentially damaging environmental change, whether by policy makers or by social professionals, is the concept of sustainability, although Marlow and Van Rooyan (2001, citing Baker *et al.*, 1997) suggest that this is differently understood by different constituencies and societies. However, Gilman (1990, p. 10) defined it as 'developing human systems, technologies and lifestyles that can provide high quality and environmentally benign ways of life for all humankind, now and many generations into the future'. Such an approach could be developed through international political initiatives to encourage a better integration between economic, social and environmental objectives, which might include at national levels, for instance, efforts to move to a low carbon economy or to harness and manage water supplies more effectively. The concept has long been familiar to many workers engaged in social and community development programmes with goals including sustainability; and this has been identified as one of the objectives of planned redevelopments following the Indian Ocean tsunami, in countries such as Thailand and Sri Lanka.

Apart from the interdependence between Western countries and the developing world in matters of the environment, the importance of international as well as local efforts is evident in individual countries. Taking one such example, Ethiopia, after suffering from a military regime for decades and also an international reputation as the poorest country in the world (with images of mass starvation in the Western media from the 1980s), is now emerging as a potential leader in regional efforts to address Africa's problems. Its population of 70 million is growing at the rate of 3 per cent per annum although a significant number of people (5–7 million each year) still depend on food aid from outside the country. It has been suggested that Ethiopia provided an early (nineteenth century) example of deforestation resulting in local climate change, which reforestation efforts are seeking to redress (Brown, 1996, cited in Lyons, 1999). Meanwhile, if the rains fail (as happened in 2002), the population needing food aid doubles: major international assistance is then required to address the problem.[2] However, some educated and experienced emigrants are returning to the country and there are a number of encouraging new developments, including in the social field, such as the establishment of the country's first masters degree programme in social work (personal communication).

Migration and International Activity as Aspects of the Professional Workforce

Although little mentioned in the professional literature, there is some contemporary evidence to suggest that social professionals are part of a wider mobile workforce. For instance, in the UK 10,000 social workers have sought verification of their qualifications from the national body regulating employment in social work in recent years (Lawrence, 2005) and 167 applications from overseas workers were accredited in Ireland in 2001 (compared with 96 in 2000 and 54 in 1999). The figure of 167 comprises largely people from the UK (many of whom would be Irish nationals returning after a period of work and training) and from Northern Ireland but also included social professionals from Germany, Canada, New Zealand and Zimbabwe.[3] As in Ireland and other countries (such as Greece) where emigration was the norm, we also know of people who have 'returned' from the UK or US (often after long periods of residence) to work as social professionals in the Caribbean, an example of a 'contraflow' which may offer its own challenges and benefits (personal communication). In addition, many professionals engage in international activities in ways which may or may not require them to relocate on a short- or long-term basis.

As well as a general lack of 'hard data' in this field (Korn-beck, 2003), individual motivations among social professionals who migrate (see Chapter 6) has barely been the subject of enquiry. In this section we draw on personal knowledge and communications, in addition to a limited range of literature, to identify some possible 'categories' of migrants and international social workers. We start from the assumption that existing skills and values, particularly if complemented by enhanced knowledge about international dimensions, make social professionals well suited to an extensive range of work in varied organizations and countries. For example, Kreitzer (2002) identified belief in social justice, community action and empowerment, as well as skills in counselling and group work, co-ordination, needs assessment, programme planning and implementation, mediation and advocacy as equipping social workers for employment in international aid agencies; and these skills might be equally relevant to work in other contexts.

Working in an INGO perhaps constitutes a first category of those who choose to work 'overseas', often for relatively short periods, either in the early stages of their careers or later. Some time ago, Rosenthal (1990) (on the basis of a study) suggested that 'despite some apparent congruence between the knowledge, skills and values required for various posts advertised as offering overseas opportunities with INGOs, only a very small proportion of American social work graduates might be interested' (cited in Lyons, 1999, p. 27). A decade later, a five-year retrospective survey of students who had completed an international social work undergraduate degree (in London) similarly found that only a very small proportion (only four of 50 respondents) had migrated or were actively seeking work in an INGO (Lyons, 2005). However, Segerstrom (1998) offers an example of work with the Swedish Save the Children in Refugee Camps in Yemen (Segerstrom, 1998); and other examples in this category include social professionals who act as 'consultants' in relation to professional education developments or volunteers who work for limited periods in particular countries (such as in a project sponsored by VSO to develop local mental health services in Romania [Lyons and Lawrence, 2006]).

Another pattern of mobility is evident in the numbers of (predominantly young, single) social workers who seek work experience in another country, and who combine an opportunity for professional development with other personal goals. Anecdotal evidence from the UK suggests that this tends to be a form of 'exchange' between Western countries. So, for examples, increasing numbers of social workers have joined the UK workforce, usually for one to two years, from Australia, New Zealand and Canada in the past decade. They currently comprise a significant proportion of the number of qualified staff from overseas in some local authority social service departments where labour shortages have been such that up to 40 per cent of staff in some such departments have been recruited from abroad. Some recruitment agencies have specifically targeted Australia and New Zealand, assuming comparable training standards and ready transfer of skills (Lawrence, 2005; Lyons and Littlechild, 2006). Meanwhile, cases are also known of UK and US social workers 'emigrating' to Australia, although little is known about the scale of these flows or whether such employment proves to be short term or the start of a 'new life' outside the country of origin.

A third category of migrants within a national workforce are those who have lived, qualified and worked in another country but who have more obviously responded to both push factors to leave (when job opportunities are limited, wages are low, the risks or frustrations are too great, or all of these factors) or pull-factors from countries where living standards are generally better and there are opportunities for work in the social professional field. So, for instance, social workers from Zimbabwe have responded to UK overseas recruitment in relatively large numbers (for instance, there are about 60 working in local authority departments in the English Midlands as well as others in London authorities) and South Africans constitute another relatively well-represented national group (Lyons and Littlechild, 2006).

Europe provides an interesting example of a region within which one might expect considerable migration and exchange, given policies which favour mobility of labour between countries (now 25) in the EU. However, the diversity of languages spoken in such a large number of countries, relative to the centrality of language and cultural understanding for competent professional practice (as well as national regulatory frameworks), has meant that mobility of social workers has not been as great as among some less skilled occupational groups (Kornbeck, 2003). But

Kornbeck also acknowledges the challenges (including linguistic) facing indigenous workers in multi-cultural societies, and he includes reference to the need for bi-lingualism in service provision in some countries, as well as the need for social professionals to develop facility in working through interpreters and/or to become more linguistically competent. It is not surprising in these circumstances to find that the majority of migrant social workers employed in the UK, for instance, have come from English speaking countries (Lyons and Littlechild, 2006).

People from minority ethnic groups who have migrated to a Western country, sometimes prior to completing education and making a career choice but often at a later stage, quite possibly as asylum seekers, constitute a fourth category. Many bring experience and qualifications from a related field and some enter the social professional field through working initially as a volunteer in a community organization or as a (paid) interpreter for local authority or health services or in voluntary agencies, such as law centres. Such personnel bring important experiential knowledge, and local agencies would be better able to tap into this valuable resource if there were more investment in 'conversion courses' and/or intensive language programmes (both in short supply in the UK). It seems likely that there are similar resources available to the workforce in other European countries as well as in North America and Australia, but again hard data is lacking.

Finally, there is a group of workers who do not choose (nor are they forced) to relocate to practice but who work for International Social Services or for an agency with a focus on refugees or asylum seekers in their home country and who might be said to be engaging in a particular form of international social work. In such cases (as in cases where people relocate), skills in working cross-culturally and particular knowledge about the impact of international events; local racism; and national immigration policies, on minority groups, are essential to good practice. It might also be worth mentioning here that some local authorities in the UK have established staff retention and development policies which recognize the value of cross-national learning and professional stimulus through enabling staff to engage in short (4–8 weeks) study visits abroad or take 'time out' to undertake longer periods of voluntary work in another country (Lyons and Littlechild, 2006).

Some of the issues raised by 'overseas recruitment' have also been identified in other professional arenas, not least medicine and the wider healthcare field, as identified in the previous chapter. Again, taking the UK as an example, there has been a long tradition of recruiting nurses and other healthcare staff from developing countries, such as Philippines, and there are serious ethical concerns, both about the principle of such a policy (depriving a developing country of large numbers of its better-educated workforce) and about specific recruitment practices. This has led to the development of a 'concordat' between British and some other national governments in the health field, but we are not aware of similar policy development in social work, in the UK or elsewhere, as yet. However, discussions in a recent symposium on the topic of social work labour mobility suggested the need for some quality-control measures in relation to recruitment policies and practices (not least to protect migrant workers themselves) (Lawrence, 2005). It also seems appropriate to consider the broader implications for professional education and for developing comparable qualifying standards.

Professional Education and Standards in Global Conditions

There has been a relative increase (over the past decade and more recently) in the literature about the benefits (and costs) of 'internationalizing' the curriculum for qualifying or specialist education of social professionals, including the value of international placements. Reference has been made in the most recent US regulations to the need to prepare all students for practice which recognizes international influences and which is 'culturally competent' (Carlsen, 2005a); and a recently established benchmark statement for the professional qualification at undergraduate degree level introduced in the UK (from 2003/4) also indicates the need for knowledge which is informed by international and comparative perspectives (Williams, 2005). However, there has been relatively little systematic study (certainly at international or cross-national level), as yet, to ascertain how such perspectives are incorporated and to what extent newly qualified social workers include international dimensions in their knowledge for practice.

Aside from the likely benefits, costs and difficulties of including international learning opportunities in qualifying programmes have also been identified in some of the literature (for instance, as discussed by Carlsen (2005a) and Williams (2005) in relation to the US and UK, respectively), and accepted wisdom suggests that many social work educators either admit to lacking knowledge and confidence to develop curricula appropriately, or, more often, consider that the existing timetables and syllabuses are already 'too full' to include new units or material. Some time ago, Healy (1986) advanced the idea that attitudes to inclusion of international perspectives could be mapped on a continuum from social work schools where there was merely 'toleration' (only sporadic activities by individual staff or students), through responsiveness (offering occasional electives or placements or independent study including at doctoral level), to commitment (with international social work being a well-articulated and regular element in the curriculum, including regular opportunities for field placements abroad). From the limited studies available and other evidence (including the low response to a recent survey carried out by IASSW [Barretta-Herman, 2005]) it would seem that, if there is any attention to international learning opportunities at all, tolerance or occasional responsiveness is the norm.

However, the picture changes somewhat if concerns are expressed in relation to the need for intercultural learning or for developing anti-oppressive approaches or cross-cultural communication skills or cultural competence, where recognition of the diversity of local populations has 'driven' some aspects of curriculum development and programme content. These subjects have obvious relevance to the development of international perspectives; and we would argue that including international perspectives, at least, at the qualifying stage, could mean some reorientation of what is taught and assessed rather than the introduction of new courses. Certainly, in the context of the European region, opportunities for (some) staff and students to participate in EU-funded multi-lateral seminars and other forms of exchange, have resulted in enrichment of the curriculum in many institutions to include at least European perspectives and comparative material on programmes in countries such as Germany, Sweden and, to a more limited extent, the UK.

There is also literature which has identified the need for inclusion of teaching in relation to particular skills or approaches, not necessarily in the context of international course development, but which seem relevant. For example, Schneider and Lester (2001) have identified 'advocacy' as a core area in which US social workers should be proficient and this would fit well with our own view of how social work education and practice might be developed both for local application and in an international context. Ramanathan and Link (1999) identify a range of areas and ways in which social work education should be reoriented to equip all social workers for practice in a 'globalized world' (including in relation to ethics), and Jones and Kumssa (1999) suggested that international perspectives can be offered through curriculum development, the awarding of dual or joint degrees, doctoral education, extra-mural activities and fieldwork abroad. Johnson (2004) describes how, in an American example, efforts to shift a social work school from 'responsiveness' to 'commitment' (to international perspectives) were built on experience gained from faculty involvement in training programmes in CEE countries, Brazil and Ghana; and she noted the importance of the establishment of a committee (including students and representatives from local agencies) to plan strategic developments and opportunities for learning about international work. Activities included 'Open Lectures'; international awareness days and informal social events, as well as more emphasis on the recruitment and integration of international students; and establishing placements overseas as well as in local agencies, which included an international and/or cross-cultural focus in their work. Curriculum developments gave attention to women's issues, AIDS, social and community development approaches and theories of poverty.

Johnson's curriculum suggestions show some overlaps with ideas put forward by Healy (2001). So, for instance, the latter argues for the inclusion of environmental studies; peace studies, human rights, multicultural education and development studies; in addition she identified core curriculum themes as comparative social policy, social development and professional development. She also identifies the desired outcomes for programmes that have a specifically international focus in terms of attitude (values), knowledge and skills. These include skills in cross-cultural work, knowledge of major global issues and efforts to address them, and opportunities for future learning (using research and cross-national literature in a specialist field as a basis for continuing professional development). Both Healy (2001) and Lyons (1999) have identified international resources for the profession as including policy statements and documents periodically produced by IASSW, ICSW and/or IFSW, as well as international conventions and reports provided by the various UN bodies and sometimes INGOs. We would also stress the potential value of attention to migration theory and policies and including reference to disaster and conflict work in the curriculum of professional education.

Other texts and articles have described the development of specific courses aiming to provide international (or regional, for example, European) and cross-cultural learning for social professionals as a main outcome of the course, and leading to appropriately named awards (occasionally at first-degree but more often at post-graduate level) and have identified the essential elements of such programmes. Among these are that the student group itself comprises people of different nationalities and cultures (and that this constitutes both a resource and a support for individual and group learning); that all students have the opportunity for some learning (whether through the college curriculum or in the field) outside their country of origin or normal residence; and that there is scope for students to develop particular areas of interest through periods of independent study or project work, as well as class presentations and assignments (Lyons and Lawrence, 2006).

There is an increasing range of literature available about the role of field placements in promoting learning and many students and staff would identify these (particularly if abroad) as providing the most challenging but rewarding way to learn about cross-cultural and international work. A chapter by Lyons and Ramanathan (1999) in an edited text provided a small number of vignettes of some of the characteristics and experiences of students who had undertaken field placements abroad in the 1990s, while a more recent text by Dominelli and Thomas Bernard (2003) included more substantial accounts in chapters authored by (ex-)students themselves. They recounted a wealth of learning about particular aspects of social work in placements outside their country of study, as well as often reflecting on the personal/professional learning such a situation affords. However, two recent American studies suggest that the numbers of students able to benefit from such opportunities are very small (Rai, 2004; Pettys *et al.*, 2005). The authors suggest that this is because of unavailability of such placements, but it may also be that there are limitations on students taking up such opportunities, even when they exist. The latter certainly seems to be the case in relation to the involvement of some UK schools in European networks, even when some funding was available for student exchange. The demand for placements in the UK from students from other European countries always outstripped the demand for placements 'abroad' from the British students. Various possible reasons were cited at the time – lack of facility in another European language; older age and domestic commitments of British students and requirements of the (then shorter) British qualifying courses. In relation to the last, expectations about the qualifications of supervisors (practice teachers) and the type of agency considered appropriate to student learning seemed quite narrow relative to the range of placements which might be judged as 'suitable' in, for example, Australia (Crisp, 2003).

Various models of providing field placement opportunities abroad for students have been advanced (Lyons and Ramanathan, 1999; Pettys *et al.*, 2005), although Razack (2002) has warned that international placements and other forms of student exchange could further disadvantage students from developing countries and constitute 'a continued form of professional imperialism' (p. 252). The latter was a concern addressed by Australian social work educators in efforts to develop international learning opportunities, specifically through a link-up with a primary health care project in Tamil Nadu (India). Tesoriero and Rajaratnum (2001), citing Ife (1997, p. 107), stated that 'internationalism can be a process underpinned by ethical considerations' (p. 32) and suggest that offering field education in overseas settings can be one way of 'promoting the social work voice with an international humanistic perspective' (p. 33). The scheme reported (based on an established relationship and a partnership model) had enabled a number of social work students to go to India (following careful selection and preparation), where they worked in pairs with selected projects, being accountable to local supervisors. The scheme included a commitment to funding for Indian project staff to pay return study visits (two so far) and Australian publication of reports (based on students' work) is copyrighted to the project. Tesero and Rajarutnum emphasize the value of learning about the strengths perspective and community development in the context of the Indian placements.

Despite the reported success of particular international programmes or placement arrangements, the small number of students participating suggests that more imaginative ways need to be found for incorporating international perspectives in the curriculum for all students and also for appreciating the international opportunities and dimensions in local practice agencies. One potential strategy has been identified in the widespread availability of ICT and the development of some distance-learning opportunities (Rafferty *et al.*, 2005). These have been progressed in relation to social work education (e.g., in Australia) and have implications both for development of nationally geared educational programmes but also for developing international links and more imaginative curricula (Healy, 2001). However, there are also concerns that such developments might constitute another aspect of the widening 'digital divide'. Additionally, as suggested, the value of personal participation in multi-cultural student groups in regional or international programmes or projects (in which learning about international or regional policies and practices is a goal) should not be underestimated (Lyons and Lawrence, 2006).

The possibility of increased opportunities for mobility, whether as students or qualified professionals, raises the question of comparability of qualifying standards between different countries. It seems evident that qualifying education must be responsible for new knowledge creation (e.g., in relation to emerging social problems and theoretical and practical responses) and equipping students for emerging areas of work (see Shera and Bogo, 2001, discussion about 'future studies' in Canada, India, South Africa and Israel). Qualifying education must also be relevant to the 'problems of the day' in the context of national socio-economic needs and resources, public and cultural expectations, and legislative frameworks. So we are clear that standards are not the same as standardization and attempts to conform to any assumed 'norms' would not be appropriate.

This, among other caveats, was recognized in work undertaken by a joint IASSW/IFSW working party to produce the document about global standards in social work education, mentioned in previous chapters. This was accepted by the general meetings of both bodies in 2004. In an editorial introducing a focus on the topic in the journal *Social Work Education* (23[5]), Sewpaul and Preston-Shoot (2004) present information about the global standards, describing them as ideals, neither defining a minimum standard nor implying homogenization. The latter danger is examined by Williams and Sewpaul (2004); while Gray and Fook (2004) identify a series of dichotomies relevant to social work education (globalization/localization, westernization/indiginization, multi-culturalism/universalization, and the universal relative to local standards). Healy identifies the danger of global standards impacting negatively on national or regional attempts to set standards and to develop educational programmes which take positive account of indigenous beliefs and practices. She bases her discussion on experience in the North American and Caribbean region, but Noble articulates similar concerns in relation to the Asia Pacific region. Such concerns are exemplified in Yip's (2004) article identifying a Western emphasis on rights, social change, equality and empowerment relative to an emphasis on responsibilities, social norms, stability and collective harmony, which might be more appropriate in Chinese society.

Apart from other articles about national and regional examples of standard setting (in Australia and Africa), the issue also includes a useful paper by Juliusdottir and Petersson (2004) which identifies the national variations in the Nordic countries between models of social work education which are based on vocational education principles relative to those countries where academic norms are more evident. They illustrate that, even within a 'subregion' of Europe – and across countries often assumed to share many common characteristics – tensions are evident between the desire to respect national traditions and freedom, and the wish for sub-regional coherence. Overall, Sewpaul and Preston-Shoot (2004) identified the rationale for attempting to articulate global standards as the need to respond to expectations regarding quality and accountability held by students and service users/communities, as well as concerns about the transferability of knowledge, values and skills across national boundaries. However, we agree with their stress on the importance of adapting such standards to local conditions and also the need to view any attempt to set standards as a process, rather than as achieving a fixed target.

Drawing Conclusions

Ife (2001b) has identified the role of social workers in promoting the idea of global citizenship as expressed through human rights, linking the personal to the political in the widest sense. This view can be linked to Healy's aspiration for '(s)ocial work as a force for humane global change and development' (Healy, 2001, p. 260) and to Van Wormer's (2004) call for social action based on the human rights of numerous minority groups who experience oppression. The corollary of human responsibility in relation to the human rights agenda is also discussed by Ife and Fiske (2006). The idea of global citizenship entails taking responsibility for issues at home and abroad and having a sense of belonging to both local and global communities. Reference to a rights-based approach casts both individuals and countries as partners and citizens rather than as service providers and users or donors and receivers (placing greater responsibility on both parties). It is important to create and utilize spaces for social work to make not only local links but also global links to address issues that 'cross' national or regional borders.

Katz (2001) has advanced the concept of trans-local counter-topographies, suggesting that different marginalized populations in different nation states present the same issues, requiring similar needs for analyses and strategies. This links with our own view that there are a growing number of social issues which have international dimensions and/or which transcend national borders, increasing the opportunities for working on a 'shared agenda for knowledge and action' (Healy, 2001, p. 105). It has also been recognized that 'countries can no longer "solve" their social problems (or protect their environments or economies) in isolation . . .' (Healy, 2001, p. 106 citing Hamilton, 1990) and it is therefore important to recognize universally relevant concepts and values as well as develop new 'globally relevant conceptual frameworks' (Healy, 2001, p. 266).

In other words, the time has come to redefine the mission and forms of social work and professional education to make them relevant to the new globalized conditions. New developments would recognize the growing importance of international civil societies and would accord with Lorenz's (1994) vision of social professionals as citizens committed to humane internationalism, integrating rights and obligations through action. Current views of globalization are often presented as an economic worldview not including global citizenship, social priorities and human rights; and one response has been localization. But as Ife (2001a) has identified, social workers are now required to work at local and global levels and to relate the two. In this sense, international social work is not a specialization but must be part of day-to-day practice. Having said this, we would also contend that there is scope for some development of specialist knowledge and personnel, and that those engaged in social work education and research, and in national and international professional associations, bear some responsibility for developing this area, as well as identifying the implications of globalization for local practice.

Given present-day social problems, we have suggested that social work needs to recognize its international opportunities and responsibilities and reassess its role in social change at national and international levels. As the IFSW states 'Globalisation is a continuing process which, while advancing global technological development and communications, also has negative impact on the balance of economic, political and cultural power between individuals and countries. Social workers see and work with the consequences of these processes' (IFSW, 2004). Interventions by social professionals which seem to us to have increasing relevance include conflict resolution, advocacy, linking with civil movements and other resources, and conducting research. We have explored how familiar concepts such as loss need to be re-evaluated in changed conditions, as well as how new conditions require the development of new concepts and fields of practice. Key themes in our discussion have been the need for increased understanding about cultural difference and international affairs, as well as expanded notions of the relevance of environmental issues and migration patterns. Knowledge of international conventions and global standards also increasingly provides important frameworks for social professionals – not just those who chose to engage in international social work but also the majority who are active in local practice.

Appendix: Acronyms and Useful Websites

Social Work Organizations

International

IASSW	International Association of Schools of Social Work	www.iassw.soton.ac.uk
ICSW	International Council on Social Welfare	www.icsw.org
IFSW	International Federation of Social Workers	www.ifsw.org
ISS	International Social Services	www.iss-ssi.org

National

AASW	Australian Association of Social Workers	http://www.aasw.asn.au/
CSWE	Council on Social Work Education (US based)-	www.cswe.org
NASW	American National Association of Social Workers	http://www.naswdc.org/

Cited Organizations

International Institutions

CSW	Commission on the Status of Women	www.un.org/women watch/daw/csw
EU	European Union	http://europa.eu.int/
FAO	Food and Agricultural Organization of the UN	http://www.fao.org/
ILO	International Labour Organization	www.ilo.org

IMF	International Monetary Fund	http://www.imf.org/
IOM	International Organization for Migration	http://www.iom.int/
INTERPOL	International Criminal Police Organization	http://www.interpol.int/
UN	United Nations	http://www.un.org/
UNDP	UN Development Programme	http://www.undp.org/
UNEP	UN Environment Programme	http://www.unep.org/
UNESCO	UN Educational, Scientific and Cultural Organization	http://www.unesco.org/
UNHCR	UN High Commissioner for Refugees	http://www.unhcr.ch/
UNICEF	UN Children's Fund	http://www.unicef.org/
UNIFEM	UN Development Fund for Women	http://www.undp.org/unifem
UNRISD	UN Research and Training Institute for Social Development	http://unrisd.org
UNWFP	UN World Food Program	http://www.wfp.org/
WB	World Bank	http://www.worldbank.org/
WFMH	World Federation for Mental Health	http://www.wfmh.org/
WHO	World Health Organization	http://www.who.int/

INGO – International Non Governmental Organizations

	Action Aid	http://www.actionaid.org/
	Amnesty International	http://www.amnesty.org/
	Caritas	http://www.caritas.org/
	Christian Aid	http://www.christian-aid.org.uk/
ECPAT	End Child Prostitution, Pornography and Trafficking International	http://www.ecpat.net/

	Global Initiative on AIDS in Africa	www.aidsinafrica.com
MSF	Médecins Sans Frontières International	http://www.msf.org/
NEPAD	New Partnership for Africa's Development	
	Oxfam	http://www.oxfam.org/
	Plan International	
	Save the Children	http://www.savethechildren.org/
	Tearfund	http://www.tearfund.org/
	Terre des Hommes	http://www.terredeshommes.org/
	The Red Cross/Red Crescent	http://www.ifrc.org/
VSO	Voluntary Service Overseas	http://www.vso.org.uk/

Other Cited Organizations

AFRUCA	Africans Unite Against Child Abuse	http://www.afruca.org/
AWHRC	Asian Women's Human Rights Council	
Casa Alianza		http://www.casa-alianza.org/
CSUCS	Coalition to Stop the Use of Child Soldiers	http://www.child-soldiers.org/
DEC	Disasters Emergency Committee	http://www.dec.org.uk
GAATW	Global Alliance Against Traffic in Women	www.gaatw.org
	Global Call to Action Against Poverty	www.whiteband.org

	La Strada	http://www.strada.cz/
	Make Poverty History (UK)	www.makepovertyhistory.org
	Make Poverty History (Canada)	www.makepovertyhistory.ca
OSCE	Organization for Security and Co-operation in Europe	http://www.osce.org/
PLAN UK		http://www.plan-uk.org/
TJM	Trade Justice Movement	www.tradejusticemovement.org.uk
USID	US Agency for International Development	http://www.USid.gov/

Useful Online Sources

ELDIS – Gateway for development issues	http://www.eldis.org/
Euromodule	http://cms.euromodule.com
One World	www.oneworl.net
Praxis – Resources for Social and Economic Development	http://caster.ssw.upenn.edu percent Erestes/praxis.html
Social Science Information Gateway	http://www.sosig.ac.uk/
Social Work Search	http://www.socialworksearch.com/
World Wide Web Resources for Social Workers	http://www.nyu.edu/socialwork/wwwrsw

Other Acronyms Used

9/11	September 11, 2001
AICs	Advanced Industrial Countries
AVR	Antiretroviral
BASIC PH	Belief System, Affect, Social Support, Imagination, Cognition, Physical
CEE	Central and Eastern Europe (states)

ICT	Information and Communication Technology
IDP	Internally Displaced Persons
LDCs	Less Developed Countries
MNCs	Multi National Corporations
PSTD	Post Traumatic Stress Disorder
STD	Sexually Transmitted Disease
STI	Sexually Transmitted Infection
TNCs	Trans National Corporations
TRIPS	Trade Related Intellectual Property Rights
TUC	Trades Union Congress
UK	United Kingdom
US	United States
USSR	Union of Soviet Socialist Republics

Notes

1 Introducing International Perspectives on Social Work

1. Pravasi Bhartiya Divas (Non-Resident Indian Day) http://www.indiaday.org/
2. www.makepovertyhistory.ca
3. Speech given by Nelson Mandela at the Make Poverty History Rally in London, 03/02/05.

2 Globalization: Fact or Fiction and Is It Relevant?

1. Richards, H. (1997) 'Global theatre', *Times Higher Education Supplement* (7/02/97) 19.
2. Ibid.

4 Loss: A Core Concept with *Universal* Relevance

1. Armas, G. (2004) 'Industrialized nations face sharp population declines', *Star Tribune* (Minneapolis, Minnesota) (18/08/04).
2. Ibid.
3. Bellaby, M. (2004) 'Girl moves from Russian orphanage to Germany's top home', *Star Tribune* (Minneapolis, Minnesota) (18/08/04) A4.
4. Fowler, G. (2003) 'Dying alone', *Far Eastern Economic Review* (05/06/03) 47.

5 Communities in Conflict

1. News Review (2003) 'War for Wealth', *Amnesty* (120) 14–15.
2. Tisdall, S. (2004) 'Stuck in France's orbit: A depressingly circular history', *The Guardian* (9/11/04) 13.
3. Meldrum, A. and Henley, J. (2004) 'French troops confront Ivorians', *The Guardian* (9/11/04) 13; Tisdall, 'Stuck in France's orbit'.
4. Fickling, D. (2004) 'If you oppress people long enough, things will erupt. Riots will happen', *The Observer* (22/02/04) 25.

5. Van Geest, H. (2004) 'Blast damages Dutch Islamic School', *The Guardian* (9/11/04) 11.
6. Porter, I. (2003) 'Britain must act to stop the slide to all-out war in Nepal', *The Guardian* (18/10/03) 24.
7. IFSW (2003) 'Special mailing to IFSW Executive' (25/03/03) subsequently on website.
8. News Review (2004) 'Rape as a weapon of war', *Amnesty* (127) 9.
9. Clayton, J. (2004) 'The rape of a nation: A doctor's despair', *The Times* (2/07/04) 10.
10. Hilsum, L. (2004) 'Rwanda's genocide could have been prevented. The UN let people die and now it watches as the survivors die', *The Observer* (28/03/04) 23.
11. News Review (2005) 'Child soldiers in 20 wars', *Amnesty* (129) 5.
12. Bone, P. (2004) 'Africa vows to stop Darfur carnage', *The Age* (Melbourne) (11/09/04) 19.
13. Ibid.
14. Anon. (2004) 'More aid staff quit', *Metro* (5/11/04) 7.
15. BBC (1999) *BBC Special Report on Sierra Leone.*
16. National News (2002) 'Australia', *IFSW Update* (8/2002) 4.
17. IFSW (2003) '40 million are starving in the shade of Iraq', *IFSW Update* (4/2003) 3.

6 Natural and Forced Migration: Causes and Consequences

1. Associated Press (2004) 'Ireland looks at new restrictions on who can claim citizenship', *Minneapolis Star Tribune* (15/6/04).
2. IFSW (2003) *IFSW Update* (8/2003) 4.
3. Ibid.
4. BBC (2004) BBC Radio News and comment programmes (6/2/04).
5. BBC Radio 4 (2003) *Today Programme*, Interview with an Italian Priest, Radio 4 (14/05/03).
6. Hogg, C. (2005) 'Sri Lanka: Helping families scarred by war', *The Supporter* (30) 6–7.

7 Child Exploitation: Local and Global Protection

1. Lovtsova, N. (2004) 'A lost generation', *Community Care* (06/05/04).
2. IFSW (2002) 'Russia: 50,000 homeless children in Moscow', *IFSW Update* (10/02) 4.

3. Lovtsova, 'A lost generation'.
4. http://webfusion.ilo.org/public/db/standards/normes/.
5. IRIN (2004) 'PAKISTAN: Child labour still widespread in NWFP', Peshawar, IRIN (13/10/04).
6. Niah, B. (2005) 'INSAF starts campaign against child labour', *Morocco TIMES* (14/11/05).
7. Those purchasing sexual services, in this case from children.

8 Spreading Disease: Global Pandemics with Local Impact and Responses

1. Horton, R. (5 October, 2005). The neglected epidemic, *The Lancet*, Published online.
2. UN Wire (2004) 'WHO counsels calm amid bird flu fears', *UN Wire*, United Nations Foundation (04/02/04).
3. Wildlife Trust (2004) *Nipah Virus Breaks Out in Bangladesh: Mortality Rates of 60 per cent-74 per cent; Human-to-Human Transmission may be Implicated* (online). available at: www.wpti.org/nipah.htm (accessed 08/04).
4. US Today (2004) 'India gears up for last mile of polio eradication' (online). available at www.UStoday.com/news/health/2004-08-28-india-polio x.htm (accessed 08/04).
5. Ibid.
6. Associate Press (2004) 'Nigerian president says vaccine for polio is safe: State holds out', *Star Tribune* (Minneapolis, Minnesota) (18/03/04).
7. Lohn, M. (2005) Polio discovered among Amish in Minnesota, *Seattle Times* (14/10/05).
8. Associated Press (2005) 'WHO: Eradication of polio to miss deadline', *New York Times* (12/10/05).
9. Wildlife Trust, *Nipah Virus Breaks Out in Bangladesh*.
10. UNAIDS (no date) *UNHRC* (online). available at: www.unaids.org/Unaids/EN/About+UNAIDS/Cosponsors/UNHCR.asp (accessed 02/05).
11. Hilsum, 'Rwanda's genocide'.
12. Haaheim, L. (2004) 'The global killer that will not die', Book review of Gandy, M. and Zumla, A., *Return of the white plague: Global Poverty and the 'new' tuberculosis*, London: Verso, *The Times Higher Education* (13/08/04).
13. BBC News (2004) 'Drugs will not stem global HIV' (online) (BBC News London). available at www.newsvote.bbc.co.uk (23/12/04) (accessed 12/04).

14. Schmickle, S. (2005) 'A dream delayed by disease', *Star Tribune* (Minneapolis, Minnesota) (31/01/05).
15. American Civil Liberties Union Report (2003) 'AIDS epidemic update', *NSW World News Update* (13/12/03) 26.
16. Ibid., p. 13.
17. UN Wire, 'WHO counsels calm amid bird flu fears'.
18. American Civil Liberties Union Report, 'AIDS epidemic update', p. 27.
19. Ibid.
20. PAHO (2003) *Homophobia shapes treatment of HIV/AIDS patients in Latin America and the Caribbean*, Washington: Pan American Health Organization (01/12/03).
21. UN Wire (2003) 'AIDS causing widening inequality in Africa, FAO study shows', *UN Wire*, United Nations Foundation (12/1/03).
22. American Civil Liberties Union Report, 'AIDS epidemic update', p. 12.
23. Ibid., p. 32.
24. UN Wire, 'AIDS causing widening inequality'.
25. PAHO, *Homophobia*.
26. American Civil Liberties Union Report, 'AIDS epidemic update', p. 33.
27. Ibid.
28. Dugger, C. (2004) 'Bridging the doctor gap in Africa', *The New York Times*, 28/12/04.
29. US Today, 'India gears up'.
30. Minnesota AIDS Project (2004) 'Housing as prevention: Housing status and HIV risk behaviours', *Minnesota AIDS Project AIDS line brief*, 10 (2).
31. Ibid.
32. Hospice Information Bulletin (2004) 'Widening our reach: Opportunities for refugee nurse placements', *Hospice Information* (London) (05/04).
33. WHPCO (2004) *£ 42 million to the Global Fund to fight AIDS, TB, and Malaria*, London: Help the Hospices (06/04) 7.
34. Minnesota AIDS Project, 'Housing as prevention', p. 7.
35. Global Initiative on AIDS (no date) *The Global Initiative on AIDS in Africa* (online). Available at: www.aidsinafrica.com (accessed 02/05).
36. WHPCO (2004) *Hospice Information Bulletin*, London: Help the Hospices (07/04).
37. Powell, J. (2004) 'A global game of chicken', *Star Tribune* (Minneapolis, Minnesota) (01/11/04), section D.

38. Becker B. (2004) *Hospice Information Bulletin*, London: Help the Hospices, WHPCO (06/04).
39. WHPCO, *E 42 million to the Global Fund.*
40. White, D. (2005) 'G8 pledges not enough', *Financial Times* (27/09/04).
41. WHPCO, *E 42 million to the Global Fund.*
42. American Civil Liberties Union Report, 'AIDS epidemic update', p. 34.

9 New Directions for Social Work in Conditions of Globalization

1. According to a BBC radio news report on (16/2/05).
2. Arnold, T. (2004) 'Time for Ireland to lead fight against hunger', *The Irish Times* (12/07/04) 14.
3. IFSW (2002) *IFSW Update* (9/2002) 4.

Bibliography

Abbott, A. (1999) 'Measuring social work values: A cross-cultural challenge for global practice', *International Social Work*, 42 (4), 455–470.

Abercrombie, N., Hill, S. and Turner, B. (1994) *The Penguin Dictionary of Sociology*, 3rd edition, London: Penguin Books.

Abye, T. (2001) 'Social work education with migrants and refugees in France', *Social Work in Europe*, 8 (3), 3–12.

Achebe, N. (2004) 'The road to Italy: Nigerian sex workers at home and abroad', *Journal of Women's History*, 15 (4), 178–185.

Adams, A., Erath, P. and Shardlow, S. (eds) (2001) *Key Themes in European Social Work: Theory, Practice and Perspectives*, Lyme Regis: Russell House Publishing.

Adepoju, A. (2002) 'Fostering free movement of persons in West Africa: achievements, constraints, and prospects for intraregional migration', *International Migration*, 40 (2), 3–28.

Admassie, A. (2003) 'Child labour and schooling in the context of a subsistence rural economy: Can they be compatible?', *International Journal of Educational Development*, 23 (2), 167–185.

Agatise, E. (2004) 'Learning from Abroad: Our Work to Address the Trafficking of African Women and Girls to Italy', Paper presented at 'The Role of the African Community in Combating Child Trafficking', *AFRUCA National Conference 2004*, 22 June 2004.

Ahmadi, N. (2003) 'Globalization of consciousness and new challenges for international social work', *International Social Welfare*, 12, 14–23.

Al-Krenawi, A. and Graham, J. (1999) 'Social work and Koranic mental health healers', *International Social Work*, 42 (1), 53–65.

Aluffi-Pentini, A. and Lorenz, W. (eds) (1996) *Anti-racist Work with Young People*, Lyme Regis: Russell House Publishing Ltd.

Anderson, B. (2003) 'A Job Like Any Other?' in Ehrenreich, B. and Hochschild, A. (eds) *Global Woman*, New York: Routledge.

Anderson, B. and O'Connell-Davidson, J. (2003) *Is Trafficking in Human Beings Demand Driven? A Multi-Country Pilot Study*, Geneva: International Organization for Migration.

Angell, G. (1999) 'Through the looking glass: Social work's challenge in the global village', *Families in Society: The Journal of Contemporary Human Services*, 80 (3), 229.

Angell, G.B., Dennis, B.G. and Dumain, L.E. (1997) 'Spirituality, resilience, and narrative: Coping with parental death', *Families in Society: The Journal of Contemporary Human Services*, 79 (6), 615–630.

Arendt, H. (1970) *Eichmann in Jerusalem: A Report on the Banality of Evil*, New York: Viking Press.

Assaad, R., Levison, D. and Zibani, N. (2001) 'The Effect of Child Work on School Enrolment in Egypt', Report presented at Workshop on the Analysis of Poverty and its Determinants in the MENA Region, Sanaa.

Axford, B. (1995) *The Global System: Economics, Politics and Culture*, Cambridge: Polity Press.

Bak, M. (2004) 'Can developmental social welfare change an unfair work? The South African experience', *International Social Work*, 47 (1), 87–94.

Barrett, D. (ed.) (2000) *Youth Prostitution in the New Europe*, Lyme Regis: Russell House.

Barretta-Herman, A. (2005) 'A Re-Analysis of the IASSW World Census 2000', *International Social Work*, 48 (6), 794–808.

Barry Jones, R.J. (1995) *Globalisation and Interdependance in the International Political Economy: Rhetoric and Reality*, London: Pinter Publishing.

Bayne, N., Uda, S. and Ullrich, H. (2004) 'The Tarten Talks, Gleneagles 2005', *LSE Magazine Winter*, 16 (2), 16–18.

Becker, J. (2004) 'Children as Weapons of War' in *Human Rights Watch World Report 2004: Human Rights and Armed Conflict*, New York and Washington: Human Rights Watch.

Bey, M. (2003) 'The Mexican Child: From Work with the Family to Paid Employment', *Childhood*, 10 (3), 287–299.

Beyrer, C. (2001) 'Shan women and girls and the sex industry in Southeast Asia: Political causes and human rights implications', *Social Science and Medicine*, 53 (4), 543–550.

Binder, M. and Scrogin, D. (1999) 'Labour force participation and household work of urban schoolchildren in Mexico: Characteristics and consequences', *Economic Development and Cultural Change*, 48 (1), 123–154.

Blair, R. (2001) 'Mental health needs among Cambodian refugees in Utah', *International Social Work*, 44 (2), 179–196.

Blass, T. (2004) *The Man Who Shocked the World: The Life and Legacy of Stanley Milgram*, New York: Basic Books.

Boss, P. (2006) *Loss, Trauma, Resilience: Clinical Work with Ambiguous Loss*, Minneapolis, Minnesota: University of Minnesota Press.

Bourdieu, P. (translated by Nice, R.) (1977) *Outline of a Theory of Practice*, Cambridge: Cambridge University Press.

Bourdieu, P. and Wacquant, L. (1999) 'On the cunning of imperialist reason', *Theory, Culture and Society*, 16 (1), 41–58.

Bramley, L., Tubman, M. and Summit Rapporteurs (1998) *Final Report – Out From the Shadows: International Summit of Sexually Exploited Youth*, Vancouver: Save the Children.

Briskman, L. and Cemlyn, S. (2005) 'Reclaiming humanity for asylum seekers: A social work response', *International Social Work*, 49 (6), 714–724.

Broad, B. (2004) 'Kinship care for children in the UK', *European Journal of Social Work*, 7 (2), 211–228.

Bruera, E., DeLima, L., Wenk, R. and Farr, W. (2004) *Palliative care in the developing world: Principles and practice*, Houston, Texas: International Association for Hospice and Palliative Care.

Brunovskis, A. and Tyldum, G. (2004) *Crossing Borders: An Empirical Study of Transnational Prostitution and Trafficking in Human Beings*, Norway: Fafo.

Bull, D. (2000) 'Forward', in Link, R. *et al.* (eds) op. cit.

Burgess, H. and Taylor, I. (eds) (2004) *Effective Learning and Teaching is Social Policy and Social Work*, London: Routledge Falmer.

Canagarajah, S. and Skyt Nielsen, H. (1999) *Child Labor and Schooling in Africa: A comparative study*, Social Protection Paper No. 9916, Washington, DC: World Bank.

Canda, E.R. (1988) 'Spirituality, religious diversity, and social work practice', *Social Casework*, 69 (4), 238–247.

Cannan, C., Lyons, K. and Berry, L. (1992) *Social Work and Europe*, Basingstoke: Macmillan.

Caragata, L. and Sanchez, M. (2004) 'Globalization and global need: New imperatives for expanding international social work education in North America', *International Social Work*, 45 (2), 217–238.

Carlsen, M. (2005a) 'International perspectives in social work education in the USA: History, the new framework and a case study', in Lyons, K. (ed.) *Internationalising Social Work Education: Considerations & Developments*, Monograph Series, London: BASW/Venture Press.

—— (2005b) '*Women, HIV/AIDS and palliative care in Tanzania: Current situation and future challenges*'. Paper presented at the International Symposium on HIV/AIDS, Gender and the Church, Moshi, Tanzania, August 2005.

Carmen, R. (1999) 'The New "Partnership" Era: But where is the third partner?', *Development*, 42 (2), 83–87.

Castells, M. (1998) *End of Millennium: The Information Age: Economy, Society and Culture*, Vol. II, Oxford: Blackwell.

Castilla, J., Sobrino, P., del Amo, J. and EPI-VIH Study Group (2002) 'HIV infection among people of foreign origin voluntarily tested in

Spain. A comparison with national subjects', *Sexually Transmitted Infections*, 78 (4), 250–255.

Castle, J. and Phillips, W. (2003) 'Grief rituals: Aspects that facilitate adjustment to bereavement', *Journal of Loss and Trauma*, 8 (1), 41–71.

Castles, S. (2000) *Ethnicity and Globalization*, London: Sage.

Centre for Human Rights (1994) *Human Rights and Social Work: A Manual for Schools of Social Work and the Social Work Profession*, Geneva: UN.

Centres for Disease Control (2004) *Update 2004: Bovine Spongiform Encephalopathy and Variant Creutzfeldt-Jakob Disease* (online) available at: www.cdc.gov/ncidod/diseases/cjd/bse_cjd.htm (accessed 02/05).

Chambers, R. (1997) *Whose Reality Counts? Putting the First Last*, London: ITDG Publishing.

Chan, C. and Ng, S. (2004) 'The social work practitioner-researcher-educator: Encouraging innovations and empowerment in the 21st century', *International Social Work*, 47 (3), 312–320.

Choi, J.S. and Choi, S. (2005) Social work intervention with migrant workers in South Korea, *International Social Work*, 48 (5), 655–665.

Christ, G. and Sormanti, M. (1999) 'The social work role in end-of-life care: A survey of practitioners and academicians', *Social Work and Health Care*, 30 (9), 81–99.

Christie, A. (2002) 'Asylum seekers and refugees in Ireland: Questions of racism and social work', *Social Work in Europe*, 9 (1), 10–17.

Clark, D. and Wright, M. (2003) 'The International Observatory on End of Life Care', *Hospice Information Bulletin*, 2 (2), 12.

Cohen, S., Humphries, B. and Mynott, E. (eds) (2002) *From Immigration Controls to Welfare Controls, Legal and Policy Developments in the UK and the US, Role of Social Workers in Immigration Controls*, London: Routledge.

Cord, C. (2003) *The Cambridge Companion to Simone DeBeauvior*, Cambridge: Cambridge University Press.

Cornwall, A. (2002) *Making a Difference? Gender and Participative Development*, IDS Discussion Paper 378, Sussex: IDS.

Council on Social Work Education (2004) 'Janice Wood Wetzel, IASSW's main representative to the UN in IASSW, represents social work education values and concerns at United Nations', *Social Work Education Reporter*, 52 (1), 17.

Craig, D. and Porter, D. (1997) 'Framing participation: Development projects, professionals, and organizations', *Development in Practice*, 7 (3), 229–236.

Cranston, J. (2004) 'Mass violence and the workplace', in Straussner and Phillips (eds) op. cit.

Crisp, B. (2003) 'Similar but not the same: Social work education in Britain from an Australian perspective', in Littlechild, B. and Lyons, K. (eds) *Locating the Occupational Space for Social Work: International Perspectives*, BASW Monograph, Birmingham: Venture Press.

CSUCS (1999a) *Use of Children as Soldiers in Africa* (online), available at: http://www.globalmarch.org/virtuallibrary/radda-barnen-child-soldiers/database/rwanda.htm (accessed 03/04).

—— (1999b) *Europe Report October 1999* (online), available at: http://www.globalmarch.org/virtual-library/csucs/country-reports/europe/uk.html (accessed 03/04).

—— (2001) *Global Report on Child Soldiers – 2001* (online), available at: http://www.globalmarch.org/virtuallibrary/childsoldiers-global-report/child-soldiers/united kingdom.doc (accessed 03/04).

—— (2003) *Child Soldier Use 2003: A Briefing for the 4th UN Security Council Open Debate on Children and Armed Conflict*, London: The Coalition to Stop the Use of Child Soldiers.

Culhane-Pera, K., Vawter, D., Xiong, P., Babbitt, B. and Solberg, M. (2003) *Healing by Heart: Clinical and Ethical Case Stories of Hmong Families and Western Providers*, Nashville, Tennessee: Vanderbilt University Press.

Currer, C. (2001) *Responding to Grief: Dying, Bereavement and Social Care*, London: Palgrave.

De Haan, A. (1999) 'Livelihoods and poverty: The role of migration – a critical review of the migration literature', *The Journal of Development Studies*, 36 (2), 1–47.

—— (2000) 'Migrants, livelihoods, and rights: The relevance of migration in development policies', *Social Development Working Paper No. 4*, London: DFID Social Development Department.

De Oliveira, W. (2000) *Working with Children on the Streets of Brazil: Policies and Practice*, New York: The Howarth Press.

De Souza, J. and Urani, A. (2002) 'Children in drug trafficking: A rapid assessment', *Investigating the Worst Forms of Child Labor, no. 20*, Brazil and Geneva: ILO, International Programme on the Elimination of Child Labour.

Deacon, A. (2002) *Perspectives on Welfare*, Philadelphia: Open University Press.

Dominelli, L. (1997) *Anti-Racist Social Work*, 2nd edition, Basingstoke: BASW and Macmillan.

—— (ed.) (1999) *Community Approaches to Child welfare: International Perspectives*, Aldershot: Ashgate/CEDR.

—— (2002) *Anti-Oppressive Social Work Theory and Practice*, Basingstoke: Palgrave Macmillan.

Dominelli, L. and Hoogvelt, A. (1996) 'Globalization and the technocratization of social work', *Critical Social Policy*, 16 (2), 45–62.

Dominelli, L. Lorenz, W. and Soydan, H. (eds) (2001) *Beyond Racial Divides: Ethnicities in Social Work Practice*, Aldershot: Ashgate.

Dominelli, L. and Thomas Bernard, W. (eds) (2003) *Broadening Horizons: International Exchanges in Social Work*, Aldershot: Ashgate.

Doña, G. (2002) 'Refugees' well-being in countries of resettlement', *Social Work in Europe*, 9 (1), 41–48.

Donnellan, C. (2000) *The Exploitation of Children*, Cambridge: Independence.

Dottridge, M. (2004) *Kids as Commodities? Child Trafficking and What to Do about It*, Lausanne: Terre Des Hommes.

Drucker, D. (2003) 'Whither international social work? A reflection', *International Social Work*, 46 (1), 53–81.

Duckett, M. (2001) *Migrants' right to health. UNAIDS and the International Organization for migration* (online), Available at: http://www.iom.int//DOCUMENTS/PUBLICATION/EN/Mig_Rights_Health.pdf (accessed 12/04).

ECPAT (2002) *The Report on the Implementation of the Agenda for Action Against the Commercial Sexual Exploitation of Children (2001–2002)*, Bangkok: ECPAT International.

Elliot, D., Mayadas, N. and Watts, T. (eds) (1990) *The World of Social Welfare: Social Welfare and Services in an International Context*, Springfield: Charles C. Thomas Publisher.

Ennew, J. (1986) *The Sexual Exploitation of Children*, Polity Press: Cambridge.

Esping-Anderson, G. (1990) *The Three Worlds of Welfare Capitalism*, Oxford: Polity Press.

Estes, R. (2001) *The Commercial Sexual Exploitation of Children in the U.S., Canada and Mexico* (online), available at http://www.caster.ssw.upenn.edu/~restes/CSEC/htm (accessed 01/04).

Etzioni, A. (1993)*The Spirit of Community Rights and Responsibilities and the Communitarian Agenda*, New York: Crown Pub.

Eyben, R. (2003) 'The rise of rights: Rights-based approaches to international development', *IDS Policy Briefing*, Sussex: IDS (17/05/03).

Falk, D. and Nagy, G. (1997) 'Teaching international and cross-cultural social work', *IASSW Newsletter*, 5.

Field, D., Hockey, J. and Small, N. (1997) *Death, Gender and Ethnicity*, London: Routledge.

Fletcher, S. (2002) 'Cultural implications in the management of grief and loss', *Journal of Cultural Diversity*, 9 (3), 86–91.

Flowers, R.B. (1998) *The Prostitution of Women and Girls*, Jefferson, North Carolina: McFarland and Co.

Fornbad, C.M. (2001) 'The crisis of confidentiality in the control of the HIV/AIDS pandemic in Botswana', *International Social Science Journal*, LIII (170), 643–656.

Fowler, G.A. (2003) 'Dying alone', *Far Eastern Economic Review*, 166 (22), 46–49.

Fox, D. (2005) *An Examination of the Implementation of Restorative Justice in Canada and Family Group Conferencing Approaches in the U.K.*, Monograph Series, London: BASW/Venture Press.

Frank, T. (2002) *One Market Under God*, London: Vintage.

Franklin, B. (ed.) (2002) *The New Handbook of Children's Rights: Comparative Policy and Practice*, London: Routledge.

Fredrick, J. and Kelly, T.L. (2000) *Fallen Angels: The Sex Workers of South Asia*, New Delhi: Poly Books.

Freire, P. (1970) *Pedagogy of the Oppressed*, New York: Continuum.

Gane, N. (2004) *The Future of Social Theory*, London: Continuum.

Garber, R. (2000) *IASSW World Consensus of Social Work Education 1998–1999* (online), available at http://www.iassw-aiets.org/ (accessed 10/05).

Garrett, P.M. (2004) 'The electronic eye: Emerging surveillance practices in social work with children and families', *European Journal of Social Work*, 7 (1), 57–71.

George, J. (1997) 'Global graying. What role for social work?', in Hokenstad, M.C. and Midgley, J. (eds) *Issue in International Social Work. Global Challenges in a New Era*, Washington: NASW Press.

Giddens, A. (2002) *Where Now for New Labour?* London: Polity Press, The Fabian Society and Policy Network.

Gilman, R. (1990) 'Sustainability – the state of the movement', *In Context*, 25, 10–12.

Glissant, E. (1996) *Introduction à une poétic du divers*, Paris: Gallimard.

Global March (2004) *World Congress* (online), available at http://globalmarch.org/worldcongress (accessed 03/04).

—— (no date) *Worst Forms of Child Labour Data*, New Delhi: Global March.

Gorkoff, K. and Runner, J. (eds) (2003) *Being Heard: The Experiences of Young Women in Prostitution*, Black Point, Nova Scotia: Fernwood Publishing and RESOLVE.

Goulet, L. (2001) *Out from the Shadows: Good Practices in Working with Sexually Exploited Youth in the Americas*, Victoria: Institute for Child Rights and Development.

Gray, M. and Fook, J. (2004) 'The quest for a universal social work: Some issues and implications', *Social Work Education*, 23 (5), 625–644.

Gregg, P., Harkness, S. and Machin, S. (1999) 'Trends in child poverty in Britain 1968–96', *Fiscal Studies*, 20 (2), 163–187.

Gresham, K., Nackerad, L. and Risler, E. (2003) 'Intercountry adoption from Guatemala and the United States', *Journal of Immigrant and Refugee Services*, 1 (3/4), 1–20.

Gutiérrez, L.M. and Lewis, E. (1999) *Empowering Women of Color*, New York: Columbia University Press.

Gutiérrez, L.M., Parsons, R.J. and Cox, E.O. (eds) (1998) *Empowerment in Social Work Practice: A Sourcebook*, Pacific Grove, California: Brooks/Cole Publishing Co.

Gysels, M., Pool, R. and Nalusiba, B. (2002) 'Women who sell sex in a Ugandan trading town: Life histories, survival strategies and risk', *Social Science and Medicine*, 54 (2), 179–192.

Haan, H.C. (2002) *Non-Formal Education and Rural Skills Training: Tools to Combat the Worst Forms of Child Labour Including Trafficking*, Bangkok: ILO Mekong Sub-Regional Project to Combat Trafficking in Children and Women.

Hamburger, F., Hirschler, S., Sander, G. and Wobke, M. (eds) (2004) *Ausbildung für Soziale Berufe in Europa*, Vol. 1, Frankfurt am Main: ISS-Pontifex.

Hamilton, J.M. (1990) *Entangling Alliances: How the Third World Shapes our Lives*, Hamilton: Seven Locks Press.

Hare, I. (2004) 'Defining social work for the 21st century: The international federation of social workers' Revised Definition of Social Work', *International Social Work*, 47 (3), 407–424.

Harris, J. and Chou, Y-C. (2001) Globalization or glocalization? community care in Taiwan and Britain, *European Journal of Social Work*, 4 (2), 161–172.

Harrop, D. (2003) 'With a little hope', *Professional Social Work* (08/2003), 7.

Harvey, J. (ed.) (1998) *Perspectives on Loss: A Sourcebook*, Washington, DC: Taylor and Francis.

Harvey, J. and Hofmann, W. (2001) 'Teaching about loss', *Journal of Loss and Trauma*, 6 (3), 263–268.

Hawken, M.P., Melis, R.D.J., Ngombo, D.T., Mandaliya, K., Ng'ang'a, L.W., Price, J., Dallabetta, G. and Temmerman, M. (2002) 'Part-time female sex workers in a suburban community in Kenya: A vulnerable hidden population', *Sexually Transmitted Infections*, 78 (4), 271–273.

Hayes, D. and Humphries, B. (2004) *Social Work, Immigration and Asylum*, London: Jessica Kingsley Publishers.

Hazan, M. and Berdugo, B. (2002) 'Child labour, fertility, and economic growth', *The Economic Journal*, 112 (482), 810–828.

Hazenkamp, J. and Popple, K. (eds) (1997) *Racism in Europe: A Challenge for Youth Policy and Youth Work*, London: UCL Press Ltd.

Heady, C. (2000) *What is the Effect of Child Labour on Learning Achievement? Evidence from Ghana*, Working Paper No. 79, Florence: UNICEF Innocenti Research Centre.

Healy, L. (1986) 'The international dimension in social work education: Current efforts, future challenges', *International Social Work*, 29 (2), 135–147.

—— (2001) *International Social Work: Professional Action in an Interdependent World*, Oxford and New York: Oxford University Press.

—— (2004a) 'Strengthening the link: Social work with immigrants and refugees and international social work', *Journal of Immigrant and Refugee Services*, 2 (1/2), 49–67.

—— (2004b) 'Standards for social work education in North American and Caribbean Region: Current realities, future issues', *Social Work Education*, 23 (5), 581–596.

Held, D. (1995) *Democracy and the Global Order: From the Modern State to Cosmopolitan Governance*, Cambridge: Polity Press.

Held, D., McGrew, A., Goldblatt, D. and Perraton, J. (1999) *Global Transformations: Politics, Economics and Culture*, Cambridge: Polity Press.

Hessle, M. (2000) 'Unaccompanied and asylum-seeking children encounter Sweden', in Callahan, M., Hessle, S. and Strega, S. (eds) *Valuing the Field: Child Welfare in an International Context*, Aldershot: Ashgate.

Hessle, S. and Hessle, M. (1998) 'Child welfare in wartime and in post-war conditions: The Bosnian case as a point of departure for social work with refugees', in Williams *et al.* (eds) op. cit.

Hickson, F., Reid, D., Weatherburn, P., Stephens, M., Nutland, W. and Boakye, P. (2004) 'HIV, sexual risk, and ethnicity among men in England who have sex with men', *Sexually Transmitted Infections*, 80 (6), 443–450.

Hill, G. and Denniston, G.C. (2003) 'HIV and circumcision: New factors to consider', *Sexually Transmitted Infections*, 79 (6), 495–497.

Hoff, M. (1997) 'Social work, the environment, and sustainable growth', in Hokenstad, M.C. and Midgley, J. (eds) op. cit.

—— (1997) *Issues in International Social Work: Global Challenges in a New Era*, Washington: NASW Press.

Hokenstad, M.C. and Midgley, J. (eds) (2004) *Lessons from Abroad: Adapting International Social Welfare Innovations*, Washington, DC: NASW Press.

Hokenstad, M.C., Khinduka, S.K. and Midgley, J. (eds) (1996) *Profiles in International Social Work*, Washington: NASW Press.

Hoogvelt, A. (1997) *Globalization and the Postcolonial World: The New Political Economy of Development*, London: Macmillan Press.

Hoyle, M. (1989) *The Politics of Childhood*, London: Journeyman.

Huegler, N. (2003) 'The situation of separated refugee children in Germany and the UK: Challenges, international standards and possibilities for social professionals to intervene', *Social Work in Europe*, 10 (2), 57–63.

—— (2005) *Care and Support for Young Separated Refuges aged 16 and 17 in Germany and the United Kingdom*, BASW Monograph, Birmingham: Venture Press.

Hui, J. and Tsui, M-S (2004) Empowerment by hotline: Experiences during the SARS outbreak, *Asia Pacific Journal of Social Work and Development*, 14 (1), 65–71.

Human Rights Watch (2004) *World Report 2004: Human Rights and Armed Conflict*, New York and Washington: Human Rights Watch.

Humphries, B. (2002) 'From welfare to authoritarianism: The role of social work in immigration controls' in Cohen, Humphries and Mynott (eds), op. cit.

Hussain, A. (2002) 'Urban poverty in China: Incidence and policy responses', in Townsend, P. and Gordan, D. (eds) *World Poverty: New Policies to Defeat an Old Enemy*, Bristol: The Policy Press.

Ife, J. (2001a) *Human Rights and Social Work: Towards Rights-based Practice*, Cambridge: Cambridge University Press.

—— (2001b) 'Local and global practice: Relocating social work as a human rights profession in the new global order', *European Journal of Social Work*, 4 (1), 15–21.

Ife, J. and Fiske, L. (2006) 'Human rights and community work – complementary theories and practises', *International Social Work*, 49 (3).

IFSW (1990) *International Policy on HIV/AIDS* (online), available at: www.ifsw.org/publications/4.5.2.pub.htm (accessed 01/05).

—— (2000a) 'Definition of Social Work', *IFSW Newsletter*, 2/2000.

—— (2000b) *International Policy on migration* (online), available at: www.ifsw.org/Publications/4.5.4.pub.htm (accessed 02/05).

—— (2004) *Policy Statement on Globalization and the Environment* (online), available at: http://www.ifsw.org/Publications/4.5.13.pub.html (accessed 02/05).

Ilahi, N. (2001)*Children's Work and Schooling: Does Gender Matter? Evidence from the Peru LSMS*, Washington, DC: World Bank.

ILO (1997) *Economically Active Population 1950–2010*, STAT Working Paper, Geneva: ILO.

—— (2001) *Good Practices in Action Against Child Labour: A Synthesis Report of Seven Country Studies (Brazil, Indonesia, Kenya, Philippines, Tanzania, Thailand, Turkey), 1997–98*, Geneva: ILO.

—— (2002) *IPEC Action against Child Labour 2000–2001: Progress and Future Priorities*, International Labour Organization, Geneva: International Programme on the Elimination of Child Labour.

INTERPOL (1998) *International Crime Statistics for 1998*, Lyon: INTERPOL.

IOM (2002) *Victims of Trafficking in the Balkans* (online), available at: http://www.iom.int/en/PDF_Files/Other/balkan_trafficking.pdf (accessed 06/02).

Irish, D., Lundquist, K., and Nelson, V.J. (1993) *Ethnic Variations in Dying, Death and Grief: Diversity in Universality*, Washington, DC: Taylor and Francis.

Irving, Z. and Payne, M. (2005) Globalization: Implications for Teaching and Learning, in Burgess, H. and Taylor, I. (eds) *Effective Learning and Teaching in Social Policy and Social Work*, London: Routledge Falmer.

Itzin, C. (2001) 'Incest, paedophilia, pornography and prostitution: Making familial males more visible as the abusers', *Child Abuse Review*, 10 (1), 35–48.

Jackson, C. (2004) 'HIV/AIDS prevention in Russia', *The BEARR Trust Newsletter*, February (41) 11.

James, A., Jenks, C. and Prout, A. (1998) *Theorizing Childhood*, Cambridge: Polity Press.

James, J. and Meyerding, J. (1978) 'Early sexual experience as a factor in prostitution', *Archives of Sexual Behavior*, 7 (1), 31–42.

Jenks, C. (1996)*Childhood*, London: Routledge.

Jessop, B. (1994) 'The transition to post-Fordism and the Schumpterian workfare state', in Burrows, R. and Loader, B. (eds) *Towards a post-Fordist Welfare State?*, London: Allen and Unwin.

Joffe, H. and Harhoff, G. (2002) 'Representations of far-flung illnesses the case of Ebola in Britain', *Social Science and Medicine*, 54 (6), 955–970.

John-Baptiste, J. (2001) 'Appropriateness of social work practice with communities of African origin', in Dominelli, L., Lorenz, W. and Soydan, H. (eds) op. cit.

Johnson, A. (2004) 'Increasing internationalization in social work programs: Healy's continuum as a strategic planning guide', *International Social Work*, 47 (1), 7–23.

Jones, J. and Kumssa, A. (1999) 'Professional growth in the global context', in Ramanathan, C. and Link, R. (eds) op. cit.

Jonker, G. (1997) 'Death, gender and memory: Remembering loss and burial as a migrant', in Field, D., Hockey, J. and Small, N. (eds) *Death, Gender and Ethnicity*, London: Routledge.

Jordan, B. with Jordan, C. (2000) *Social Work and Third Way: Tough Love as Social Policy*, London: Sage Publications.

Juliusdottir, S. and Petersson, J. (2004) 'Nordic Standards revisited', *Social Work Education*, 23 (5), 567–580.

Jurgens, K. (2004) 'Almost home houses: A special Dutch model', *Hospice Information Bulletin*, 2 (2), 11–12.

Ka'opua, L.S. and Mueller, C.W. (2004). 'Treatment adherence among native Hawaiians living with HIV', *Social Work*, 49 (1), 55–63.

Kaseke, E. (2001) 'Social Development as a model of social work practice: The experience of Zimbabwe', in Dominelli, L., Lorenz, W. and Soydan, H. (eds) op. cit.

Kasiram, M.I. and Partab, R. (2002) 'Grieving through culture and community: A South African perspective', *Maatskaplike Werk/Social Work*, 38 (1), 39–44.

Katz, C. (2001) 'On the grounds of globalization: A topography for feminist political engagement', *Signs*, 26 (4), 1213–1234.

Kaufman, M. (2001) 'The white ribbon campaign: Involving men and boys in ending global violence against women', in Pease, B. and Pringle, K. (eds) op. cit.

Kawewe, S. (2001) 'The impact of gender disempowerment on the welfare of Zimbabwean women', *International Social Work*, 44 (4), 471–485.

Kearl, M.C. (1989) *Endings: A Sociology of Death and Dying*, Oxford: Oxford University Press.

Kebaabetswe, S., Lockman, S. and Mogwe, S. (2003) 'Male circumcision: An acceptable strategy for HIV prevention in Botswana', *Sexually Transmitted Infections*, 79 (6), 214–219.

Kebebew, A. (1998) *Statistics on Child Labour: A Brief Report*, Bulletin of Labour Statistics 3, Geneva: ILO.

Kelly, L. and Regan, L. (2000) *Stopping Traffic: Exploring the Extent of, and Response to, Trafficking of Women for Sexual Exploitation in the UK*, Police Research Series, Paper 125, London: Home Office.

Kennedy, M.A., Klein, C., Gorzalka, B.B. and Yuille, J.C. (2004). 'Attitude change following a diversion program for men who solicit sex', *Journal of Offender Rehabilitation*, 40 (1/2), 41–60.

Khan, P. and Dominelli, L. (2000) 'The impact of globalization on social work in the UK', *European Journal of Social Work*, 3 (2), 95–108.

Kindhauser, M.K. (ed.) (2004) *Global Defence Against the Infectious Disease Threat*, Lyon: WHO.

Kingsley, C. and Mark, M. (2000) *Sacred Lives: Canadian Aboriginal Children and Youth Speak Out about Sexual Exploitation*, Vancouver: Save the Children Canada.

Korn, D. (1999) *Exodus within Borders: An Introduction to the Crisis of Internal Displacement*, Washington: Brookings Institution Press.

Kornbeck, J. (ed.) (2003) *Language Teaching in the Social Work Curriculum*, Mainz: Logophone.

Kreitzer, L. (2002) 'Liberian Refugee Women: A qualitative study of their participation in planning camp programmes', *International Social Work*, 45 (1), 45–58.

Krugman, P. (1997) *Pop Internationalism*, London: The MIT Press.

Krzyszkowski, J. (2003) 'Social care and social work in Poland since 1989: Evidence for recent research', *Social Work in Europe*, 10 (3), 71–75.

Kubler-Ross, E. (1969) *On Death and Dying*, New York: Macmillan Publishing Company.

Lague, D. and Saywell, T. (2003) 'The new war on disease', *Far Eastern Economic Review* (24/04/03) 19–21.

Laing, R.D. (1990) *The Politics of Experience*, London: Penguin Books.

Laird, S. (2004) 'Inter-ethnic conflict: A role for social workers in Sub-Saharan Africa', *Social Work Education*, 23 (6), 693–709.

Lamis, A.S. (2002) 'The courage to re-discuss ourselves: The politics of justice', *Development*, 45 (2), 71–75.

Larsen, P.B. (2003) *Indigenous and Tribal Children: Assessing Child Labour and Education Challenges*, Child Labour and Education Working Paper, Geneva: ILO, International Programme on the Elimination of Child Labour.

Lavinas, L. (2001) *The Appeal of Minimum Income Programmes in Latin America*, Geneva: ILO, InFocus Programme on Socio-Economic Security.

Lawrence, S. (2005) 'International mobility of labour in social work: Support and training implications, Symposium Report', *European Journal of Social Work*, 8 (2), 209–213.

Lawson, C. and Katz, J. (2004) 'Restorative justice: An alternative approach to juvenile crime', *Journal of Socio-Economics*, 33 (2), 175–188.

Lee, E.S. (1966) 'A theory of migration', *Demography*, 3 (1), 47–57.

Leonard, M. (2004) 'Children's views on children's right to work: Reflections from Belfast', *Childhood*, 11 (1), 45–61.

Lev-Wiesel, R. and Friedlander, D. (1999) 'Role perceptions among social workers living in politically uncertain areas', *International Social Work*, 42 (1), 67–78.

Liebel, M. (2003) 'Working children as social subjects: The contribution of working children's organizations to social transformations', *Childhood*, 10 (3), 265–285.

Link, R., Bibus, A. with Lyons, K. (2000) *When Children Pay: US Welfare Reform and Its Implications for UK Policy*, London: Child Action Poverty Group.

Lloyd-Williams, M. (2003) *Psychosocial Issues in Palliative Care*, Oxford: Oxford University Press.

Lorenz, W. (1994) *Social Work in a Changing Europe*, London: Routledge.

Loury, G. (1977) 'A dynamic theory of racial income differentials', in Wallace, P. and LeMund, A. (eds) *Women, Minorities, and Employment Discrimination*, Lexington: Lexington Books.

Lowman, J. (2000) 'Violence and the outlaw status of (street) prostitution', *Violence against Women*, 6 (9), 987–1011.

Lum, D. (2000) *Social Work Practice and People of Color: A Process-Stage Approach (4th edn)*, Belmont, California: Brooks/Cole Thomson Learning.

Lyons, K. (1999) *International Social Work: Themes and Perspectives*, Aldershot: Ashgate.

—— (2005) 'International perspectives' in Burgess, H. and Taylor, I. (eds) op. cit.

—— (2006) 'Globalization and social work: International and local implications', *British Journal of Social Work*, 36 (3).

Lyons, K. and Lawrence, S. (eds) (2006) *Social Work in Europe: Educating for Change*, Birmingham: IASSW/Venture Press.

Lyons, K. and Littlechild, B. (eds) (2006) *International Labour Mobility in Social Work*, BASW Monograph, Birmingham: Venture Press. In press.

Lyons, K. and Ramanathan, C. (1999) 'Models of field practice in global settings', in Ramanathan, C. and Link, R. (eds) op. cit.

Lyons, K. and Stathopoulos, P. (2001) 'Migration and refugees in Europe: Greek and British perspectives on implications for social work practice and education', *European Journal of Social Work*, 4 (1), 55–63.

MacDonald, T. (2005) *Third World Health: Hostages to First World Wealth*, Oxford: Radcliffe Publishing.

Machel, G. (1996) *The Impact of Armed Conflict on Children*, Geneva: UN Centre for Human Rights.

—— (2000) *The Impact of Armed Conflict on Children: A Critical Review of Progress Made and Obstacles Encountered in Increasing Protection for War-Affected Children*, Winnipeg: UNIFEM and UNICEF.

MacInnes, R.A. (1998) *Children in the Game: Child Prostitution – Strategies for Recovery*, Canada: Street Teams.

Macionis, J. and Plummer, K. (2002) *Sociology a Global Introduction*, 2nd edn, Harlow: Pearson Education Ltd.

Manderson, L. (2004) 'Disability, global legislation and human rights', *Development*, 47 (2), 29–35.

Manion, H.K. (2002) 'Trafficking in women and children for sexual purposes: A growing threat in europe', *Social Work in Europe*, 9 (2), 11–22.

—— (2004) *Commercial Sexual Exploitation of Children: Models of Good Practice in Biopsychosocial Rehabilitation*, Monograph Series, London: BASW/Venture Press.

—— (2005) 'A global perspective on intellectual property rights: A social work view', *International Social Work*, 48 (1), 77–87.

Mänsson, S.-A. (2001) 'Men's practices in prostitution – The Case of Sweden', in Pease, B. and Pringle, K. (eds) op. cit.

Marlow, C. and Van Rooyen, C. (2001) 'How green is the environment in social work?' *International Social Work*, 44 (2), 241–254.

Martin, P. (2003) 'Sustainable labor migration policies in a globalizing world', Paper for *Globalization, the State, and Society Conference*, Washington University, St. Louis, 13–14 November 2003.

Martinez-Brawley, E. (1999) 'Social work, postmodernism and higher education', *International Social Work*, 42 (3), 333–346.

Mathiason, N. (2005) 'Brown plan will cut aid by $108bn, says study', *The Observer*, 06/02/05.

Matz, P. (2003) *Costs and Benefits of Education to Replace Child Labour*, Working Paper, Geneva: ILO, International Programme on the Elimination of Child Labour.

McEnhill, L. (2004) 'National network for the palliative care of people with learning disabilities', *Hospice Information Bulletin*, 2 (4), 11.

McIntyre, S. (2005) *Under the Radar: The Sexual Exploitation of Young Men*, Edmonton: Government of Calgary.

McLuhan, H.M. (1967), *The Medium Is the Message*, New York: Bantam.

Mead, M. (1963) *Coming of Age in Samoa: A Psychological Study of Primitive Youth for Western Civilization*, Harmondsworth: Penguin.

Mehta, V. (1997) 'Ethnic Conflict and Violence in the Modern World: Social Work's Role in Building Peace', in Hokenstad, M.C. and Midgley, J. (eds) op. cit.

Melrose, M. (2000) *Ties that Bind – Young people and the Prostitution Labour Market in Britain*, 4th European Feminist Research Conference: Bologna, September 2000.

Meuse, R. (2003) 'Away from home: Reflections on working with asylum seekers in the Netherlands', in Dominelli, L. and Thomas Bernard, W. (eds) op. cit.

Michie, J. (ed.) (2003) *The Handbook of Globalization*, Cheltenham: Edward Elgar.

Midgley, J. (1995) *Social Development: The Development Perspective in Social Welfare*, London: Sage.

—— (1997a) *Social Welfare in Global Context*, Thousand Oaks, CA: Sage.

—— (1997b) 'Social work and international social development', in Hokenstad, M.C. and Midgley, J. (eds) *Issues in International Social Work: Global challenges in a New Era*, Washington: NASW Press.

—— (2000) 'Globalization, capitalism and social welfare: A social development perspective', in Rowe, B. (ed.) *Social Work and Globalization*, Ottawa: Canadian Association of Social Workers.

Minnesota AIDS Project (2004) *Annual Report*, Minneapolis: Minnesota.

Mishra, R. (1999) *Globalization and the Welfare State*, Cheltenham: Edward Elgar.

Mlczoch, M. (2002) 'Voluntary work and research in an accommodation centre for asylum seekers in Switzerland', *Social Work in Europe*, 9 (1), 32–40.

Modelski, G. (1972) *Principles of World Politics*, New York: Free Press.

Montgomery, H. (2001) *Modern Babylon? Prostituting Children in Thailand*, Oxford: Bergham Books.

Morris, S., Neidecker-Gonzales, O., Carletto, C., Munguia, M., Medina, J. and Wodon, Q. (2001) 'Hurricane mitch and the livelihoods of the rural poor in Honduras', *World Development*, 30 (1), 49–60.

Msimang, S. (2003) 'HIV/AIDS, globalization and the international women's movement', *Gender and Development*, 11 (1), 109–113.

Muntarbhorn, V. (1996) *Sexual Exploitation of Children*, New York and Geneva: Centre for Human Rights, UN.

Mupedziswa, R. (2001) 'The quest for relevance: Towards a conceptual model of developmental social work education and training in Africa', *International Social Work*, 44 (3), 285–300.

Mwabu, G., Ugaz, C. and White, G. (2001) *Social Provision in Low-Income Countries: New Patterns and Emerging Trends*, Oxford: Oxford University Press.

Nagy, G. and Falk, D. (2000) 'Dilemmas in international and cross-cultural social work education', *International Social Work*, 43 (1), 49–60.

Nair, P.R.G. (1999) 'Return of overseas contract workers and their rehabilitation and development in Kerala (India): A critical account of policies, performance and prospects', *International Migration*, 37 (1), 209–242.

NASW (2004) *Social Justice: Issue Fact Sheet* (online), National Association of Social Workers, available at http://www.socialworkers.org/pressroom/features/issue/peace.asp (accessed 12/04).

Ng, H. (2003) 'The "social" in social work practice: Shaman and social workers', *International Social Work*, 46 (3), 289–301.

Nieuwenhuys, O. (1994) *Children's Lifeworlds: Gender, Welfare and Labour in the Developing World*, London: Routledge.

Noble, C. (2004) 'Social work education, training and standards in the Asia Pacific region', *Social Work Education*, 23 (5), 527–554.

Noyoo, N. (2004) 'Human rights and social work in a transforming society: South Africa', *International Social Work*, 47 (3), 359–369.

Nussbaum, M. (2000a) 'Beyond the social contract: Capabilities and global justice', *Oxford Development Studies*, 32 (1), 3–18.

—— (2000b) *Women and Human Development. The Capabilities Approach*, Cambridge: Cambridge University Press.

Nyambedha, E.O., Wandibba, S. and Aagaard-Hansen, J. (2003) 'Changing patterns of orphan care due to the HIV epidemic in western Kenya', *Social Science and Medicine*, 57 (2), 301–311.

Nyaywa, R. (17/11/2003) 'Tanzania: Rapists in the family', *Women's Feature News Services*, New Delhi, India, available at http://proquest.umi.com (accessed 25/03/05).

Oakley, A. (2002) *Gender on Planet Earth*, Cambridge: Polity Press.

O'Connell-Davidson, J. (1998) *Prostitution, Power and Freedom*, Michigan: University of Michigan Press.

—— (2001) *The Sex Exploiter: Paper for the Second World Congress against Commercial Sexual Exploitation of Children*, Japan, Bangkok: ECPAT International.

O'Gorman, T. (1992) *Charity and Change: From Bandaid to Beacon*, Melbourne: World Vision.

Olofsgard, A. (2003) 'Incentives for secession in the presence of mobile ethnic groups', *Journal of Public Economics*, 87 (9), 2105–2128.

O'Neill, O. (2002) *Reith Lectures 2002 – A Question of Trust* (online), available at: http://www.bbc.co.uk/radio4/reith2002/ (accessed 12/04).

O'Neill, T. (2003) 'Anti-child labour rhetoric, child protection and young carpet weavers in Kathmandu, Nepal', *Journal of Youth Studies*, 6 (4), 413–431.

Orme, J. (2001) *Gender and Community Care: Social Workers and Social Care Perspectives*, Basingstoke: Palgrave.

Otto, H-U. and Lorenz, W. (1998) 'Editorial: The new journal for the social professions', *European Journal of Social Work*, 1 (1), 1–4.

Palma, G. (2003) 'National inequality in the era of globalization: What do recent data tell us?', in Michie, J. (ed.) op. cit.

Palmer, I. (1985) *The Impact of Male Out-Migration on Women in Farming*, West Hartford: Kumarian Press.

Parkes, C.M., Laungani, P. and Young, B. (1997) *Death and Bereavement Across Cultures*, London: Routledge.

Patricola-McNiff, B. (2002) 'Loss reflected', *Journal of Loss and Trauma*, 7, 83–86.

Patterson, E. (2004) 'Impact of globalization on social work practice in Romania', in Tan, N.-T. and Rowlands, A. (eds) op. cit.

Pearson, E. (2001) *Human Rights and Trafficking in Persons: A Handbook*, Bangkok: GAATW.

Pease, B. and Pringle, K. (eds) (2001) *A Man's World?: Changing Men's Practices in a Globalized World*, London: Zed Books.

Penna, S., Paylor, I. and Washington, J. (2000) Globalization, social exclusion and the possibilities for global social work and welfare, *European Journal of Social Work*, 3 (2), 109–122.

Pepin, J. and Mabey, D. (2003) 'Editorial: sexually transmitted infections in Africa: Single dose treatment is now affordable: There remains no financial obstacle to rapid and effective syndromic treatment of STIs in developing countries', *Sexually Transmitted Infections*, 79 (6), 432–435.

Perlas, N. (2000) *Shaping Globalization: Civil Society, Cultural Power and Threefolding*, Pasig City, Philippines: Centre for Alternative Development Initiatives.

Pettys, G., Panos, P., Cox, S. and Oosthuysen, K. (2005) 'Four models of international field placements', *International Social Work*, 48 (3), 273–284.

Phillips, D. and Berman, Y. (2001) 'Social quality and community citizenship', *European Journal of Social Work*, 4 (10), 17–28.

Plan (2005) *Universal Birth Registration – a Universal Responsibility*, London: Plan International.

Post, N. (1994) *The Disappearance of Childhood*, New York: Vintage Books.

Potocki-Tripody, M. (2002) *Best Practices for Social Workers with Refugees and Immigrants*, New York: Columbia University Press.

Prigoff, A. (1999) 'Global social and economic justice issues', in Ramanathan, C. and Link, R. (eds) op. cit.

Pugh, R. and Gould, N. (2000) 'Globalization, social work and social welfare', *European Journal of Social Work*, 3 (2), 123–138.

Putnam, R. (2001) *Bowling Alone: The Collapse and Revival of an American Community*, New York: Simon and Schuster.

Queiro-Tajalli, I., McNutt, J. and Campbell, C. (2003) 'International social and economic justice and on-line advocacy', *International Social Work*, 46 (2), 149–161.

Rabinov, P. (ed.) (1991) *The Foucault Reader: An Introduction to Foucault's Thoughts*, London: Penguin Books.

Rafferty, J., Ashford, M. and Orton, S. (2005) 'Towards e-learning: Opportunities and challenges', in Burgess and Taylor (eds) op. cit.

Rai, G. (2004) 'International fieldwork experience', *International Social Work*, 47 (2), 213–226.

Ramanathan, C. and Link, R. (eds) (1999) *All Our Futures: Principles and Resources for Social Work Practice in a Global Era*, Pacific Grove, CA: Brooks Cole.

Rammohan, A. (2000) 'Interaction of child labour and schooling in developing countries: A theoretical perspective', *Journal of Economic Development*, 25 (2), 85–99.

Rando, T. (1984) *Grief, Dying and Death: Clinical Interventions for Caregivers*, Illinois: Research Press.

Ravallion, M. and Wodon, Q. (2000) 'Does child labour displace schooling? Evidence on behavioural responses to an enrolment subsidy', *Economic Journal*, 110 (2000), 158–175.

Ravlolomanga, B. and Schlemmer, B. (2000) ' "Unexploited" Labor', in Schlemmer, B. (ed.) *The Exploited Child*, London: Zed Books.

Razack, N. (2002) 'A critical examination of international student exchanges', *International Social Work*, 45 (2), 251–265.

Reality of Aid Network (2004) *Reality of Aid 2004 – Asia Report*, Manila: Ibon Foundation.

Reed, H. and Keely, C. (2001) *Forced Migration and Mortality*, Washington: National Research Council.

Rees, J. (2004) 'Drops of gold', *LSE Magazine*, 16 (2), 9–11.

Reflex (2004) *Paladin Child: The Safeguarding Children Project*, London: London Heathrow UK Immigration Service, ADSS, NSPCC, Hillingdon.

Reichert, E. (2003) *Social Work and Human Rights: A Foundation for Policy and Practice*, New York: Columbia University Press.

Resl, V., Kumpova, M., Cerna, L., Novak, M. and Pazdiora, P. (2003) 'Prevalence of STDs among prostitutes in Czech border areas with Germany in 1997–2001 assessed in project "Jana" ', *Sexually Transmitted Infections*, 79 (6), E3.

Rose, N. (1992) 'Governing the enterprising self', in Heelas, P. and Morris, P. (eds) *The Values of the Enterprise Culture: The Moral Debate*, London: Routledge.

Rosenberg, J., Gonzales, M. and Rosenberg, S. (2005) 'Clinical practice with immigrants and refugees: An ethnographic multi-cultural approach', in Congress, E.P. and Gonzales, M.J. (eds) *Multicultural Perspectives in Working with Families*, 2nd edn, New York: Springer Publishing Co. Inc.

Rosenthal, B. (1990) 'US social workers' interest in working in the developing world', *International Social Work*, 33 (3), 227–232.

Rowlands, A. (2004) 'Reappraising social work's contribution to recovery from disaster and trauma: Applying a strengths perspective', *Asia Pacific Journal of Social Work and Social Development*, 14 (2), 67–85.

Rubin, S., Malkinson, R. and Witztum, E. (2003) 'Trauma and bereavement: Conceptual and clinical issues revolving around relationships', *Death Studies*, 27 (8), 667–690.

Ryan, S. and Groza, V. (2004) 'Romanian adoptees: A cross-national comparison', *International Social Work*, 47 (1), 53–80.

Schlemmer, B. (ed.) (2000) *The Exploited Child*, London: Zed Books.

Schneider, R. and Lester, L. (2001) *Social Work Advocacy: A New Framework for Action*, Belmont, CA: Brooks/Cole.

Second World Congress (2001) *Trafficking in Children for Sexual Purposes: An Analytical Review*, Paper for the Second World Congress against Commercial Sexual Exploitation of Children, Yokohama, Japan, 17–20 December.

Segerstrom, E. (1998) 'Collective action in a refugee camp: A case study', in Williams *et al.* (eds) op. cit.

Seibel, F. and Lorenz, W. (eds) (1998) *Social Professions for a Social Europe*, Frankfurt: IKO.

Seipel, M. (1994) 'Disability: An emerging global challenge', *International Social Work*, 37 (2), 165–179.

—— (1999) 'Social consequences of malnutrition', *Social Work*, 44 (5), 416–425.

—— (2005) Social consequences of emerging and re-emerging infections diseases, *International Social Work*, 46 (1), 35–48.

Selman, P. (1998) 'Intercountry adoption in Europe after the Hague convention', in Sykes, R. and Alcock, P. (eds) *Developments in European Social Policy: Convergence and Diversity*, Bristol: Policy Press.

Selye, H. (1956) *The Stress of Life*, New York: McGrawHill.

Sen, A. (1982) *Choice, Welfare and Management*, Oxford: Basil Blackwell.

—— (1997) 'Editorial: Human Capital and Human Capability', *World Development*, 25 (12), 1959–1961.

—— (1999) *Development as Freedom*, New York: Oxford University Press.

Sepulveda, C., Habiyambere, V., Amandua, J., Borok, M., Kikule, E., Mudanga, B., Ngoma, T. and Solomon, B. (2003) 'Quality care at the end of life in Africa', *British Journal of Medicine*, 327 (7408), 209–213.

Sewpaul, V. (2004) 'Globalization, African governance and the new partnership for Africa's development', in Tan, N.-T. and Rowlands, A. (eds) op. cit.

Sewpaul, V. and Preston-Shoot, M. (2004) 'Editorial', *Social Work Education*, 23 (5), 491–492.

Shamai, M. and Boehm, A. (2001) 'Politically oriented social work intervention', *International Social Work*, 44 (3), 343–360.

Shera, W. and Bogo, M. (2001) 'Social work education and practice: Planning for the future', *International Social Work*, 44 (2), 197–210.

Simmonds, J. (2003) *Every Child Matters – Consultation Response*, London: British Association of Adoption and Fostering.

Somerset, C. (2001) *What Professionals Know: The Trafficking of Children into, and through, the UK for Sexual Purposes*, London: ECPAT UK.

Somerset, C. (2004) *Cause for Concern? London Social Services and Child Trafficking*, London: ECPAT UK.

Sopheab, H., Gorbach, P.M., Gloyd, S. and Leng, H.B. (2003) 'Rural sex work in Cambodia: Work characteristics, risk behaviours, HIV, and syphilis', *Sexually Transmitted Infections*, 79 (4), 335–341.

Soumpasi, N. (2003) 'Pilot project in Kosovo: Training the trainers in tolerance, a social work perspective', *Social Work in Europe*, 10 (1), 32–37.

Soyden, H. (1998) 'Understanding migration', in Williams *et al.* (eds) op. cit.

Straussner, S. and Phillips, N. (2004) *Understanding Mass Violence: A Social Work Perspective*, New York: Pearson Education, Inc.

Stroebe, M. and Schut, H. (1999) 'The dual process model of coping with bereavement: Rationale and description', *Death Studies*, 23 (3), 197–224.

Stroebe, M.S., Hansson, R.O., Stroebe, W. and Schut, H. (eds) (2001) *The Handbook of Bereavement Research: Consequences, Coping, and Care*, Washington DC: American Psychological Association.

Suanda, M. (2003) 'Democratizing Education', *Changemakers*, 5 (1), 7–13.

Sunderland, D. (2004) *The British International Development Sector: A Panorama Study* (online), Coordination SUD, France, available at: http://www.coordinationsud.org (accessed 02/05).

Szasz, T. (1970) *The Manufacture of Madness*, New York: Harper and Row.

Tajfel, H. and Turner, J. (1979) 'An integration theory of intergroup conflict', in Austin, W. and Worchel, S. (eds) *The Social Psychology of Intergroup Conflict*, Montery, CA: Brooks Cole.

Tan, N.-T. and Rowlands, A. (eds) *Social Work Around the World III*, Bern: IFSW Press.

Tasse, A. (2001) 'Social work education with migrants and refugees in France', *Social Work in Europe*, 8 (3), 3–12.

Taylor, Z. (1999) 'Values, theories and methods in social work education: A culturally transferable core?', *International Social Work*, 42 (3), 309–318.

Teeple, G. (2000) *Globalization and the decline of social reform: Into the 21st century*, 2nd Edition, Aurora, ON: Garamond Press.

Tesoriero, F. and Rajaratnum, A. (2001) 'Partnership in education: An Australian school of social work and a South Indian primary health care project', *International Social Work*, 44 (1), 31–41.

Thompson, N. (ed.) (2002) *Loss and Grief: A Guide for Human Services Practitioners*, London: Palgrave.

Trevillion, S. (1997) 'The globalization of European social work', *Social Work in Europe*, 4 (1), 1–9.

Tucker, N. (2005) *Love in the Driest Season: A family memoir*, New York: Crown.

Tyler, T., Boeckmann, R., Smith, H. and Hua, Y. (1997) *Social Justice in a Diverse Society*, Boulder: Westview Press.

UN (2004) *A More Secure World: Our Shared Responsibility, Report of the Secretary-General's High-level Panel on Threats, Challenges and Change, Executive Summary*, New York: UN.

UNAIDS (2004a) *UNAIDS 2004 Report on the Global AIDS Epidemic – Executive Summary*, Bangkok: UNAIDS.

—— (2004b) *2004 Report on the Global AIDS Epidemic. Fourth Global Report*, Bangkok: UNAIDS.

UNDP (1999) *Human Development Report* (online), available at http:// www.globalmarch.org/worstformsreport/world/links/hdr1999/ hdr99-contents.htm (accessed 03/04).

UNFPA (2004) *State of the World Population Report 2004* (online), available at http://www.unfpa.org/swp/swpmain.htm (accessed 12/04).

UNHCR (2000) *Refugees and Others of Concern to UNHCR: 1999 Statistical Overview*, Geneva: Registration and Statistical Unit, UNHCR.

—— (2005) *UNHCR Global Appeal 2005*, Geneva: UNHCR.

UNICEF (1996)*Declaration and Action for Agenda of the World Congress Against Commercial Sexual Exploitation of Children* (online), available at: http://www.unicef.org/events/yokohama/ (accessed 04/04).

—— (1997) *The Promotion and Protection of Children's Rights in Post-Genocide Rwanda*, Italy: UNICEF.

—— (2003) *End Child Exploitation: Stop the Traffic*, New York: UNICEF.

—— (2004a) *Voicing our Views* (online), available at: http://www. unicef.org/voy (accessed 03/04).

—— (2004b) *What Young People are Saying: Children and Work* (online), available at: http://www.unicef.org/voy/news (accessed 03/04).

—— (2005) *State of the World's Children 2005: Children Under Threat*, New York: UNICEF.

—— (no date) *Girls Education* (online), available at: http://www. unicef.org/girlseducation (accessed 03/04).

UNICEF UK (2003) *End Child Exploitation: Stop the Traffic!*, London: UNICEF UK.

US Dept. of State (2004) *Human Trafficking: 4th Annual Trafficking in Persons Report*, Washington, DC: US Department of State.

USID (2001) *Trafficking in Persons: USID's Response* (online), available at: http://www.USid.gov/wid/pubs/trw0la.htm (accessed 06/02).

Van Wormer, K. (1997) *Social Welfare – A World View*, Chicago: Nelson Hall.

—— (2004) *Human Behaviour and the Social Environment*, Oxford: Oxford University Press.

Wallerstein, I. (1974) *The Modern World System*, New York: Academic Press.

Walter, N., Bourgois, P. and Loinaz, H.M. (2004) 'Masculinity and undocumented labor migration: Injured latino day laborers in San Francisco', *Social Science and Medicine*, 59 (6), 1159–1168.

Walters, G. (2003) 'Msc module for palliative care chaplains', *Hospice Information Bulletin*, 2 (3).

Ward, M. and Roby, J. (2004) Commercial Sexual Exploitation of Children in the Philippines, *Asia Pacific Journal of Social Work and Development*, 14 (2), 19–31.

Warren, G. (1939) 'International social work' in Kurtz, R. (ed.) *Social Work Yearbook*, New York: Russell Sage Foundation.

Webb, S. (2003) 'Local order and global chaos in social work', *European Journal of Social Work*, 6 (2), 191–204.

Welsby, P. (1998) 'The real or perceived losses for a patient with HIV infection or AIDS', in *Palliative Aspects of AIDS*, Oxford: Oxford University Press.

Welsby, P. and Richardson, A. (1999) 'Palliative aspects of adult acquired immune deficiency syndrome', in Doyle, D., Hanke, W.C. and MacDonald, N. (1999) *Oxford Textbook of Palliative Medicine*, Oxford: Oxford University Press.

WHO (2000a) *Fact Sheets #242: Women and AIDS* (online), available at: www.who.int/medicentre/factsheets/fs242/en/print/ (accessed 04/04).

—— (2000b) *Fact Sheet #247: Women and AIDS* (online), available at: www.who.int/mediacentre/factsheets/fs247/en/print/ (accessed 04/04).

—— (2002) *Factsheet # 267: Plague* (online), available at: www.who.int/mediacentre/factsheets/fs267/en/print.html (accessed 11/04).

—— (2003) *Communicable Diseases Cluster: Highlights of Communicable Disease Activities*, Geneva: WHO.

—— (2004a) *A Global Emergency: A combined response*, Geneva: WHO.

—— (2004b) *The World Health Report 2004* (online), available at: http://www.who.int/whr/2004/ (accessed 12/04).

WHPCO (2004) *Worldwide Hospice and Palliative Care Online*, Help the Hospices, Hospice House, 33–44, Britannia St., London, SE1.

Wikan, U. (1988) 'Bereavement and loss in two Muslim communities: Egypt and Bali compared', *Social Science and Medicine*, 27 (5), 451–460.

Williams, C., Soydan, H. and Johnson, M. (eds) (1998) *Social Work and Minorities: European Perspectives*, London: Routledge.

Williams, J. (2005) 'Developing international perspectives in UK curricula: Opportunities and challenges', in Lyons, K. (ed.) *Internationalising Social Work Education: Consideration and Developments*, BASW Monograph, Birmingham: Venture Press.

Williams, L. and Sewpaul, V. (2004) 'Modernism, postmodernism and global', *Social Work Education*, 23 (5), 555–565.

Women's International Network (2001) 'Women and violence', *Women's International Network News*, 27 (3), 33–46.

Woodward K. (ed.) (2000) *Questioning Identity: Gender, Class, Nation*, London: Routledge.

World Guide (1998) *The World Guide; A View From the South, 1997–1998*, London: New Internationalist.

Yip, K. (2004) 'A Chinese cultural critique of the global qualifying standards for social work education', *Social Work Education*, 23 (5), 597–612.

Zapf, M.K. (2005) The spiritual dimension of person and environment: Perspectives from social work and traditional knowledge, *International Social Work*, 48 (5), 633–642.

Zimmerman, W. and Fix, M. (2002) 'Immigration and welfare reforms in the United States through the lens of mixed status families', in Cohen, S. *et al.* (eds) op. cit.

Zinner, E.S. and William, S.M.B. (eds) (1999) *When a Community Weeps: Case Studies in Group Survivorship*, Ann Arbor, MI: Taylor and Francis.

Zuniga, M. (2004) 'Mexican immigrants: Would you sacrifice your life for a job?' in Drachman, D. and Paulino, A. (eds) *Immigrants and Social Work: Thinking Beyond the Borders of the United States*, New York: Howarth Press.

Index

Note: Names of organisations, projects, papers and initiatives have been italicized. Country names appear in bold. Entries with multiple page numbers will have key pages bolded where appropriate.